AN EXISTENTIALIST THEOLOGY

A Comparison of
Heidegger and Bultmann

JOHN MACQUARRIE

With a Foreword by
RUDOLF BULTMANN

SCM PRESS LTD
BLOOMSBURY STREET LONDON

To my Father and Mother

FIRST PUBLISHED 1955
SECOND IMPRESSION 1960
FIRST CHEAP EDITION 1965
© SCM PRESS LTD 1960
PRINTED BY OFFSET IN GREAT BRITAIN BY
WILLIAM CLOWES AND SONS, LIMITED
LONDON AND BECCLES

CONTENTS

CONTENTS

FOREWORD

THE author gives a picture of an 'existentialist theology' by showing how the hermeneutic principle which underlies my interpretation of the New Testament arises out of the existential analysis of man's being, given by Martin Heidegger in his work, *Being and Time*. In addition, the author pursues the question of whether and to what extent there is justification for such an 'ontological' method in the interpretation of the New Testament.

The book is distinguished by great clarity in the unfolding of the problem and in the sequence of thought; also by great care and objectivity, and by independent judgment.

The author rightly maintains that the existentialist philosophy, as represented by Heidegger's *Being and Time*, is not a speculative philosophy, but an analysis of the understanding of existence that is given with existence itself. He also affirms—and rightly so, I am convinced—that the understanding of man developed in existentialist philosophy possesses a certain kinship with the understanding that is contained implicitly in the New Testament. Thus he acknowledges my interpretation of the New Testament to be one that is valid in principle. He then makes a careful examination of my interpretation, and comes to the conclusion that on the one hand I make relevant and intelligible many important ideas, especially in the Pauline and Johannine writings; but that on the other hand I sometimes overstep the limits that are set to an existentialist interpretation, and that justice is not done to the transcendent reality towards which faith is directed in the New Testament.

I cannot agree with the author's criticism at all points. But I must concede that the criticism is not only fair and perceptive, but also touches upon points that are really problematic and must be cleared up in future discussion. The author's criticism is not dogmatically introduced from outside, but arises from the inner understanding of the existential interpretation, as the author takes part in it and, through his participation, seeks to recognize its justification and limits. Thus the criticism is a fruitful one.

I have seldom found so unprejudiced and penetrating an understanding of my intentions and my work as in this book. It also evidences a penetrating and, as I believe, an essentially correct understanding of Heidegger, as well as a rare capacity for unfolding simply and clearly this philosopher's ideas, which are often hard to understand.

So I must give my opinion that the author's book is a distinguished performance. He shows himself to be a thinker of high rank, with outstanding power of exposition. I am happy that the theological discussion of the present has been enriched by this contribution which both clarifies it and carries it further; and I set great hope on the future work of the author.

Marburg   RUDOLF BULTMANN

PREFACE

THE aim of this work is to make some contribution towards understanding the influence of existentialist philosophy upon contemporary theological thought. I have concentrated, however, on the particular case of the relation between two German scholars—Professor Martin Heidegger, the philosopher, and Professor Rudolf Bultmann, the theologian. I have chosen this particular case for two reasons: firstly, the relation here is a very close one; and secondly, it is a very interesting one, for both of these men—even if we disagree with their teaching sometimes—appear to me to be, in their own fields, really original and outstanding thinkers.

In the Introduction the problem is stated, and a sketch is given of the existential approach to theology. This approach is defended on three grounds. These are: the right of the apologist to make use of current philosophical concepts; the claim that there is a special relation between the philosophy of existence and the work of theology; and an affinity between the concepts of existentialism and those of biblical thought.

The main body of the work falls into two parts, reflecting a division found both in Heidegger's *Sein und Zeit* and in Bultmann's *Theologie des Neuen Testaments*. The first part considers Heidegger's analysis of inauthentic existence in relation to Bultmann's exposition of the New Testament teaching on man without faith, showing the close connection between the two, and making critical comment where necessary. The second part is concerned with Heidegger's idea of an authentic existence in relation to Bultmann's exposition of the Christian life as a new understanding of the self.

The Conclusion attempts to summarize the results of the enquiry. Bultmann's place in the development of twentieth-century theology is indicated, and the value of his contribution is assessed.

I have referred to the German editions of Bultmann's *Theologie* and of *Kerygma und Mythos*, since these were the only ones available at the time of writing, but I would like to draw the reader's attention to the fact that there is now an English translation of Bultmann's work, entitled *Theology of the New Testament* (S.C.M. Press, vols. I and II), and that a selection of essays from *Kerygma und Mythos* has been translated under the title, *Kerygma and Myth* (S.P.C.K.).

It is a pleasant duty to acknowledge my indebtedness to Professor Ian Henderson, whose advice on many points has been quite invaluable, and whose work, *Myth in the New Testament* (S.C.M. Press, 1952), pioneered this field for English-speaking readers. My thanks are due also to Professor J. G. Riddell, who gave me every facility and encouragement to prosecute this work.

University of Glasgow   J. M.
  October 1954

NOTE TO 1965 EDITION

PROFESSOR Macquarrie referred in this book to the German editions of Bultmann's *Theologie des Neuen Testaments* and Heidegger's *Sein und Zeit* since these were the only editions available at the time of writing, but both books are now available in English. *Theology of the New Testament* by Rudolf Bultmann, translated by Kendrick Grobel in two volumes, is now included among the cheap editions of the S.C.M. Press. *Being and Time* by Martin Heidegger, translated by John Macquarrie and Edward Robinson, was published in 1962 in the S.C.M. Press Library of Philosophy and Theology, the series in which *An Existentialist Theology* appeared in 1955. That series now also includes Professor Macquarrie's survey of the world-wide theological discussion aroused by Bultmann's ideas, *The Scope of Demythologizing* (1960), and his *Twentieth-Century Religious Thought* (1963).

Rudolf Bultmann has summed up his teaching in *Jesus Christ and Mythology* (S.C.M. Press), and essays by him are collected in *Existence and Faith* and *Primitive Christianity in its Contemporary Setting* (both in the Fontana Library). Recent discussions of his thought include *The Christian Message and Myth* by a Belgian Catholic, L. Malevez (S.C.M. Press); *Gospel and Myth in the Thought of Rudolf Bultmann* by an Italian Protestant, G. Miegge (Lutterworth); *A Gospel without Myth?* by Professor D. Cairns of Aberdeen (S.C.M. Press); and *Christ without Myth* by S. M. Ogden, an example of American interest (Collins).

INTRODUCTION

I

THE RELATION OF THE PHILOSOPHY OF EXISTENCE TO THEOLOGY

1. *Philosophical Influences upon Theological Thought*

WHETHER for good or ill, it is a fact that throughout its history Christian theology has fallen at various times under the influence of different secular philosophies. Even in the New Testament there are passages which seem to betray Gnostic influence. From Justin Martyr to Augustine, the early theologians drew freely on Greek sources, especially Plato, for their theological work. Thomas Aquinas made use of the philosophy of Aristotle in his exposition of the Christian faith. Butler shows in his writings the influence of eighteenth-century rationalism. In the nineteenth century theology fell under the spell of Hegelian idealism, and later it was influenced by ideas stemming from the new scientific theories.

In all these cases we see an apologetic motive at work. The theologians were trying to find a point of entry into the contemporary mind in order that they might be able to present the Christian faith in terms intelligible to their own age. They therefore made use of current philosophical concepts even when these were drawn from systems of thought quite alien to Christianity.

The apologetic purpose of the theologians who have been mentioned was, in general, successfully accomplished. The early apologists were faced with the challenge of pagan philosophy; Thomas Aquinas by that of the Averroism of the medieval universities; Butler by that of deism. All of them

3

by the skilful use of contemporary philosophical ideas restated the historic Christian faith in such a way as to win a hearing for it in their own time. But more than that, it may be said also that all of them made contributions of permanent value to theological thought, because they themselves won a deeper understanding of Christian truth through their work.

Clearly, however, there are grave dangers inherent in this way of theologizing. The peril is threefold. Preoccupation with a secular philosophy and the employment of it in the interpretation of the Christian faith may easily lead to the distortion of Christian teaching through the over-emphasis of those elements in it which happen to be specially congenial to the philosophy concerned. Or again, ideas quite foreign to Christianity may slip into its theology while masquerading under the guise of traditional Christian terminology. At worst, there may be a plain accommodation of the Christian faith to the prevailing philosophical fashion of the age.

It can be argued that these dangerous possibilities were, in fact, realized when Christian theology fell under the influence of Hegelian idealism, and it can be even more forcibly contended that much in the movement known as liberal modernism was motivated by the idea that, at all costs, the Christian faith must be so interpreted that it would not give offence to the popular scientific outlook. It is understandable, therefore, that in the twentieth century there should have arisen among theologians a sharp reaction against philosophical influences. Of Barth it has been said that he 'is always the theologian criticizing the philosophers, and the theologians who allow their teaching to be determined by philosophical notions'.[1] It is maintained that the concern of theology is solely with the revealed Word of God, and that human philosophies can only obscure and distort the Christian faith when they are allowed to influence its interpretation. The endeavour is to derive theological teaching entirely from the divine revelation of biblical religion, and to exclude from it all elements of human speculation.

Thus to say that the thought of such a theologian as

[1] R. Birch Hoyle, *The Teaching of Karl Barth*, S.C.M. Press, p. 57.

4

Bultmann shows the influence of existentialist philosophy might seem sufficient to condemn it right away in the eyes of many contemporary theologians who have come to have a profound distrust of philosophy. Is not Bultmann falling into the old error of making Christian teaching conform to the trends of current secular thought? And will not Christian theology be again misled and distorted through this alien influence?

We might, of course, defend Bultmann on the lines on which the great apologists of earlier times could be defended, and say that he is seeking, not unsuccessfully, to present Christianity as a relevant issue in the mid-twentieth century. Existentialism has appeared as a philosophical reaction against the scientific humanism that prevailed in the early part of the century. It denies the claim of that school of thought that the only knowledge is that which can be scientifically verified, and affirms, on the contrary, that scientific knowledge is only one kind of knowledge, not privileged but specialized, and subordinate to the fundamental knowledge, which is knowledge of existence. On the face of it, this philosophical movement does seem to offer to the Christian theologian a way of access to the contemporary mind. It has apologetic possibilities, and, rightly used, these might prove to be of considerable value. It may be that through his preoccupation with existentialist ideas Bultmann on occasions misrepresents some Christian teaching, and where that can be shown to happen, it will be a weakness in his theological position. But it still remains arguable that the contemporary apologist, like his predecessors, has a right to use, with proper care, such current philosophical concepts as will enable him to present the Christian faith as a living and intelligible issue in his own generation.

This, however, is not the main line of defence for Bultmann's position. He is not primarily concerned to expound Christian thought in the language and concepts of what may prove to be a passing philosophical mood, but makes the more far-reaching claim that the philosophy of existence stands in a special relation to theology. If existentialism has

2   5

influenced the theology of Bultmann, it is not as an external influence, like much of the influence of Greek and western philosophy upon theology in the past. Theology is understood by Bultmann as the clarification of the content of faith, and the bringing of it to conscious knowledge. [2] That is to say, theology is a kind of phenomenology of faith, through which that which is implicit in Christian belief is exhibited in a connected system of thought. Further, he says that this analysis of faith must be undertaken from the standpoint of faith itself. Bultmann, just as much as Barth, is oriented in his thought to the faith which has its origin in the Christian revelation. His primary concern is to interpret faith itself, to let it show itself and speak for itself. His authentic intention is to exhibit the thought of the New Testament as such. Where, then, does the influence of existentialism come in? Can it be anything other than an extraneous and distorting influence in the exegesis of New Testament thought, even when that thought is to be shown in its relevance to the present day? But we have said that existentialism is not an external influence upon theology, but stands in a special relation to it. What, then, is that relation?

2. *Theology and Ontology*

Every inquiry has its presuppositions, and that is as true of theological inquiry as of any other. These presuppositions delimit the field of the inquiry, determine its basic concepts, and give it direction. [3] In some way they already determine the result of the inquiry—not the content of the result, but the kind of result that will be obtained. These presuppositions are ontological, that is to say, they consist in a preliminary understanding of the being of the entities into which the inquiry is being made. For example, the theologian may ask, 'What is man in his relation to God?' For the doctrine of man, that is to say, the content of the theological concept of man, he will go to the Christian revelation in search of his answer.

2 *Theologie des Neuen Testaments*, Tübingen, p. 187.
3 Cf. Heidegger, *Sein und Zeit*, Tübingen, pp. 9-12.

6

But what about the 'is' in his question? That already implies some understanding of the being of man—among other things, that the being of man is such that he can have a relation to God. Is the being of man, for instance, already conceived as substance? Or is it conceived existentially? Or in some other way? Whatever the presupposition—and there must be some presupposition, even if it is not explicit—it will influence both the inquiry and its result.

Thus we see the possibility of a pre-theological inquiry into the being of the entities discussed in theology. This pre-theological inquiry is not itself theology, though intrinsically related to theology. It is rather philosophy or, more strictly speaking, ontology. It is the critical examination and analysis of the understanding of being from which the inquiry sets out. Prior to every ontical inquiry, there lies an ontological inquiry.

As an illustration, let us return for a moment to the Christian doctrine of man. It is sometimes said that Saint Paul taught a trichotomy of man's being as opposed to the dualism of Greek philosophy. Man is body, soul and spirit, and we find this content for the concept of man by going to the New Testament writings.[4] But how we understand this doctrine of man depends on the preliminary understanding of his being, which we already have before we begin our inquiry into the New Testament teaching about man. If we conceive man's being substantially, then we may conclude that, according to Saint Paul, he is made up of three parts or elements. On the other hand, if we conceive the being of man existentially, then we may conclude with Bultmann[5] that man consists neither of two elements nor of three, but is a unity with different possible ways of being, here indicated by the terms body, soul and spirit.

The question of being, as Heidegger points out,[6] is one that has long been neglected or treated as superfluous, not only by theologians, but by philosophers, scientists and historians as well. What is meant by the being of anything is supposed to be either indefinable or self-evident. We do not

[4] I Thess. 5.23.   [5] *Th. des NT*, p. 205.   [6] *S. u. Z.*, p. 2.

7

pause to ask what we mean when we say that anything is.
Yet as Heidegger shows, it needs little thought to realize that
the idea of being is obscure in the extreme, and since some
understanding of being is assumed in every inquiry, that
initial obscurity is bound to have its consequences in the
ontical inquiry into which it is carried. On the other hand,
Heidegger thinks,[7] the progress of a science consists in the
constant revision and clarification of the first principles and
basic concepts from which it sets out—a view with which the
historian of science would probably agree.[8] On the special
problem of theology, Heidegger remarks:

> 'Theology is seeking a more primordial interpretation
> (than formerly) of the being of man in relation to God,
> prescribed by the meaning of faith itself and remaining
> within it. It is slowly beginning to understand once more
> Luther's insight, that its system of dogma rests on a foun-
> dation which is not itself a matter of faith, and the concepts
> of which are not only inadequate for theological problems,
> but obscure and distort them.'[9]

Bultmann has taken up this challenge. Before proceeding
to the interpretation of what is contained in the Christian
faith, he has paused to examine the presuppositions of
theological thinking. And he has come to believe that these
presuppositions are clarified and secured by a philosophy
of the existentialist type. For existentialism is a philosophy
of being. It has been argued by Heidegger[10] that in the
approach to the problem of being in general, precedence
belongs to the problem of the being of man, because man's
being is such that with it there is given some understanding
of his being. As existing, man is disclosed to himself. Thus
existentialism claims that it is not a speculative philosophy,
but an analysis of that understanding of existence which is
given with existence.

We can now see why it may be claimed that the influence

[7] *S. u. Z.*, p. 9.
[8] Cf. Dampier, *A History of Science*, C.U.P., pp. 457 and 491.
[9] *S. u. Z.*, p. 10. [10] *S. u. Z.*, p. 7.

of existentialism upon Bultmann's theology is not an external influence like that of a metaphysical system. It is an intrinsic influence, and it may well be in some respects at least a legitimate one, for it is the influence of a pre-theological—or ontological—inquiry into the idea of being which theology assumes. If it is claimed for any theologian that he is entirely free from the influences of secular philosophy, that may simply mean that he has not troubled to examine the implicit ontological assumptions from which his theology sets out and which are necessarily carried into all his inquiries.

The argument which we have put forward here is admirably summarized by Tillich:

'Theology, when dealing with our ultimate concern, presupposes in every sentence the structure of being, its categories, laws and concepts. Theology, therefore, cannot escape the question of being any more easily than can philosophy. The attempt of biblicism to avoid non-biblical, ontological terms is doomed to failure as surely as the corresponding philosophical attempts. The Bible itself always uses the categories and concepts which describe the structure of experience. On every page of every religious or theological text these concepts appear: time, space, cause, thing, subject, nature, movement, freedom, necessity, life, value, knowledge, experience, being and non-being. Biblicism may try to preserve their popular meaning, but then it ceases to be theology. It must neglect the fact that a philosophical understanding of these categories has influenced ordinary language for many centuries. It is surprising how casually theological biblicists use a term like "history" when speaking of Christianity as a historical religion or of God as "the Lord of history". They forget that the meaning they connect with the word "history" has been formed by thousands of years of historiography and philosophy of history. They forget that historical being is one kind of being in addition to others and that, in order to distinguish it from the word "nature", for instance, a general vision of the structure of being is presupposed. They forget that the problem of history is tied up with the problems of time, freedom, accident and so on, and that each of these concepts has had a development similar to the concept of history. The theologian must take seriously the meaning of the terms he uses. They must be known to him in the whole depth and breadth of their meaning. Therefore, the systematic theologian must be a philosopher in critical understanding even if not in creative power.'[11]

3. The Existential Approach to Theology

Bultmann states his claim for the special relation of existentialist philosophy to the work of the theologian in the following terms: 'The "right" philosophy'—and that, we take it, means the philosophical outlook proper to theological study—'is quite simply that philosophical work which endeavours to develop in suitable concepts the understanding of existence that is given with human existence.'[12] Believing as he does, that the work of the theologian as the interpreter of the content of faith is dependent on his philosophical outlook, because consciously or unconsciously he brings to the exegesis of the sacred writings presuppositions derived from the tradition of secular thought, Bultmann holds that he must examine these presuppositions to ensure that he has the 'right' philosophy, and he claims further that it is the philosophy which analyses man's understanding of his own existence that especially clarifies the basic concepts that are of particular interest to the theologian.

The existential approach to theology—if we may call it such—will only be fully exhibited in the detailed examination of Bultmann's thought, but his position can be made clearer at this stage by a discussion of two preliminary conceptions that are of considerable importance for both Heidegger and Bultmann. Since there are no precise English equivalents to express these conceptions, we may be per-

11 *Systematic Theology*, Nisbet, vol. I, pp. 24-25.
12 *Kerygma und Mythos*, Hamburg, vol. II, p. 192.

mitted to use the German terms rather than to para-phrase in English, provided that the meaning is first made clear.

The first term is *Fragestellung*—literally, the putting of the question. The way in which a question is asked has its conse-quence in determining the answer. To give an extreme illustration, a man on the verge of despair who has come to the end of his own moral and spiritual resources and who asks himself whether there is a God has obviously a very different *Fragestellung* from that of the philosopher who, reclining in his study, asks whether there is a God as the ground of the natural world. The former is inquiring about something that is of concern to his own existence, while the latter is asking an academic or speculative question. Both may come to the conclusion that there is a God, but their concepts of God will differ so widely that it might almost be said that they had come to believe in different entities. One will have found the God of prayer and worship, the other the God of metaphysical speculation. But the difference was already there in the manner in which each of them asked the question. The theologian also must have his *Fragestellung*. Bultmann tells us that when he goes to the Bible, the question to which he is seeking the answer is the question of human existence.[13] No doubt he is also asking about God, but about God in so far as he is significant to man as existing.[14] There may be depths of being in God beyond his significance to us, but, if so, they are inaccessible and not the concern of theology.

Because of this *Fragestellung*, it follows that, in the existential approach to theology, man and his being are central in all theological problems. The statements of the New Testament will be interpreted as statements significant for my existence. (This point, incidentally, is fundamental for Bultmann's views on demythologizing.) The centrality of human existence in this type of theology may be illustrated from Bultmann's description of the conversion of Saint Paul as his entering into a new understanding of himself.[15] One could equally well speak of a new understanding of God, but Bultmann, in

[13] *K. u. M.*, II, p. 191.   [14] *Th. des NT*, p. 186.   [15] *Th. des NT*, p. 184.

accordance with his *Fragestellung*, prefers to speak of it as primarily a new understanding of man's own existence in relation to God. Again, we see the centrality of man's existence for Bultmann's thought in his exposition of the entire Pauline theology as an anthropology or doctrine of man.[16] Doubtless the Pauline theology could be expounded in other ways, but this is the typical existential approach.

Bultmann claims, of course, that in making his theology centre in the question of man's existence, he is simply following the precedent of the New Testament. In the most systematic exposition of his own thought, the Epistle to the Romans, Saint Paul begins by describing the situation of man, and relates all his teaching to that.[17] Bultmann's claim that his own existential approach to theology is identical with, or at least very sympathetic towards, the approach of the New Testament writers themselves is one that will require closer examination later. But perhaps enough has been said here to make out a preliminary case for the existential approach to theology as a possible and legitimate one, for where else are we to begin, if not with out own existence which lies open to us, and what question is more urgent than the question of deciding about our own existence? But if this is so, then we see again the need to clarify the initial assumptions about human existence that are already there in the *Fragestellung* and which, therefore, underlie the inquiry and give to it its direction. This *Fragestellung* does not, of course, as Bultmann indicates, prejudice the content of the answer which we seek, or decide in advance the exegesis of the biblical writings from which the Christian theologian seeks to interpret the faith; but it does, he claims, 'open our eyes to the content of the text'.[18]

This leads us to the second of our preliminary conceptions, expressed by the term *Begrifflichkeit*. Sometimes this means no more than a terminology, as when Bultmann says that Gnosticism provided Christian missionaries to the Hellenistic world with a terminology familiar to their hearers, or that the Jewish sacrificial cult offered a terminology to express the

16 *Th. des NT*, p. 188.   17 *Th. des NT*, p. 296.   18 *K. u. M.*, II, p. 191.

significance of the death of Jesus.[19] But more typically the *Begrifflichkeit* is the context of ideas expressed in the terminology. The *Begrifflichkeit* of any inquiry is the system of basic concepts which it employs in the understanding of its subject-matter. Biology, mathematics, history and every other study have each a special *Begrifflichkeit*. In the widest sense the *Begrifflichkeit* can be a system of categories, that is to say, the basic formal concepts under which we understand what confronts us in experience. The most familiar example of such a system of categories is that elaborated by Kant in *The Critique of Pure Reason*. It is dominated by the category of substance, as every traditional *Begrifflichkeit* in western philosophy has been since the time of Aristotle. These traditional categories make it possible for us to understand the natural world, and to classify its phenomena. According to Heidegger, the merit of Kant's work is that it provides 'a concrete logic of the field of nature'.[20] But the important question raised by the existentialist philosophers is whether this traditional *Begrifflichkeit* is appropriate to the phenomena of human existence. While the natural sciences have steadily advanced, the human sciences remain in obscurity and confusion. May the reason be that, whereas the natural sciences have in the traditional categories a *Begrifflichkeit* which is appropriate to their subject-matter, the idea of being which these categories imply is quite inapplicable to human existence? Convinced that this is indeed the case, the existentialist philosophers have tried to think out a new *Begrifflichkeit* that will enable us to have a true understanding of the being of man. The categories applicable to the natural world are replaced by new categories—or rather, existentials, as Heidegger calls them—applicable to human existence.

Let us take a simple example. The basic constitution of the being of man, according to Heidegger, is 'being-in-the-world'. This expression uses the terminology of spatial relations. (It may be noted in passing that Heidegger makes the curious claim that originally the preposition 'in' had not spatial but existential meaning, and he quotes Grimm as his

[19] *Th. des NT*, pp. 163, 290.   [20] *S. u. Z.*, p. 11.

authority on this linguistic point.[21] This claim, if true, is interesting, but of course does not alter the fact that in modern usage we would normally understand the expression 'being-in-the-world' in a spatial sense.) But Heidegger is at pains to make it clear that this expression is to be understood in an entirely different *Begrifflichkeit* or context of ideas from that of spatial relations. Here 'being-in' (*Insein*) does not mean the relation of, say, water in a glass or a coat in the cupboard. It signifies not a spatial but an existential relation. It means not that man is located in the world, but that he is bound up with the world in his existence.[22] Through his existential analytic, Heidegger seeks to show the structure of the being of man, and how his being differs from the being of objects in nature, and must be differently understood and described. Now all this must be of the greatest interest to the theologian, especially if, like Bultmann, he approaches theology with the question of human existence in the forefront of his thought. The theologian undertakes his task with a *Begrifflichkeit* (be it conscious or unconscious) as well as a *Fragestellung*. If he lacks an appropriate *Begrifflichkeit*, then his interpretation of Christian doctrine will force it into unsuitable categories of thought, and this will lead to obscurity and distortion.

We now have before us the two main distinguishing characteristics of the existential approach to theology: (*a*) the *Fragestellung*, or manner of putting the question, which treats theological questions as primarily questions of man's existence in relation to God, and interprets the sacred writings as statements which primarily concern man's existence; (*b*) the *Begrifflichkeit*, or system of basic concepts derived from the philosophy of existence, which claims to have analysed in suitable concepts the understanding of existence which is given with existence.

4. *Existentialism and Biblical Thought*

At an earlier point in the argument it was shown how Saint Paul's analysis of the being of man as body, soul and

[21] *S. u. Z.*, p. 54. [22] *S. u. Z.*, p. 53 ff.

spirit could be understood in two distinct ways according as we conceive the being of man substantially or existentially. We deliberately refrained at that stage from asking an important question which no doubt occurred to the reader, namely, how did Saint Paul himself understand what he had written? That is the type of question that must be raised now. We must test the existential approach to theology in another way, by asking how far it is likely to reveal to us the authentic thought of the New Testament writers. True, as Tillich's remarks on uncritical biblicism showed us, we can never completely enter into the outlook of the biblical writers, for some two thousand years of thought lie between us and them. Yet we must have as large a measure of sympathy with their outlook as possible, and approach as near as we can to their standpoint if we are making the claim to interpret their thought. However interesting and attractive the existential approach to theology might appear, it would be nothing other than a mistake if it makes us read into the New Testament thoughts which were never in the minds of the men who wrote the New Testament.

The business of the theologian, it has been already stressed, is not to construct or invent a philosophy of religion, but to exhibit clearly, systematically, and intelligibly for his own age the genuine content of historic Christian faith. Our principal source for the Christian faith is the New Testament. The theologian, then, is the interpreter of the thought of the New Testament. But the writers of the New Testament must also have had their presuppositions, their preliminary understanding of being. If existentialist philosophy is to be helpful to the theologian in his work of throwing light on the teaching of the New Testament, it should be possible to show that there is some sympathy and affinity between the idea of being made explicit by this philosophy, and the idea of being that is implicit in the thought of the New Testament writers. If no such affinity can be shown, then indeed it might be justly said that the existential approach to theology obscures and distorts authentic Christian teaching by compelling it to assume the forms of a way of thought which is quite foreign. Bultmann's theology would not then be what it claims to be, namely, the theology of the New Testament.

Are we embarking on an absurd enterprise when we set out to look for affinities between biblical thought and this secular twentieth-century philosophy of existentialism? Is it ridiculous to speak of existentialism in biblical thought? Are we falling into the same kind of trap as the victims of the Piltdown skull hoax, who are said to have explained a pre-historic human skull in conjunction with the jaw of a modern ape? That might be our first reaction, and when, for instance, Bultmann interprets Saint Paul's concept of the body as meaning that man in his being is related to himself, we might without further consideration conclude, as one recent writer has done in what is otherwise a most useful book,[23] that this is a 'glaring example' of the importation of contemporary philosophy into the New Testament. But this judgment may be too hasty.

Existentialism is not a philosophy but a type of philosophy, and a type so ·flexible that it can appear in such widely differing forms as the atheism of Sartre, the Catholicism of Marcel, the Protestantism of Kierkegaard, the Judaism of Buber, and the Orthodoxy of Berdyaev. And again, though the name of existentialism is relatively new, it does not follow that this type of philosophy is new. Mounier has constructed a family tree of existentialism with its roots going far back into the pre-Christian era.[24] The contemporary existentialists look back to Kierkegaard. But before him there were Pascal and Maine de Biran, who both showed marked affinities with existentialism. Father Copleston claims that there was a school of thought with resemblances to existentialism in the late Middle Ages.[25] Brock finds traces of existentialism in Augustine's reflections on 'the ceaseless unrest which marks the temporal life of the individual'.[26] There were undoubted

[23] Robinson, *The Body*, S.C.M. Press, p. 12, note.
[24] *Existentialist Philosophies: an Introduction*, Rockliff, p. 3.
[25] In his paper, *Existentialism and Modern Man*, Blackfriars.
[26] *Contemporary German Philosophy*, C.U.P., ch. on Heidegger.

stirrings of the existentialist type of thought in ancient Greece, for example, in Socrates,[27] though it was not the dominant trend in classical philosophy. Thus existentialism, it is claimed, is not merely a phenomenon of modern times. It appears rather to be one of the basic types of thought that has appeared from time to time in the history of philosophy. It stresses the difference between the individual being of man (*Existenz*) and the being of objects in nature (*Vorhandenheit*) that lends itself to generalization and classification, and it asserts the importance of the former as against the latter.

Now what is the understanding of being that is implicit in the thought of the New Testament writers? The assumptions of their thought stemmed in the main from Hebrew thought, and the New Testament can only be properly understood against the background of the Old Testament. And even where we discern Hellenistic influences in the New Testament, it is worth noting that they come primarily from an element in Hellenistic thought that was non-Hellenic—namely, from Gnosticism. In fact, there is a great gulf fixed between the basic concepts of the New Testament, taken over principally from Hebrew thought, and those of Greek philosophy, and therefore of the western philosophy which is descended from it.

As a preliminary evidence of this difference, we may refer to a subject which has recently received attention—the form of the biblical writings. Broadly speaking, it has been assumed in Greek and western thought that knowledge is capable of being expressed in general statements, and its typical form is the systematic scientific or philosophical treatise. There is hardly anything of that in the Bible. Are we then to say that the Bible does not convey knowledge? Or is it that the biblical writers communicate a different kind of knowledge—the knowledge of individual human existence before God, which defies the kind of classification and generalization which are appropriate only to the knowledge of objects in nature? In other words, did Hebrew thought grasp what, in the main,

[27] Cf. Robin, *Greek Thought*, K. Paul, p. 159.

17

traditional western thought has failed to grasp—the fundamental distinction between *Existenz* (the being of man) and
Vorhandenheit (the being of things) as different ways of being?
'Recital' is the broad term suggested by a recent writer[28] to
describe the form of the biblical writings. The sacred authors
employed poetry, prophecy, histories of national heroes and
men of God, myths, and so on, to convey knowledge. They
did not make general statements, but confronted their readers
with individual human beings in *existentiell* situations. That is
understandable if their approach to the subject was existential. It is significant that many modern existentialists have
reverted to a method of teaching similar to that used by the
biblical writers. While Heidegger has attempted the systematic
description of the structures of human existence, Sartre has
used the forms of the novel, the journal and the drama to
convey his existential teaching through *existentiell* situations.
As has been said, there is presented a situation in order to
suggest *the* situation.[29]

Obviously, so vast a subject as the biblical understanding
of the being of man can be treated only very briefly here.
Yet before proceeding any further with the examination of
Bultmann's theology, it will be necessary to show that the
philosophy of existence is not only the 'right' philosophy from
the point of view of theological method, but also—which is
more important if we are aiming, so far as possible, at the
elucidation of the genuine thought of the New Testament—
that this is the philosophy which, more than any other
philosophy, expounds an understanding of the being of man
which has affinity with the understanding of his being
implicit in the thought of the biblical writers.

It may be asserted first that, on the biblical understanding
of his being, man is not simply a part of nature. While both
man and nature are the creation of God, and while man in
his existence is bound up with the world, the being of man, as
made in the image of God,[30] is conceived as quite distinct
from the being of nature. 'Man cannot be submerged in

[28] Wright, *God Who Acts—Biblical Theology as Recital*, S.C.M. Press.
[29] Remark attributed to T. S. Eliot.   [30] Gen. 1.26.

18

nature, or merged in the laws of the cosmos, so long as he remains true to his destiny. The Creator's greatest gift to man, that of the personal "I", necessarily places him, in analogy with God's being, at a distance from nature.'[31] This understanding of the being of man is far removed from Greek attempts to determine and classify his place within the unity of the cosmos, for instance, as a rational animal. It is equally far removed from the Cartesian notion of *res cogitans*, which, however distinct from *res extensa*, still remains *res*, an objective concept which fails to do justice to the personal 'I' that is made in the image of the Creator. And it is poles apart from modern endeavours to understand man scientifically, as though he were nothing but an unusually complicated phenomenon of nature that may, with patience, be ultimately explained in the same kind of way as science explains the rest of nature. But on the other hand, the teaching of the existentialists who maintain that *Existenz* and *Vorhandenheit* are fundamentally different ways of being which must be differently conceived seems to have a certain kinship with the biblical understanding of man. The philosophy of existence does not depersonalize man, as any philosophy which objectifies him must do. It does justice to the claims of the individual personal 'I', and in this important respect we are entitled to say that there is a definite similarity between existentialism and the understanding of the being of man in biblical thought.

Confirmation of the affinity between the two may be obtained from a consideration of some of the main themes in the biblical teaching about man. Among these may be mentioned: individual responsibility before God—which Eichrodt well illustrates from the reiterated demands of the prophets for personal obedience to God, and their protest against the reduction of religion to a collective impersonal cult[32]; man's fall from his true destiny into concern with the creature; his consciousness of guilt; the call for decision; the fleeting nature of man's temporal existence, and its

[31] W. Eichrodt, *Man in the Old Testament*, S.C.M. Press, p. 30.
[32] Eichrodt, *op. cit.*, p. 21.

19

termination by death.[33] But these are remarkably similar to the main themes of existentialist philosophy. The responsibility of the individual confronted with the possibility of being himself and the possibility of losing himself, fallenness, guiltiness, resolve, temporality, death—these are prominent among the phenomena which such a philosopher as Heidegger considers to be constitutive structures of the being of man. It would be strange indeed if the biblical writers and the existentialist philosophers both concentrated attention on the same characteristics—so often neglected—of human life, were there not some fairly close relation between them in their understanding of the being of man.

The biblical concept of God may be adduced as further evidence for the kinship between biblical thought and existentialism. Since the philosophy of existence analyses the understanding of existence which is given with existence, and since this existence is always my existence,[34] that is to say, a human existence, it follows that this philosophy does not directly give an account of the being of God. That it raises the question of God indirectly we shall endeavour to show later, so that we would give only a modified assent to Copleston's contention that 'the problem of God cannot be raised on the plane of the phenomenological analysis of man.'[35] Yet in any case we must understand the being of God as somehow analogous to our own, if we are to speak of him at all. The Bible certainly does so. It thinks of God as personal and historical—'the living God' is a typical and significant expression.[36] This concept is utterly different from the concepts of God which have been current in Greek and western philosophy—the Unmoved Mover, the First Cause, the Timeless Absolute and so on. Where these concepts have influenced theological thought, they have obscured the authentic biblical understanding of God. The

---

[33] These points may be illustrated by, e.g., Gen. 3.6; Ps. 51.3; Josh. 24.15; Ps. 103.15-16.
[34] Cf. Heidegger, *S. u. Z.*, p. 42.
[35] *Existentialism and Modern Man*, Blackfriars, p. 18.
[36] E.g., Ps. 42.2.

difference between such concepts of God and the biblical concept may be expressed by saying that the former understand his being under the categories of substantiality, the latter understands his being under the categories of existentiality.

When someone claims, let us say, that he finds the doctrines of socialism in the New Testament, it is only too easy for him to read into the text what is not there, and to be guilty of the wildest anachronisms. We must, therefore, be very careful when we speak of existentialism in biblical thought. All that we have claimed here is that there is a certain kinship or sympathy between the understanding of being implicit in biblical thought and the understanding of being made explicit by the philosophy of existence. But this is sufficient for our present purpose, which is to show that the ontological presuppositions of a theology such as Bultmann's are not alien to those of the New Testament writers, who took them over from the Old Testament tradition. As a consequence, Bultmann's existential approach to the teaching of the New Testament should not be found to impose upon it ideas foreign to the minds of the writers, but should reveal to us not only how Bultmann understands it, but, so far as possible, its authentic meaning as understood by the New Testament writers themselves.

5. *Existentialism and the Teaching of Jesus*

This subject will be treated here partly because it will supplement the argument of the preceding section, and partly because the teaching of Jesus, like that of the Old Testament, is preliminary to the theology proper of the New Testament.[37] There will be the further advantage that a discussion of Bultmann's treatment of the teaching of Jesus will introduce a line of criticism of his position, which will be more fully developed later.

It is not difficult to find elements in the teaching of our Lord which invite comparison with the teaching of the

[37] Cf. *Th. des NT*, p. 1.

3

existentialists. He protested against the deadening influence of tradition, which had made observance of the law formal and external, so that in the Sermon on the Mount he was able to draw a contrast between the law and the will of God, though these two should have been identical.[38] As against this formal observance, Jesus demanded authentic individual obedience. Rather similarly we find the existentialists protesting against the blind acceptance of the traditions and customs of collective humanity—*das Man*, in Heidegger's expression—and insisting that the individual must understand and decide for himself.

The worst that can happen to a man, Jesus taught, is to lose himself. This he does when he sets his heart on the world and in the process loses his own soul. On the other hand, he is saved when he comes to himself, and through a renunciation of the world finds his true being.[39] With this we compare the existentialist teaching that man is confronted with the basic possibilities of an authentic existence, in which he finds himself, and an inauthentic existence, in which the self is lost and scattered in concern with the world.

Thus man is pressed to a radical decision. He must choose between God and the world—that is to say, between being his true self in a life of obedience to his Creator, and losing himself in serving the creaturely. The whole eschatological teaching of Jesus stresses the urgent need for decision. But in existentialist teaching, also, radical decision has an important place. It is resolve which unifies the self and makes its existence authentic.

So far as this line of thought goes, it may fairly be claimed that there is some affinity between existentialism and the teaching of Jesus, and again Bultmann is cleared of the charge that his philosophical assumptions are foreign to the New Testament. But the question may be raised whether this presentation of the teaching of Jesus goes nearly far enough. According to Bultmann, this would appear to be

[38] E.g., Matt. 5.21-22; cf. *Th. des NT*, p. 12.
[39] E.g., Mark 8.36; Luke 15.17; Matt. 10.39.
[40] Cf. Matt. 6.24.

the essence of what our Lord taught, but to many it will seem a very attenuated account of the matter. Did Jesus have no consciousness of being the Messiah? Was there no reflection of such a consciousness in his teaching? Would men have believed in him apart from it? Was his teaching not closely connected with his own person? These questions are surely not unimportant, but Bultmann does not seem to take them very seriously. They are somewhat dogmatically brushed aside, and it is asserted that Jesus had no consciousness of being the Messiah. Now Bultmann, as a great New Testament scholar, has, of course, been led to this conclusion by his own critical studies. But, on the other hand, his negative attitude to these questions compared with his preoccupation with the existentialist elements in the teaching of Jesus suggests that Bultmann may be unconsciously biased in his presentation because of the influence of existentialism in his thought.

It is very doubtful whether the Christian faith could have been built upon the foundation of a historic Jesus who, as Bultmann presents him, was little more than a teacher of a practical philosophy with certain resemblances to existentialism, and who is stripped of the numinous characteristics which the Gospels ascribe to him. 'There must have been something,' says Professor Henderson, 'about the actual Jesus at the time at which he was on earth, to make the New Testament witnesses summon men to decide for or against him. And if it is so, the historical facts about Jesus, and the mythological element in his life, cannot have quite the subordinate role that Bultmann allots to them.'[41]

We might say that of the three pitfalls mentioned earlier as lying in the path of the unwary theologian who approaches the work of interpreting the Christian faith with certain philosophical presuppositions in his mind, we have sought to show that Bultmann is in little danger from the second and third of these, which were the importing of alien ideas into Christian theology, and the accommodating of that theology to a prevailing philosophical fashion. But his treatment of the

[41] *Myth in the New Testament*, S.C.M. Press, p. 49.

ministry of our Lord indicates that Bultmann may be in considerable danger from the first of the three, which was the over-emphasis of those elements in Christian teaching which are specially congenial to the theologian's philosophical outlook, accompanied by neglect of anything that is not so congenial, with consequent distortion of the whole. This line of criticism will be followed up when we come to consider Bultmann's interpretation of the New Testament theology proper.

6. *A Preliminary View of Bultmann's Position*

Apart from the note of criticism struck in the preceding section, we have so far been principally concerned to defend Bultmann against some of the more obvious and superficial charges that might be made against him for permitting the secular philosophy of existentialism to influence his theological work. We have based this defence on three grounds. The first, and least important, is that Bultmann is simply following the precedent of some of the greatest theologians of the past in making use of contemporary philosophical concepts in his presentation of the Christian faith. It is obvious that there are apologetic possibilities in existentialism which has reinstated in the province of philosophy problems which 'logical positivism would declare to belong to the province of feeling'.[42] The second and more important ground is that since existentialism is specially concerned to analyse the constitution of the being of man, and since the theologian must make certain ontological assumptions about man, this philosophy stands in a special relation to the theologian's work. The third ground is that what existentialism teaches about the being of man has a certain kinship and sympathy with the understanding of his being implicit in biblical thought, so that the theologian who approaches the Bible with an existentialist understanding of being is likely to interpret its teaching in a way which would be faithful to the authentic thought of the biblical writers themselves. If,

[42] Copleston, *Existentialism and Modern Man*, Blackfriars, p. 6.

then, we have succeeded in making out a case for the existential approach to theology as exemplified by the work of Bultmann, we may proceed to the examination of his thought in the knowledge that here we have a serious, legitimate and possibly valuable contribution to the problems of a genuinely Christian theology.

It will be understood, of course, that a purely existential approach to theology is almost impossible, even if it were supposed to be desirable. Consciously or unconsciously, other influences from the long tradition of theological and philosophical thought will enter into any presentation of the Christian faith. This is quite obviously the case in Bultmann's work, where we can detect other influences besides that of the philosophy of existence. Among them we note a strong evangelical and Protestant influence. Like Barth, Bultmann attaches great importance to the concept of the Word. As we shall see, the preaching and hearing of the Word are accorded a key position in his theology. His distinctively Protestant outlook may be illustrated from his interpretation of the sacraments as 'only a special mode of the proclamation of the Word'.[43] Another influence which exerts itself quite noticeably is that of liberal modernism. While Bultmann differs from its positions at many points, it would be surprising if its influence were entirely absent in one who has been known for many years as a radical New Testament critic. In his treatment of the resurrection of Christ, for instance, it appears to me that this influence is combined with the influence of existentialism, and the two must be carefully disentangled if the existential element is to be properly evaluated.

It may seem surprising that in the preceding pages, apart from one passing but not unimportant reference,[44] nothing appears to have been said on the subject of demythologizing. There are two reasons for this. The first is that the notoriety given to this part of Bultmann's work in recent controversy may obscure the fact that it is, after all, only a part of his work, and may detract attention from much of his theology

[43] *Th. des NT*, p. 309.   [44] *Supra*, p. 11.

which is not directly connected with demythologizing but which seems to me of very considerable value. The second reason is that demythologizing can only be properly understood in the light of Bultmann's general theological position. Demythologizing is only a consequence—albeit a very important one—of Bultmann's existential approach to theology, and as such it will be treated in its proper place.

Bultmann holds that there is, strictly speaking, no unitary theology of the New Testament, but a number of theologies, each with its own terminology and distinctive emphasis. He gives pride of place to the Pauline theology which, as was stated already, he expounds as a doctrine of man. This exposition falls into two parts—the life of man without Christ, and the life of man in the Christian faith. In a similar fashion Heidegger, in the exposition of his philosophy, describes first what he calls everyday or inauthentic existence, and then goes on to the problem of an authentic existence. We shall follow the same order in the present inquiry, taking the Pauline theology as the main source for illustrations from the New Testament, but referring also to the Johannine and other writings where necessary. First we shall consider how far the ontological analysis of everyday inauthentic existence, as we find it expounded in existentialist philosophy, throws light on the New Testament teaching on man without faith—the natural man. Then we shall go on to consider how far the idea of an authentic existence elucidates the theology of the life of faith in Christ.

PART ONE

EXISTENCE
AS INAUTHENTIC AND
FALLEN

II

EXISTENCE IN THE WORLD

7. *The Concept of Existence*

OUR subject is the relation of existentialist philosophy to theological thought, and to make the argument concrete it will be illustrated especially from the work of Martin Heidegger, the philosopher, and Rudolf Bultmann, the theologian. Bultmann is probably the most noted exponent of this type of theology; Heidegger fairly represents the existentialist school of philosophy; and further there is, as will be shown, a particularly close connection between these two thinkers. In what follows, therefore, we are confronted with a twofold task: first, to follow Bultmann to the pages of the New Testament, and to determine exactly where and how his interpretation of its teaching is influenced by his ontological assumptions derived from Heidegger's philosophy of existence; and next, to assess the value of such an interpretation, that is, to answer the question whether, as Bultmann himself claims, his eyes have been opened to the meaning of the text, or whether, on the contrary, he has been misled. The most interesting method of accomplishing this task will be to consider side by side and step by step the existential analytic of Heidegger on the one hand, and Bultmann's exposition of the New Testament theology as a doctrine of man on the other. But first we must examine more closely some of the leading ideas of existentialist philosophy, and define more exactly some of its technical terms, already introduced in the preceding pages, and freely used by Bultmann in his theological writings.

Strictly speaking, it might be said that Heidegger is not so much an existentialist as an ontologist. His concern is with the problem of being in general, and his exposition of the being of man was intended to be only an introduction to the wider problem. But Heidegger has not fully carried out this ambitious programme, for his principal work, *Sein und Zeit*, breaks off at the end of the analysis of human existence, and has not been completed. While of his later writings, in which he attacks his main problem, even so acute an interpreter of the thought of Heidegger as H. J. Blackham remarks that they are 'oracular in tone, and one can have no confidence in interpreting the cryptic sentences in which his thought is condensed'.[1] In view of this, it is therefore not unfair to regard Heidegger as primarily an existentialist philosopher, while recognizing his intention to go beyond existentialism.

We begin by noting the distinction between being as such (*Sein*) and being in the sense of that which is (*Seiendes*). The former, in Heidegger's view, is the proper subject of philosophical inquiry; the latter is the subject both of scientific and everyday knowledge. It follows that we can make two kinds of statement about anything. A statement may be ontological (*ontologisch*), that is to say, it will tell us about the being of something and its range of possibilities. Or a statement may be ontical (*ontisch*), that is to say, it will tell us about some entity in its actual relations with other entities. But every ontical statement carries ontological implications, for to say that A is, in fact, B implies that A has the possibility of being B. This is a statement about the being of A, namely, that its being is such that A can be B. Hence arises Heidegger's insistence on the need to examine the ontological assumptions of all ontical inquiries.

Let us now try to clarify these points with an illustration from theology. When Saint Paul says that 'all have sinned' he is making an ontical statement.[2] He is claiming that, in fact, the entity (*das Seiende*) which we call man has fallen into the relationship which we call sin, and that this is true of all men. But clearly this ontical statement can only be properly understood if it is clarified ontologically. Both its subject and predicate remain little more than vague words unless we

[1] *Six Existentialist Thinkers*, Routledge, p. 103.   [2] Rom. 3.23.

30

understand how the being (*das Sein*) of man is such that sin can be a possible way of being for him. On a materialistic and mechanistic view of man, sin, as Saint Paul understood it, would be an illusion. On certain idealistic views of man, it might be possible to construct some concept of sin, but it would be open to question whether or not it represented the genuine Christian understanding of sin. In both cases, however, these are speculative theories, and the Christian theologian is under no obligation to conform to their views. If they teach a view of man which does not allow for the possibility of sin, as the New Testament understands it, then so much the worse for these theories, for they have failed to take into account a fact of Christian experience. An academic theory of being cannot be set up as a standard by which ontical statements are to be tested. Yet we have said, on the other hand, that the ontical must be clarified ontologically, that the fact must be shown to fall within the possible ways of being of the entity about which the statement is made. How, then, do we arrive at this ontological understanding which is necessary for the proper understanding of an ontical statement?

Returning to our example, 'all have sinned', we may say that this statement can be clarified ontologically in two ways. Partly it may be clarified in the light of the whole Pauline theology. That theology not only makes statements about man's actual relationships, but discloses an understanding of his being. The important concept of σῶμα, for instance, with which we shall shortly be occupied, is primarily an ontological concept. Saint Paul's ontical statements about man are made in the light of his own ontological understanding of man. Yet we do not find, and we would not expect to find, a systematic ontology of man explicitly stated in the Pauline writings. That is not the business of the theologian, but of the philosopher. It is to the latter that we must go for a full account of the possibilities of man's being. We are not concerned with speculative philosophies, whether idealistic or materialistic, which try to fit man into some comprehensive world-view. The theologian has no need to adjust his thinking to their teaching. But we are concerned with the existentialist type of philosophy, which is not a speculative metaphysic but simply the philosophical analysis of man's own understanding of his being. Man not only is— he understands that he is, his being is open to himself, and this understanding of being which belongs to man in virtue of his being, however vague it may be at ordinary levels, is capable of being analysed and clarified. It is such an analysis that Heidegger claims to have accomplished in *Sein und Zeit*.

Heidegger prefers to speak not of man but of *Dasein*, a term which he thinks expresses man's peculiar way of being—man considered ontologically. *Dasein* means literally 'being-there', and the reasons for this choice of terminology will become clearer as we proceed. *Dasein* is said to exist, and it is important that we should be clear about the meaning of this basic term, existence (*Existenz*). It does not merely mean to be extant, the traditional sense of *existentia*. For that way of being, Heidegger uses the term *Vorhandenheit*. An inanimate object, such as a stone, is extant, it occurs, but it does not exist in the sense in which Heidegger uses the term. What, then, are the distinctive characteristics of existence?[3]

These may best be explained by contrasting the being of man with the being of a thing (*Vorhandenheit*), for to say that man exists means that in some way he stands outside (*ex-sistere*) the world of things. (*a*) Man has a relation to himself in a way that is peculiar to him as existing. A cricket-ball, as we understand it, is purely an object. But man is not an object. He is at once subject and object to himself, or as is said, he transcends the subject-object relationship. He understands himself, is open to himself in his being. He can be at one with himself or at war with himself, he can be himself or lose himself. The examination of this relation of *Dasein* to himself is one of the main concerns of existentialist philosophy. (*b*) Man is possibility. He is always more than he is, his being is never complete at any given moment. He therefore has no essence as an object has. The essential

[3]Cf. *S. u. Z.*, p. 41 ff.

properties of a cricket-ball are a certain size and weight, redness, rotundity, resistance, and so on. These give a more or less complete description of it. But because man as existing is possibility, and is never fixed or complete in his being, he is not to be described in terms of the 'objective properties of something merely extant, but his possible ways of being, and only these'.[4] It will be understood, of course, that by possibility the existentialist does not mean mere contingency, something that may happen (for in that sense a thing also would have infinite possibilities), but a possibility of decision, a way of being which man, because he exists, can choose for himself. (c) Man is individual. This is the characteristic of existence which Heidegger terms *Jemeinigkeit*—existence is always mine. One cricket-ball is pretty much like another. They are all made to a standard pattern, and while there are no doubt minor differences, it is true to say that if we have seen one, we have seen them all. Things can be classified—indeed not only science but everyday life would be impossible were we unable to classify and expect that one object will behave in the same way as others in the same class. But man as existing is an individual and defies classification. This is a point on which existentialism does justice to the biblical understanding of men as individual creatures of the Father[5] and sets itself in opposition to the tendency of modern scientific humanism to regard the being of man as at bottom no different from the being of things, and therefore amenable to study by scientific methods. Of course, this is not to deny value to the social sciences. But it is to indicate their severe limitations. We read, for instance, that 'loose thinking and prejudice are extremely prevalent in matters of politics, economics, religion, crime and the like ... yet the social sciences, such as psychology and sociology, are endeavouring to study these subjects rationally and impartially, in the same manner as the physicist studies the atom, or the physiologist the workings of the body.'[6] The sciences mentioned are highly abstract, since they must select as their data such

[4] *S. u. Z.*, p. 42.   [5] Cf. Matt. 10.29-31.
[6] Vernon, *The Measurement of Abilities*, Univ. Lond., Pref., pp. v-vi.

facts about man as are measurable, either statistically or in some other way. The information thus gained is valuable, but we should understand that what has been excluded in this 'impartial' investigation is precisely that which is distinctively human. It is interesting to know that a family of 2·3 children is necessary to maintain the population of these islands at its present level, or that the average American woman has 3·7 romances in her life. But, of course, this says absolutely nothing about the human phenomena of the family and love. The distinctively human is characterized by *Jemeinigkeit*—existence is always my existence, individual, unique, personal. It is never as such a classifiable object.

This last point raises the question whether and how existence can be described. If *Dasein*'s existence is always his own, then is it not futile to attempt an analysis of the being of *Dasein* which would be true for every *Dasein*? To answer this question, we must note the distinction which is made between what are termed *existentiell* (*existenziell*) and 'existential' (*existenzial*) possibilities. The concrete practical possibilities of the individual *Dasein* are his *existentiell* possibilities. But there are horizons to *Dasein*'s possibilities—limits within which every individual existence must fall. These wide possibilities are called existential, and their investigation is the subject of the existential analytic of *Dasein*. What we have, then, is not an attempt to describe universal properties of *Dasein*—which would be impossible, since *Dasein* is not an object, but exists—but an attempt to show the horizons of possibility within which the concrete possibilities of every individual *Dasein* must fall. Used as a noun, the term 'existential' (*Existenzial*) denotes one of the broad fundamental possibilities of *Dasein*'s being, in analogy to the term category which denotes one of the basic formal characters of an object. The systematic description of all the fundamental possible ways of being of *Dasein* is called the existentiality (*Existenzialität*) of existence.

By what method is the task of an existential analytic of *Dasein* to be carried out? The scientific method which discovers the general properties and behaviour of an object

34

has already been ruled out, as unsuitable to the study of that which exists. The method used by Heidegger is that of phenomenology, and while we cannot go fully into this subject here, something must be said about it, more particularly as we already suggested that Bultmann might be said to regard theology as a kind of phenomenology of faith. The phenomenological method stems from Husserl,[7] who developed it in reaction against the scientific positivism which had begun to prevail at the end of the nineteenth century. He pointed out that the knowledge of nature gained by science never attains certainty or finality. It is subject to constant revision and correction. Further, the scientific method is not itself a piece of scientific knowledge. The scientist must make in his investigation of nature assumptions and presuppositions which science itself cannot establish. Husserl believed that certainty is attained when the attention is directed to the experiences of the self which stands outside nature, without raising the question of the reality to which these experiences are supposed to refer. The exploration of the experiences of the self consists not in reasonings but in descriptions of what shows itself, namely, the phenomenon.

Heidegger has adapted the phenomenological method to his own purposes,[8] but substantially it remains as we have described it. For Heidegger phenomenology is directed to being—the being which shows itself in *Dasein*'s own understanding of himself. The existential analytic consists in the descriptive analysis of that which is revealed to *Dasein* in his own self-disclosure as existing. And this method of investigation, the phenomenologists would claim, yields in its own field results more securely based than any knowledge that we can have of nature.

On the subject of the relation of phenomenology to theology, Tillich claims that:

'theology must apply the phenomenological approach to all its basic concepts, forcing its critics first of all to see

[7] See his own art., 'Phenomenology', *Enc. Britt.* 14th Edn.
[8] Cf. *S. u. Z.*, pp. 27-39.

35

what the criticized concepts mean, and also forcing itself to make careful descriptions of its concepts and to use them with logical consistency, thus avoiding the danger of trying to fill in logical gaps with devotional material. The test of a phenomenological description is that the picture given by it is convincing, that it can be seen by anyone who is willing to look in the same direction, that the description illuminates other related ideas, and that it makes the reality which these ideas are supposed to reflect understandable.'[9]

These points are worth bearing in mind, particularly in assessing Bultmann's treatment of the Pauline theology.

Returning, however, to Heidegger's phenomenological method, we find dozens of examples of this careful analysis in his work—indeed the minute detailed descriptions become somewhat tedious as the method is applied to one phenomenon after another. We will give one illustration here, the analysis of fear,[10] which shows very clearly this method of descriptive analysis of the constitutive structures of a phenomenon which is open to *Dasein* as understanding himself. Heidegger begins with that which is feared, and carefully analyses its characteristics: it is injurious, its harmful character is directed on a certain area which it renders insecure, it is not yet present but is approaching, it is uncertain in the sense that it may pass by, but this uncertainty does not lessen the fear but fosters it. He then proceeds to the description of fearing. This is the discovery of something as terrible, which implies, Heidegger thinks, that the world is understood *a priori* to be such that out of it something terrible may appear. And, finally, Heidegger turns to *Dasein* himself, who fears for the sake of himself, and asks what this phenomenon reveals in the being of *Dasein*. It reveals his possibility of danger, and incidentally throws light on Heidegger's choice of the term *Dasein* since it draws attention to the sheer fact of *Dasein's* being situated in a world where his being is threatened—he simply is there.

This illustration of fear, as well as showing us Heidegger's

9 *Systematic Theology*, Nisbet, I, p. 118.   10 *S. u. Z.*, pp. 140-142.

method of phenomenological analysis, may be used also to show the distinctive nature of the existential analytic. For it may be asked whether the being of man is not already analysed and described for us in psychology, history, theology and other subjects which make a study of man in his various activities. But how other disciplines differ from the existential analytic may be illustrated if we consider, for instance, how the psychologist, might describe fear. He would tell us[11] about the organic state of the fearing subject, the action of the sympathetic nervous system and the endocrine glands, the effect upon the action of the heart, stomach and other organs, the preparation of the entire organism for sudden action in the emergency which has arisen, and so on. Quite clearly, what we have here is an ontical account of fear, whereas Heidegger has given us an ontological or existential account. He has analysed fear as a way of being of *Dasein*, and the whole existential analytic is of the same kind. It describes *Dasein* in respect of his being, and is more fundamental than any ontical or scientific description of human activity, and is indeed required for the proper interpretation of the latter.

We now have before us a preliminary view of the concept of existence, and the method by which existence may be analysed and described. The existentialist philosopher claims that man must always be understood as a 'who' and not as a 'what', and further that, because existence implies with it the understanding of existence, there is open to man the possibility of a knowledge of the 'who' more certain and more fundamental than any knowledge that he can reach of the 'what'. We now proceed to the existential analytic proper, and its bearing on theology.

8. *Man and the World*

Man exists, in the sense which we have endeavoured to explain in the preceding pages, that is to say, he has a relation to himself, he is confronted with possibilities, and he is

11 Cf. e.g., Woodworth, *Psychology*, Methuen, p. 419 ff.

individually unique in his being. This concept of existence carries with it two implications which are important for our purpose.

The first is that man is in a world. Heidegger is never tired of attacking the notion of a pure ego, or a bare subject.[12] Man is always already in a world which is, so to speak, his *Spielraum*, the field within which his possibilities confront him. Whether the world is ideal or material, or whether there are both ideal and material worlds, are speculative questions which need not be raised on the level of the existential analytic. The point is simply this, that with the understanding of his own existence there is given to man the idea of the world, something other than himself, an environment in which he is set. Biologists, psychologists and educationists all understand the importance of the relations of man to his environment, but their interest in these relations is naturally confined to certain ontical aspects. Heidegger is interested in the problem from the ontological point of view.

He has little difficulty in showing the obscurities which beset philosophies which begin with the notion of a self-contained subject and seek to relate it to an object. Descartes' *res cogitans* and *res extensa* come in for special criticism. This philosophy—and other traditional philosophies share the defect—is bedevilled by the idea of substance, which, Heidegger claims, is a category inapplicable to the being of man. Man exists, and the world is already given with his existence, so there is no need to work out the problem of how a world of objects can be known to the mind—indeed the attempt to do so rests on a misunderstanding of the being of man. Kant thought that it was a scandal to philosophy and human intelligence that there was lacking a cogent proof for the reality of a world outside ourselves. Heidegger's reply is that the true scandal of philosophy is not that such a proof is lacking, but that it was ever looked for.[13] Man as existing is always already in a world. And if he were not in a world—whether it be this world of space and time, or some other world beyond our ken—then he would no longer exist. The

[12] Cf. *S. u. Z.*, pp. 114-117.   [13] *S. u. Z.*, p. 203 ff.

pure ego, the thinking substance, is a fiction, for if I think, I already have an object for my thought. Heidegger would restate the famous argument, '*Cogito ergo sum*', in some such words as, 'I think something, therefore I am in a world.'[14]

This fundamental character of existence Heidegger denotes by the hyphenated expression 'being-in-the-world' (*In-der-Welt-sein*). This being-in-the-world is a unity within which we may distinguish through analysis the self on the one hand and the world on the other, but from which we may not separate either of them. We said already that Heidegger's interest in being-in-the-world is ontological or existential. It follows, therefore, that the preposition in the expression must be understood in an existential, not a spatial, sense. To call man 'being-in-the-world' is to say something about him quite different from saying, for instance, that the Isle of Arran is in the Firth of Clyde. 'Being-in' (*Insein*) is an existential, a way of being. Being-in-the-world expresses the character of man that as existing he is bound up with the world, he has to do with it, he is occupied with it. The general term used by Heidegger to express this relation of *Dasein* to his world is concern (*Besorgen*). To be in the world does not mean for man merely to be located in it, as a rock is, but to be concerned with it in his existence.

We now turn to the second implication contained in the concept of existence. It is that existence can be either authentic (*eigentlich*) or inauthentic (*uneigentlich*). These are the fundamental possibilities which confront man in his existence. What exactly is meant by these terms?

Heidegger's view at this point could almost be expressed in Johannine terminology by saying that man is in the world but not of the world.[15] He is in the world in the sense already explained—so long as he exists, his existence is bound up with the world and he has to do with it. But being-in-the world is quite different from being within the world (*Innerweltlichkeit*) in the sense of belonging to the world, being a part of it, as a physical object is. This is once again the difference between *Existenz* and *Vorhandenheit*. Man is

[14] Cf. *S. u. Z.*, p. 211.   [15] John 17.15-16.

always in the world, and yet he is quite distinct from it in his way of being. But in his intimate concern with the world, claims Heidegger, '*Dasein* can lose himself to the being that meets him in the world, and be taken over by it.'[16] Because he has a relation to himself, man can become an object to himself, and can understand himself as one object among the other objects in his world. This is what is meant by an inauthentic existence—man becomes merged in the world. He exists authentically when, instead of being enslaved to the world, he is free for his world, in Heidegger's phrase. In that case he resolves to be himself in the face of a world the being of which is alien to his own being. These fundamental possibilities of authenticity and inauthenticity may be expressed in another way by saying that man can either gain himself or lose himself.

'But what,' it may be asked, 'has all this to do with the faith once delivered to the saints—or with the interpretation of it which is the business of the theologian?' Admittedly we have made a fairly long excursus at this point into the technicalities of existentialism, but that was necessary if we are to follow Bultmann's exposition of New Testament teaching and assess the value of his work. However, we now return to the theological problem, and first to the Pauline concept of σῶμα which Bultmann treats as an ontological concept and believes to be of first-class importance for the understanding of the whole Pauline theology, and therefore of much of Christian theology in general.

Bultmann says that the concept of σῶμα is the most comprehensive of the Pauline anthropological concepts, and also the most complicated and difficult to understand.[17] It will be understood, therefore, that here we have a key concept, and that much of Bultmann's subsequent exposition of the New Testament teaching rests upon his interpretation of σῶμα. The term is used in various senses by Saint Paul. We leave aside for the present all passages in which he speaks of 'the body of Christ', since that is a specialized usage. Again, in passages such as that in which he speaks of the destruction

16 *S. u. Z.*, p. 76.　　　　17 *Th. des NT*, p. 189 ff.

40

of the 'body of sin',[18] he uses the term σῶμα to express a concept for which he more commonly uses the term σάρξ, which will also be treated later. For Saint Paul did not share the Gnostic view that the body is necessarily evil. On the contrary, he taught that 'the body is not for fornication but for the Lord . . . it is the temple of the Holy Ghost.'[19] But when special usages have been set aside, there is still a bewildering range of statements and phrases from which the characteristic meaning must be sought.

Bultmann's own discussion of the concept of σῶμα is fairly complicated. Broadly speaking, he approaches the problem with the assumption that σῶμα stands for a way of being, and more particularly, a way of being in virtue of which man is in a world. While guarding against the dangers of over-simplification, we will endeavour to expound his interpretation of σῶμα as three fundamental propositions concerning the being of man.

(a) Man's existence is always somatic. The body is constitutive of the being of man, and Saint Paul cannot conceive him without a body. Even in the life to come, man will still be a body[20]—not indeed a body of flesh and blood, but nevertheless a body of some kind. Saint Paul follows the Hebrew rather than the Greek understanding of man. For him man is a unity, and the body is his characteristic way of being. There is no hint here of man's being compounded of a material substance called a body and an immaterial substance called a soul. The body, as Saint Paul uses the term, is a way of being—not a substance or a thing. It can, of course, be considered as a purely physical structure, but that is the concern of the anatomist. When Saint Paul says, 'Let not sin therefore reign in your mortal body,'[21] he is obviously not thinking of tissues of bone and muscle and so on, but of man's way of being in a world where sin is possible. To be a body means that man does not exist as a bare discarnate ego—he is always in a world where possibilities confront him.

There are, of course, some passages in Saint Paul's writings

[18] Rom. 6.6.
[20] I Cor. 15.35 ff.
[19] I Cor. 6.13, 19.
[21] Rom. 6.12.

which suggest another point of view. The most obvious is that in which he seems to speak of absence from the body as equivalent to presence with the Lord.[22] This rather looks like the Gnostic view of the liberation of the soul from the body. Yet a glance at the preceding verses shows that Saint Paul believed that on the dissolution of the earthly body the believer would be 'clothed' anew, that is to say, his existence would still be somatic. In speaking of his own mystical experience of the risen Lord, Saint Paul says that he does not know whether this experience were 'in the body, or out of the body'.[23] This, however, is an exceptional way of speaking, and seems to mean simply that he did not know whether his vision was perceived by the bodily senses or by some super-natural insight. In any case, neither of these passages is sufficient to overthrow the characteristic interpretation of somatic existence as found in Saint Paul's writings.

(b) Man in his being has a relation to himself. 'He can make himself the object of his own action.'[24] And to express this reflexive action, if we may so call it, Saint Paul customarily uses the term $\sigma\hat{\omega}\mu\alpha$. Thus he says that man can abuse himself or master himself; that he can surrender himself to sin; or that he can offer himself to God.[25] In these examples $\sigma\hat{\omega}\mu\alpha$ stands for the object-self, yet it is the same man who is at once subject and object to himself, so that we have here expressed the relatedness of man to himself in his being.

(c) Man has two fundamental possibilities: he can be at one with himself or he can be estranged from himself. This follows from what has been said about man having a relation to himself. He may master himself or he may lose himself and live at war with himself. When Saint Paul does on occasion seem to approach to the Gnostic understanding of the being of man as a soul imprisoned in an alien body, it is, Bultmann suggests, because he had become so acutely aware of the split within the self in a sinful existence that his thought assumes a dualistic form—or at least appears to come very close to it.[26] When the body has fallen completely into sin it

22 II Cor. 5.8.   23 II Cor. 12.2.   24 *Th. des NT*, p. 192.
25 Cf. I Cor. 9.27; Rom. 6.12 ff; 12.1.   26 *Th. des NT*, p. 195 ff.

becomes 'the body of death'[27] from which man must be rescued—but this means deliverance from the σάρξ, the evil possibilities of somatic existence, and not from the body as such, the possibilities of which may be either good or bad. The Gnostic view that the body is alien, an encumbrance to man's true being, leads naturally either to asceticism or to libertinism. The body does not matter. But if the body is man's necessary way of being, both of these extremes are excluded, and that is surely the typical Pauline and Christian view.

The three propositions, that man's existence is always somatic, that therefore he has a relation to himself, and that he is confronted with the two basic possibilities of either being at one with himself or estranged from himself, clearly constitute an existential interpretation of the concept of σῶμα. This interpretation which Bultmann puts forward immediately invites comparison with Heidegger's teaching that man is always being-in-the-world, that he exists in the sense of being related to himself, and that his existence can be authentic or inauthentic. But what are we to say of Bultmann's exposition of the concept? If it is valid, then it is a further confirmation of what has been already suggested, namely, that there is a kinship between existentialism and New Testament thought, so that what we have called the existential approach to theology is likely to lead us to the authentic thought of the New Testament writers. On the other hand, it may be contended that this interpretation of the concept of σῶμα is due simply to the ascendancy of existentialist influences in Bultmann's thinking. If the question is raised whether the text itself supports the interpretation of σῶμα which Bultmann expounds, I do not think that a conclusive answer can be given either way. There is insufficient exegetical evidence to prove conclusively that Bultmann's interpretation is the right one, yet on the other hand he can adduce sufficient evidence to show that his view is at least a reasonable and possible interpretation.

The validity of Bultmann's exposition may, however, be

[27] Rom. 7.24.

tested from another angle. If it can be shown that Bultmann's existential interpretation of the concept of σῶμα throws light on any difficult passage of Pauline theology, and enables us to make better sense of it than other interpretations of σῶμα do, then that would weigh the balance significantly in Bultmann's favour. As an example we take the notoriously difficult doctrine of the resurrection of the body, as Saint Paul teaches it in his First Epistle to the Corinthians.

It is generally agreed that this doctrine, as opposed to a belief in the survival of a soul apart from the body, is intended to teach the continuation of the entire personality into the life to come. But that in itself does not answer the question of what can be meant by the resurrection of the body. The crucial element in Saint Paul's teaching on this subject is contained in the verse: 'It is sown a natural body; it is raised a spiritual body. There is a natural body, and there is a spiritual body.'[28] How do we understand this?

Normally, western man understands the body to be a substance. About the natural body there is no difficulty—it is the mortal body of flesh and blood, the physical organism. But what of the spiritual body? The trouble is that he understands spirit to be a substance also, but an immaterial substance, entirely different in its nature from the substance of the body. The idea of these two substances of which man is supposed to be compounded comes not from the New Testament but from Greek thought, yet it has become so much a part of the western outlook that it is used to interpret the New Testament. Hence the difficulty with the spiritual body. At first sight this looks like a contradiction in terms. If spirit and body are two entirely different kinds of substance, how can there be a spiritual body? An attempt is made to get round the difficulty by imagining some kind of ethereal stuff, midway between spirit and body. This seems to be the view taken by commentators who work with the concept of substance, and are forced to imagine the spiritual body as a kind of ghostly replica of the natural body, differing from it only in 'being freed from some of its previous limitations'[29]—

[28] I Cor. 15.44. [29] Evans, *Corinthians*, O.U.P., p. 139.

that is to say, not subject to all the laws which normally govern the behaviour of physical bodies. This is a far from satisfactory interpretation. Not only is it highly speculative, but it seems also to be materialistic or animistic in its tendencies. Moreover, it may be questioned whether such an interpretation would really ensure that continuity of personality which is implied in the doctrine of the resurrection of the body. And similar difficulties will beset any interpretation which, explicitly or implicitly, understands the body under the category of substance.

But now let us set aside the notion of substance, and try to understand the natural body and the spiritual body existentially. That means that we must understand the natural body and the spiritual body as ways of being. The first describes man's way of being upon earth, the second the Christian believer's way of being in the world to come. Ontologically, his being is the same in both cases—he is a body, he exists in a world. Thus the principle of continuity is safeguarded. But ontically there is a difference. On earth he is always more or less estranged from himself, in the life to come he is at one with himself. For πνεῦμα, like σῶμα, is to be understood not as a substance but as a way of being. It is that way of being in which man is truly himself, as opposed to σάρξ, in which he loses himself to the world. Thus understood, there is no contradiction and, indeed, no difficulty in Saint Paul's mention of the spiritual body. The passage, when it is interpreted in an existential context of ideas appropriate to its subject-matter, which is man, becomes simple and intelligible.

It may be objected that we have made the interpretation too simple, by those who still hanker after some metaphysical explanation of the life to come. But to that objection it may be replied that Saint Paul wrote to answer concrete questions of human existence, not to satisfy the curiosity of philosophers, and that must be remembered in the interpretation of his writings. His theology is not philosophical construction but the exposition of the content of faith—it is existential in the sense that it exhibits man's way of being as believing. If an

45

existential explanation seems inadequate and we look for some abstruse metaphysical doctrine in his treatment of the resurrection of the body, his reply might well be: 'Eye hath not seen, nor ear heard, neither have entered into the heart of man, the things which God hath prepared for them that love him. But God hath revealed them unto us by his Spirit.'[30] Saint Paul is not concerned to solve intellectual problems but to set before men *existentiell* possibilities. The risen life in Christ is not a philosophical conception but a possibility for which men are asked to decide. Thus it may be claimed that Bultmann's existential interpretation of somatic existence not only renders intelligible a difficult passage in Saint Paul's writings, but brings it from the realms of speculation to the actual problems of human existence.

We have so far confined our attention almost exclusively to the Pauline theology. But Bultmann extends his existential approach to the other New Testament writings also, and before we leave this general discussion of the concept of existence in the world and its implications, we must look at the Johannine theology also. Attention was already drawn to the significance of the Johannine way of speaking of being in the world but not of the world. There is, however, in the Johannine writings no key ontological concept comparable to the Pauline $\sigma\tilde{\omega}\mu\alpha$. The argument for an existential interpretation here must, therefore, rest on the question how far it makes the Johannine theology intelligible, and how far the implicit understanding of the being of man which can be discerned in the Johannine writings is akin to the concept of existence. So far as the Johannine writings take over the same assumptions derived from Hebrew thought as did Saint Paul, we would expect to find a similar understanding of man's existence in the thought of both. That this is indeed so Bultmann argues from his consideration of what he calls the Johannine dualism. By this he means the contrasted concepts which occur throughout the Johannine writings—light and darkness, truth and falsehood, life and death, freedom and enslavement.[31] This dualistic way of speaking suggests a

[30] I Cor. 2.9.   [31] E.g., John 1.5; 6.33; 8.32, etc.

Gnostic provenance. But whereas Gnosticism attributed darkness, falsehood and the other negative concepts to the working of evil powers, and rested on an ultimate metaphysical dualism, in the Johannine writings in which God is acknowledged as Creator of the world they must be interpreted in the light of some such concept of existence as we have described. They are possibilities of decision. These concepts 'gain all their meaning from the question of human existence, and express the double possibility in man's existing.'[32] That double possibility is to live from God, or to live from human resources—for man to be himself as the child of God, or to lose himself in the world.

9. *The World*

We saw that man is always in a world, and that Heidegger uses the expression being-in-the-world to indicate a fundamental characteristic of human existence, namely, man's intercourse in the world with entities belonging to the world.[33] 'Being-in' here meant an existential relation, and is to be distinguished from the physical relation of being within the world, which characterizes the things with which man is concerned in the world. They belong to the world, whereas man as existing stands apart from it. To reach the existential understanding of the world we begin with the consideration of the things within the world (*das innerweltliche Seiende*) which confront man in his practical concern as being-in-the-world.

'The Greeks,' says Heidegger, 'had an appropriate name for things, namely, πράγματα, that is, what we have to do with in πρᾶξις or active intercourse.'[34] He goes on to say that, unfortunately (from his point of view), when the Greeks came to philosophize they neglected the pragmatic character of things and considered them as mere things (*blosse Dinge*) objects of theoretical study rather than of practical concern. This led them to explain the being of what is within the world in terms of substantiality, extension and so on, and to understand the world as a self-contained cosmos. In constructing

32 *Th. des NT*, p. 367.   33 *S. u. Z.*, p. 67.   34 *S. u. Z.*, p. 68.

47

the existential concept of the world Heidegger returns to the pragmatic character of the entities within the world as they confront man in his concern. They are characterized as *zuhanden* rather than merely *vorhanden*—they are to hand, immediately present to my concern, rather than mere objects for contemplation or observation. The German term *Zuhandenheit* conveys the further sense of being handy or useful. What is in the world is of use to me, it is an instrument (*Zeug*).

This applies not only to things like writing materials, garden implements, vehicles and the like, which are obviously instrumental in character, but to objects in nature which might at first sight seem to be remote from man's concern. The forest is timber, the mountain is a quarry, the river is a canal, all are actually or potentially instruments. Even the celestial bodies can be used as instruments for telling the time, finding the way and so on. To quote one of Heidegger's own examples,[35] the south wind may be considered as purely an object (*vorhanden*), namely, a stream of air with a given geographical direction. When the farmer makes use of the south wind as an indication of rainy weather to come, this is not just an additional property of the wind, it is man's discovery of its instrumental character so that it ceases to be merely *vorhanden* and becomes *zuhanden*. The mere thing, Heidegger maintains, is potentially an instrument not yet understood, and as man learns to use it, he also discovers it in its being.

Does this look like pure subjectivism? We reserve this point for discussion later. Meantime we are coming into view of the existential concept of the world as an instrumental system. That which is immediately to hand has the character of escaping notice (*Unauffälligkeit*). My attention is not directed to the pen in my hand but to what I am writing, not to the telephone I use but to the person at the other end of the line. The instrument immediately to hand only comes into the focus of attention when something goes wrong with it—for instance, the pen runs dry or the telephone goes dead. Then we suddenly become aware of its place in an entire

[35] *S. u. Z.*, pp. 80-81.

instrumental system. For each individual instrument carries with it its implications (*Bewandtnisse*).[36] The fountain-pen in my hand implies ink to fill it and paper on which to write, the paper implies the paper-mills and the raw materials and so on. As an instrument, everything has a reference (*Verweisung*) to something else, and the totality of these references constitutes the significance (*Bedeutsamkeit*) of the world. These references are brought into a unity in that they are all directed to one end—they are for the sake of *Dasein*. Now, since every instrument implies a reference to the whole system, the idea of the world is already present implicitly in the understanding of the individual instrument. Thus the world, as Heidegger understands it, is an *a priori* concept of an instrumental system founded in man's practical concern.

The world, in Heidegger's view, is therefore not primarily an objective cosmos, the laws of which are to be discovered by the intellectual activity of science, but a workshop[37] which man, as being-in-the-world, constructs in his practical concern. The implications of this concept of the world will be more fully clarified when we go on to discuss Heidegger's view of understanding. Meanwhile, to complete the picture, we note briefly the existential concept of spatiality. The pure extension of geometrical science is an abstraction prior to which comes the space of practical concern. This is conceived as a system of places, analogous to the system of instruments which constitutes the world. A place (*Platz*) is not a mere location (*Raumstelle*).[38] It is to be understood in relation to man's practical concern—everything that he uses has its place where he will find it to hand. He constructs for himself a system of places in which he moves in his everyday concerns. This system also escapes notice until something forces our attention upon it—for instance, we remove from one house to another, nothing can be found in its place, and we realize for the first time how much we relied upon the system of places which we had constructed. Distance also is primarily understood in relation to concern. The interlocutor at the other end of the telephone line is near to my concern, even

36 *S. u. Z.*, p. 83 ff.   37 *S. u. Z.*, p. 75.   38 *S. u. Z.*, p. 102.

49

if, in terms of the objective measurement of distance, he is a hundred miles away. Man has a tendency to annul space and bring things nearer to himself, for instance, in speedier transport and telecommunications of various kinds. It is true that the distance in terms of miles remains the same, but it is reduced from the point of view of man's concerns, and in Heidegger's view the space of practical concern is prior to the space of geometry and exact measurement, and the condition of it. While time is considered by Heidegger to be quite different in its character from space, the primary reckoning of time is also in terms of my concern. There is a time to get up, a time to go out to work and so on.

In his everyday inauthentic existence, man is absorbed in his concern with the world. He is at home (*vertraut*) in the world, he understands himself and his possibilities from the world, he seeks his security in it.[39] He loses himself in the world and regards himself as belonging to the world. But in that case has not man ceased to exist, since existence was defined by distinguishing the being of man from the being of what is within the world, the objects of the world? Heidegger himself answers this objection. It could only hold, he says, if man were an isolated subject, and the world his object. Then to be lost in the world would mean that he, too, had become an object. But man is always already being-in-the-world, and even inauthenticity is a possibility of being-in-the-world. Man can only lose himself because he exists, and stands before the possibility of losing himself.[40]

The complete existential concept of the world has therefore two sides to it: (*a*) The world is an instrumental system, a workshop, to be understood in relation to man's practical concern. (*b*) The world is a threat to man's authentic existence, in so far as he can lose himself in it, and conceal from himself the difference between his own being and the being of what is within the world.

The New Testament term for the world of things is generally not κόσμος, as in Greek philosophy, but κτίσις, the creation. Sometimes in the Johannine writings κόσμος means

[39] Cf. *S. u. Z.*, p. 54.   [40] *S. u. Z.*, p. 179.

the created world, but both there and in the Pauline writings this term usually has a different significance, as we shall see later. In any case, the Greek concept of a self-contained rational cosmos is one that is quite alien to biblical thought. The Old Testament writers speak often enough of the world of nature, but they appear to have no interest in what might be called the scientific view of nature. The New Testament writers, accepting this tradition of thought, are equally indifferent to anything like a scientific view of nature.

What, then, is their concept of the world? The term used by Saint Paul for the world is, as was mentioned already, κτίσις, the creation. Bultmann points out that this term has a twofold significance for Saint Paul:[41] (a) The creation is the work of God, made by him for man's use and enjoyment. 'The earth is the Lord's, and the fulness thereof.'[42] As such, the creation is good. Here Saint Paul is following the Old Testament teaching. God himself is author of the creation, and he considered it to be good; it is a garden for man to cultivate; it is the sphere over which man has been set.[43] Clearly what we have here is something like a religious interpretation of the existential concept of the world as a workshop, primarily to be understood in relation to man's practical concerns. (b) But the creation can also be conceived as hostile. It has fallen under the dominion of evil powers[44]— and here presumably we see a Gnostic influence combining with the Old Testament tradition in the Pauline concept of the created world. But while Saint Paul sometimes uses Gnostic terminology, it seems clear that in his view the creation (which is God's creation) can be hostile not because it belongs to evil powers external to man, but because man himself has given to it these possibilities of evil. The real trouble is that man has 'worshipped and served the creature (κτίσις) more than the Creator'.[45] Because he has done so, the creation has, so to speak, gone corrupt in his hands, and instead of being a thing of use it becomes a threat to his being. It can become 'a hostile destroying force if man has decided

41 *Th. des NT*, p. 226.   42 I Cor. 10.26.
43 Gen. 1.31; Gen. 2.8 ff; Ps. 8.6.   44 Rom. 8.22.   45 Rom. 1.25.

for it instead of for God, that is, if he founds his life upon it instead of upon God'.[46] Man as existing stands apart from the world. He is between the world and God, and he can decide to build his life on the one or the other. Again we have here something like a religious statement of the second side of the existential concept of the world as the alien being in which man can lose himself.

The corresponding Johannine teaching may be summarized in Bultmann's phrase as 'the perversion (*Verkehrung*) of the creation into the world.'[47] As an illustration there may be quoted the double use of the term κόσμος in the verse, 'the world was made by him, and the world knew him not.'[48] Here we have together the thought of the world as the creation of God and the thought of the world as hostile power. But since we have here been principally concerned with the term κτίσις, further discussion of the term κόσμος will be deferred until later.

The foregoing discussion has shown how the existential concept of the world is used by Bultmann to interpret the New Testament concept of the creation. The problem is related to the possibilities of human existence, and the New Testament teaching on this subject is expounded within the horizon of these possibilities. The interpretation offered by Bultmann appears to be intelligible and satisfying, and it does not seem to do violence to the text of the New Testament. But is the existential concept of the world a valid one? Is it not subjective, or even fanciful, in its thought of an instrumental system, or a world which tempts man to lose himself? Over against it stands the scientific attitude to the world with its claim to be objective, impersonal and unprejudiced. Is that not the true picture, and the one in the light of which we should seek to interpret the biblical concept of the world? But if we do seek so to interpret it, we seem to find that there is no point of contact. The biblical concept of the world seems to be as far removed from the scientific view as is the existential concept, and to be equally fanciful and unrealistic from the viewpoint of one accustomed to look upon nature

[46] *Th. des NT*, p. 226.   [47] *Th. des NT*, p. 372.   [48] John 1.10.

scientifically. Or, on the other hand, does the existentialist concept of the world represent the rediscovery of truths long neglected, and which are present also in the biblical concept of the world? To these questions we must now address ourselves, and this will involve a consideration of what we mean by understanding.

III

THE DISCLOSURE OF
EXISTENCE

10. *Understanding*

WHEN we speak of understanding, we commonly think of an intellectual activity which leads to theoretical knowledge. To understand anything means to know its properties and behaviour, and the most exact understanding is of the kind which we call scientific. Against this excessive intellectualism, however, Heidegger and other existentialist thinkers protest. For Heidegger, 'understanding always touches on the whole constitution of being-in-the-world'.[1] That is to say, it is not purely or even primarily theoretical, but is rooted in man's way of being as practically concerned with his world. We all know that theoretical understanding is not the only kind of understanding. I may understand the working of the internal combustion engine, the principles of transmitting power and so on, but that in itself will not enable me to drive a car. For that I need a different kind of knowledge which must be acquired by practice. Yet the latter seems to be at least equally as important as the former, and is equally entitled to be called understanding. I may be thoroughly conversant with the rules of cricket, but it does not follow that therefore I can emulate Sir Donald Bradman with the bat. That would require a practical understanding of the same kind as I need for driving a car. It is worth noting that a child's first question about any novel object is usually, 'What is it for?' That is the question of practical concern. The child seeks to understand things in terms of their use. An infant may be

[1] *S. u. Z.*, p. 144.

54

said to have understood a spoon when he lifts it to his mouth. He has discovered its serviceability, though he is still ignorant of its objective properties—for instance, whether it is of wood or horn or silver. To quote one of Heidegger's own illustrations, consider the sentence, 'The hammer is heavy.'[2] For everyday understanding this does not mean that a certain object, called a hammer, has a certain property, namely, heaviness. It is understood in relation to practical concern, and it issues in changing the unsuitable instrument for a lighter one. Indeed the understanding is there in the act of substitution, even if nothing is said. It need not be formulated in words at all. The world is not primarily an object of contemplation but the field of my concern, and my everyday understanding of it and statements about it relate to that concern. Things are understood as *zuhanden* rather than *vorhanden*, to use the terms which we met in connection with the existential concept of the world.

The practical understanding which we have described is regarded by Heidegger as the fundamental understanding, the understanding which touches on the whole constitution of man as being-in-the-world. It is the condition which makes theoretical understanding possible. Theoretical or scientific understanding is held to be a special case of understanding in general. In that special case entities are abstracted from all practical concern and viewed as purely objective.

Did men play cricket before they formulated the rules of the game? No doubt the rules were subsequent in time to the playing of the game, and were framed in accordance with the way in which the game was actually played. On the other hand, it might be contended that the rules, in some form, were logically prior to the game, because as soon as men began to play the game, they must have had already some accepted conventions in their minds. If the question were whether $\theta\epsilon\omega\rho\acute{\iota}\alpha$ or $\pi\rho\hat{\alpha}\xi\iota\varsigma$ comes first, it might seem as insoluble and as fruitless to attempt an answer as to decide

[2] *S. u. Z.*, p. 157.

55

between the rival claims to precedence of the hen and the egg. Each seems to imply the other.

However, the contrast in Heidegger is not strictly between theory and practice, but rather between the purest theory (which, in his view, is never quite pure, that is to say, never entirely aloof from practical concern) and that other understanding, itself a kind of implicit theory even if it cannot be formulated, which belongs to everyday activities. To return to our illustration, as well as the rules of cricket there is what the Americans would call the 'know-how' of the players. They cannot formulate that as they formulate the rules, though perhaps it is communicable in other ways, but it is knowledge or understanding, possessed by those who play the game. And this type of understanding, Heidegger claims, is our most fundamental understanding of the world. Our closest intercourse with the world is not percipient knowledge, but the practical concern which uses, handles, and so on, and has its own knowledge.[3]

Before we go on to the further exposition of Heidegger's treatment of understanding, let us pause to consider briefly the implications of this line of thought for theology. Heidegger has attempted to show that, as well as the theoretical knowledge which reaches its purest expression in science, there is another knowledge which is much more difficult to formulate but which should not on that account be overlooked. Indeed, if Heidegger is right, scientific knowledge is subordinate to and derivative from this fundamental existential knowledge, as it is frequently called. (The expression 'existential knowledge' is not used by Heidegger, but as it has become current, we accept the usage while noting that the term 'existential' is here used in a looser sense than the one already defined.[4]) Now it is with this existential kind of knowledge that theology is primarily concerned. The knowledge of God is different from our knowledge of nature. It is not a set of propositions about God, as if God were an object to be viewed with academic detachment, but the knowledge which is implicit in our faith in God. 'He judged the cause

[3] *S. u. Z.*, p. 67.   [4] *Supra*, p. 34.

of the poor and needy; then it was well with him: was not this to know me? saith the Lord.'[5] The knowledge spoken of here, like Heidegger's understanding of the hammer, did not issue in a statement but in a pattern of action. This knowledge is not theoretical in the usual sense of that term, but it is a genuine θεωρία, an insight or understanding implicit in the experience of faith in God. Contemporary theologians, whether or not they use the expression 'existential knowledge', seem to have grasped the peculiar status of religious knowledge much more clearly than did the theologians of a century ago. Dr William Temple, for instance, has dealt very faithfully with the difference between a mere theistic philosophy and the genuine knowledge of God in his criticism of Descartes.[6]

Two consequences follow from recognizing that the knowledge of God is of the kind that we call existential. The first is that we can no more speak intelligently about God without the experience of faith than we can talk intelligently about cricket without ever having handled a bat or bowled a ball. Theological knowledge must be from the inside, it must be faith interpreting itself. Here, of course, the difficulty of communication arises. We saw already that the biblical writers used poetry, myth and historical narrative rather than the systematic treatise for the communication of their thought. Action and example are other important ways in which an existential understanding of any kind may be communicated. But in any case the communication must be made by someone who has the existential knowledge. To quote Tillich:

'If the word "existential" points to a participation which transcends both subjectivity and objectivity, then man's relation to the gods is rightly called existential. Man cannot speak of the gods in detachment. The moment he tries to do so, he has lost the god and has established just one more object within the world of

---

[5] Jer. 22.16.
[6] *Nature, Man, and God*, Macmillan, Lectures II and III.

objects. Man can speak of the gods only on the basis of his relation to them.'[7]

It may be asked in view of this whether the work of the theologian does not, therefore, break down on the difficulty of communicating knowledge which is of an existential kind, for the theologian is expected, so far as possible, to dispense with myth, poetry and the other ways of communicating existential knowledge that were mentioned, and to set out his teaching systematically in the plainest language that he can find. This, however, is precisely the same question that was asked and answered in connection with the existentialist philosopher's attempt to give a systematic account of the being of man after he had maintained that existence is always my own or someone's own—the principle of *Jemeinigkeit*[8], and therefore defies generalization and classification. The being of neither man nor God can be objectively set down as are the properties of the natural world in scientific analysis. But there is still the possibility of the phenomenological method, which in the case of theology would mean the descriptive analysis of the self's experience of God in faith.

The second consequence of recognizing that the knowledge of God is existential knowledge is to give to it its own certainty. If we accept Heidegger's analysis of understanding, the understanding which is implicit in πρᾶξις is as much entitled to respect as is the purest theory, and is indeed, he would claim, more fundamental. This is, of course, altogether contrary to the prevailing popular view that the highest degree of certainty belongs to scientific knowledge alone, and that other kinds of so-called knowledge, religious knowledge among them, are really only matters of opinion, or perhaps matters of feeling. Many reasons could be adduced for the rise of that popular view—or popular delusion, we might say —such as the amazing success of science in explaining nature on the one hand, the difficulties of communicating knowledge of the existential kind on the other, and the frequent con-

[7] *Systematic Theology*, Nisbet, vol. I, p. 238.   [8] *Supra*, p. 33 ff.

58

fusion in the past (especially in the disputes between theology and science) of existential understanding with what we may call objective understanding. All these factors have contributed to the development of a scientific positivism which, of course, has its influence on the unreflective popular outlook of the twentieth century. Heidegger—and in this he remains faithful to Husserl—opposes the exclusive claims made for the scientific method as the only avenue to genuine understanding and knowledge, and in the quest for certain foundations on which to build his philosophy, he directs attention away from nature to the analysis of the self as existing, that is to say, standing outside nature. And the self differs from every object in nature precisely in this, that to the self belongs what Heidegger calls disclosure (*Erschlossenheit*). Man not only is, he understands that he is, he is open or disclosed to himself in his being. This disclosure, which is a fundamental structure of existence, Heidegger identifies with the traditional doctrine of a 'light of nature'.[9] This is the fundamental understanding which makes possible all other understanding and knowledge. It has already been pointed out how this teaching of Heidegger differs from the '*cogito ergo sum*' of Descartes, to which it bears a superficial resemblance.[10] Descartes also was looking for a certain foundation on which to erect his philosophy, and he thought that he had found it in the pure subject, the doubting self which cannot doubt the reality of its own doubt. Heidegger, we saw, rejects the notion of a bare subject. What is disclosed by the 'light of nature'— that is, by the very structure of man's existence as open to himself—is 'being-in-the-world'. The self and the world are given together. 'Truth in the most original sense is the disclosure of *Dasein*, to which belongs the discovery of nature.'[11] But if this be so, then the phenomenological analysis of the experiences of the self as being-in-the-world should be able to yield knowledge which is more fundamental, certain and indubitable than any scientific understanding of nature. And if, among the possible ways of being which are disclosed to man in the analysis of his own existence, we find the way of

[9] *S. u. Z.*, p. 133.   [10] *Supra*, p. 39.   [11] *S. u. Z.*, p. 223.

being which we call religious faith, then the analysis of it—
that is, theology—can lay claim to the same truth that
belongs to all phenomenological analysis. Theological
statements are not, therefore, merely matters of opinion,
still less expressions of feeling, neither true nor false, as the
logical positivist might say. They are statements which
communicate that existential knowledge to which the most
original truth belongs. That original truth is not the correspondence of statements to facts (a very difficult theory in
any case) but the 'light of nature', the disclosure of being-in-
the-world to itself, which makes all understanding and
knowledge possible.

Let us now consider further the view of understanding
which Heidegger sets forth. Understanding is an existential,
a possible way of being. Its characteristic structure is the
project (*Entwurf*).[12] The term project, as used by Heidegger,
seems to contain two ideas. As related to man's possibilities,
it suggests intention or purpose. By this we do not mean that
a project is a plan which has been thought out and is then
put into operation—indeed Heidegger explicitly says that a
project does not mean this for him. But when the child lifts
a spoon to his mouth, he has understood the spoon in the
sense that he has discovered its instrumental character. He
is making it serve his possibilities in projecting his possibilities
upon it.

This brings us to the second idea contained in the notion of
a project. This is analogous to projection in mathematics.
Meaning is projected upon things by the understanding.
In themselves, Heidegger holds, they are meaningless. But
this implies that the world itself is an existential. That is not
to say that there is nothing apart from what is understood,
for Heidegger is not a follower of Berkeley. What is (*das
Seiende*) is there, whether it is understood or not, but it only
becomes a world and acquires significance through the projecting activity of man's understanding. The world is thus
itself a way of being which man as understanding constructs
in projecting his possibilities.

[12] *S. u. Z.*, p. 145.

This brings us once again to the question whether the existentialist view of the world as an instrumental system constructed by man's projects is subjectivism, even in spite of the fact that Heidegger strenuously opposes the notion of a pure subject, and contends that the being of man is always being-in-the-world. Does he really escape subjectivism? It may, I think, be fairly claimed that Heidegger's account of the world is neither more nor less subjective than, let us say, the account given by Kant on the one hand, or by a modern physicist on the other. Kant's categories of substance and accident, cause and effect and so on, were, in his own view, forms imposed upon phenomena by the understanding. The mathematical formulae of the scientist are equally constructions of the understanding which he finds convenient for the interpretation of natural phenomena. These two cases are projects, in Heidegger's sense of the term, but they are highly specialized projects—the projects of theoretical understanding. The categories of substantiality, causality and so on, or their modern equivalents, are the basic concepts (*Begrifflichkeit*) for the project of a scientific understanding of the world. Heidegger's categories, for instance, *Zuhandenheit, Vorhandenheit, Innerweltlichkeit*—and we must remember that his categories are to be distinguished from his existentials[13]—differ from those of Kant or the scientist in being the categories of everyday understanding, and not of that specialized type of understanding which we call theoretical or scientific. And this everyday understanding which relates to practical concern is, of course, far more fundamental to man's existence and occupies him for a far greater part of his time than theoretical understanding. Even a philosopher or a physicist, when he turns a door handle, thinks of it as a handy instrument, not as a metal object or a pattern of molecules and atoms. In other words, he conceives it under the category of *Zuhandenheit*, not under the categories of philosophy or science which are related to theoretical understanding, whether they be Kantian or more recent.

These different ways of understanding the world are not

[13] *Supra*, p. 13.

antagonistic to one another, and it is most unfortunate that existentialism is sometimes regarded as anti-scientific or even irrational. The different ways of understanding arise from the projecting of different possibilities of man's being—the possibilities of his practical concern, or the possibilities of his theoretical reasoning. There could only be conflict if it were claimed that the true understanding of the world belongs exclusively to one of these projects—a claim which might be made by the logical positivists on behalf of the scientific project. But we have already dwelt at some length on Heidegger's arguments against such a claim, and his demonstration of the importance of existential understanding over against theoretical understanding.

What further light does the foregoing discussion throw on the New Testament understanding of the world as the κτίσις, the creation of God? We noted already that this understanding of the world is more akin to the existentialist than to the scientific concept of the world. The world, as created by God, is of use to man, who is God's creature, but it has also the possibility of being hostile to man when he prizes the creation above the Creator. This understanding of the world is the project of religious faith. It is not a theoretical but an existential understanding. That is to say, we do not reason from the world and its usefulness to a Creator. Such arguments may have some force, but they lead to the God of metaphysics, an object of theoretical knowledge, and can never lead to the living God of religious faith, who is never an object. In religious faith, God is disclosed immediately with the self and the world. Heidegger teaches that in the original disclosure of *Dasein* the self and the world are disclosed together. Religious thought must go beyond that and assert that God also is disclosed—or rather, discloses himself. In the light of that disclosure, the world is understood as creation and the self as the creature who may use the creation or be lost in it. It is through the existential knowledge of God, who discloses himself to man in his way of being which we call faith, and not through any theoretical reasoning that we understand the world as creation. 'Through faith we understand that the worlds were framed by the word of God, so that things which are seen were not made of things which do appear.'[14] Only so do we apprehend the Creator as the living God, and not as merely some shadowy First Cause.

But if God discloses himself together with the self and the world, why then, it may be asked, is there no mention of God in Heidegger's existential analytic, which Bultmann seems prepared to accept, in its broad outlines at least, as an adequate analysis of that 'understanding of existence which is given with existence' and therefore as a suitable ontological *Begrifflichkeit* for the problems of theology? This is, in fact, the question which Schumann has raised about Bultmann's approach to theology.[15] Can there be a trustworthy analysis of human existence which does not see that existence in relation to God? In answer to this objection, it may be replied that the religious bearing of Heidegger's philosophy is by no means simple. This question will be raised again later, but for the present we may say that even if God is not disclosed in the phenomenological analysis of understanding, so far as we have pursued it, there is still another very important mode of disclosure of which Heidegger treats, that which is given in affective states or moods (*Befindlichkeiten*) which have their own understanding, and especially the state of dread or anxiety (*Angst*). This topic will occupy us in the next section, and there we shall see that Heidegger's existential analytic comes very near to becoming a religious philosophy. It will be argued at that point that the existential analytic should become religious for its completion, and that God is disclosed with the self and the world, as has been already asserted.

Before leaving the subject of understanding, there are some further points that remain to be discussed. The doctrine of creation, which is of fundamental importance in the New Testament as well as in the Old Testament, has been one of the principal battle-grounds in the conflicts which have arisen over the question of the relations of religion and science. It should be clear from what has been said that the scientific

[14] Heb. 11.3.   [15] *K. u. M.*, vol. I, p. 220.

and biblical accounts of the world arise from different projects, and there can be no question of conflict between them—unless, indeed, one or the other asserts to itself exclusive truth as the only possible understanding of the world. The scientific view of the world is the project of the theoretical understanding, the doctrine of creation is the project of the existential understanding which belongs to faith.

There are, of course, now very few who would hold that, let us say, the Genesis accounts of the creation are to be regarded as science, or who would attempt the harmonizing of these accounts with the teaching of science, as was once done. But what is not so clearly understood is that these accounts are not primarily theism either, even if they imply theism. They are not, that is to say, mythological symbols intended to teach a philosophy of cosmic origins or a theistic world-view. Their teaching goes far beyond any metaphysical doctrine of a First Cause, which, like science, would belong to the sphere of theoretical understanding. The biblical accounts of the creation are to be understood existentially. They are vehicles for the communication of the existential understanding of the living God—the saving knowledge of God, if we may so speak—which belonged to the sacred writers and was disclosed or revealed to them in the experience of faith. Thus Adam's dependence and creatureliness is both the writer's and mine when I read his story and understand it as something which touches my existence. Adam's disobedience is the writer's disobedience and my disobedience; Adam's fall is the writer's fall and my fall. Here is neither science nor philosophy, but something much more important for myself confronted with the problems of existence, namely, a disclosure of myself as a creature who has fallen into sin. So also with the account of the creation of the world of nature. It does not teach me how to understand the world considered as an object for theoretical study, as science teaches me, but it does teach me to understand the world as a constant factor in my existence as being-in-the-world, that the world is good and for my use, but that at the same time I lose myself in the world in preferring the creature above the Creator as Adam did. Thus understood, there can be no possible conflict between the teaching of these accounts and the teaching of science or cosmology, and thus understood it is clear also that these accounts of the creation touch a level of truth more fundamental and important for my existence than any theory of cosmic origins could be.

To complete this discussion of understanding, it is necessary finally to consider the New Testament passages which explicitly speak of understanding or knowledge, and to ask whether they confirm the existential view of religious understanding which has here been expounded. And first let us consider the Pauline concept of νοῦς, with reference to Bultmann's interpretation of it.[16]

Passages such as 'be ye transformed by the renewing of your mind (or understanding)' and 'God gave them over to a reprobate mind (or understanding), to do those things which are not convenient'[17] clearly indicate that for Saint Paul νοῦς does not stand for theoretical understanding but for a practical understanding closely connected with willing and doing. Indeed, Bultmann suggests that, in the two verses quoted, νοῦς might almost be rendered by character.[18] Ontologically this practical understanding is the 'light of nature' which discloses to me my possibilities for good or evil, and makes possible my decisions—it is 'the law of my mind (or understanding)'.[19] But, ontically, the understanding may be fallen or 'reprobate' and therefore misleading— and, of course, both Saint Paul and Heidegger teach that the understanding is, in fact, generally fallen.

If understanding bears this practical or existential sense in the New Testament, it justifies the reiterated use by Bultmann (and in this usage he also follows Heidegger) of the expression self-understanding (Selbstverständnis) in his interpretation of Christian theology. He can say that Jesus taught men a new understanding of themselves; that Saint Paul's conversion was a new self-understanding; that the Christian life is a new

16 *Th. des NT*, p. 207 ff.   17 Rom. 12.2; 1.28.
18 *Th. des NT*, p. 209.   19 Rom. 7.23.

understanding of the self. If by understanding Bultmann meant primarily a theoretical activity, then to speak of a new understanding of the self would seem to be a very inadequate account alike of the teaching of Jesus, the conversion of the apostle, and the Christian life. But in the sense of understanding which has been explained, and which seems close to the New Testament meaning of the term, a new understanding of the self means nothing less than a complete reorientation of the entire personality. It is equivalent to a new life.

In the Johannine writings it might seem that there is a bias in the direction of intellectualism. Frequently recurring concepts such as 'knowledge', 'truth', 'light' are reminiscent of Greek philosophy. Commenting on this affinity with Greek thinking, E. F. Scott remarks that the Fourth Gospel 'lays stress on knowledge as the chief factor in the attainment of life.'[20] But is knowledge understood even here, in spite of the affinity with Greek thinking, as theoretical or speculative knowledge? The same commentator goes on to say that 'a native Hebrew strain in John's thinking blends itself with the Greek, and essentially modifies it.' The effect of this modification, we would say, is to bring knowledge and truth from the sphere of the theoretical to that of the practical. Christ himself is the truth[21]—not his discourses only, but primarily himself in his life and death and resurrection. Another commentator on the Fourth Gospel says, 'Christ did not answer all our speculative questions, but his life itself is the answer to all the final questions'[22]—and by 'final questions' we may suppose are meant the ultimate questions of man's existence. Whatever affinities we may trace with Greek speculation, the Johannine concept of the knowledge of God which is 'life eternal'[23] is essentially like the concepts of knowledge and understanding which we find in the other biblical writers. It is a knowledge of the kind which we call existential.

[20] Cf. *The Fourth Gospel*, T. & T. Clark, pp. 256-257.
[21] John 14.6.
[22] C. J. Wright, *Mission and Message of Jesus*, Nich. & W., p. 881.
[23] John 17.3.

11. *Anxiety*

It was mentioned before that Heidegger teaches that man is disclosed to himself in his being not only by understanding but also by affective state (*Befindlichkeit*). All understanding is coloured by some emotional mood, while every mood of the emotions has its own understanding.[24] We suggested that this mode of disclosure which comes with feeling is of special importance for religious thought, and it is to this problem that we turn now.

The affective states which Heidegger proposes to analyse ontologically are, he says, familiar to us ontically as moods. Man always has some mood. Both the undisturbed equanimity and the frustrated discontent of everyday existence, and the passing over from one to the other, have, in Heidegger's view, their ontological significance, even if these phenomena are commonly supposed to be the most fugitive elements in the being of man. Mood has its own understanding—not in the sense of an explicit knowing, but in the sense that it discloses man to himself as 'being-there'. It lights up being-in-the-world, and discloses together both the self and the world in their inseparable relationship with one another. Heidegger maintains that (from the ontological point of view at least) the disclosures which scientific knowledge makes fall far short of the original disclosures of mood. Theory seeks a uniform unchanging knowledge of the world, but it is just in the unsteady flickering disclosures of mood that there is revealed the nature of the world, which is never the same on two successive days.[25]

We have already considered, as an example of Heidegger's phenomenological method, his ontological analysis of one such affective state, namely, fear.[26] Heidegger regards fear as an inauthentic mood. As we saw, fear always has as its object something within the world, and it belongs, therefore, to that inauthentic way of being in which man is absorbed in concern with the world and seeks his security there. An authentic existence, claims Heidegger, knows no fear, for it is

[24] Cf. *S. u. Z.*, p. 134 ff.   [25] Cf. *S. u. Z.*, p. 138.   [26] *Supra*, p. 36 ff.

67

not oriented to the world. It is worth noting here that the New Testament also characterizes the life without Christ, that is, the life founded on the world, as a life of fear, from which Christ brings deliverance. 'Ye have not received the spirit of bondage again to fear,' says Saint Paul to the Roman converts.[27]

Can we discern the fundamental affective state (*Grundbefindlichkeit*) of which fear is an inauthentic mode? In his inauthentic way of being, man loses himself in the world, and understands himself in terms of the world. This may be regarded as a kind of flight from himself as existing, that is, standing apart from the world. It might be called a flight from the responsibilities of existence. It is from a consideration of this flight that Heidegger approaches the problem of the mood which above all discloses man in his being, and which he calls anxiety (*Angst*).[28] (Following Tillich, we here translate '*Angst*' by 'anxiety', in preference to the terms 'dread' and 'anguish' which have been used by English translators of Kierkegaard and Zehrer respectively.) Bultmann also suggests that Jewish legalism and pagan speculation alike, characterized in the New Testament by 'confidence in the flesh', arise from man's flight from his own being as disclosed in anxiety.[29]

But if man, in his inauthentic way of being, flees before the disclosure of himself in anxiety and seeks to allay the feeling, how can we know what that disclosure is? Heidegger replies that man can only flee before himself in so far as he has been brought before himself in the disclosure which belongs to anxiety. The flight itself is evidence for what is disclosed, and what is thus ontically disclosed may possibly be ontologically conceived. In one of his works,[30] Sartre has set down a careful day-to-day description of changing moods, and leaves the reader with the impression of man's helplessness in the world, which, as we shall see, is not far removed from the disclosure of anxiety, as Heidegger interprets it. Genuine anxiety would appear to be a much rarer phenomenon

27 Rom. 8.15.
28 *S. u. Z.*, p. 184 ff.
29 *Th. des NT*, p. 239.
30 *La Nausée*, Paris, 1938.

than fear, with which it must not be confused, but it belongs to man's existence as such, even if the majority of men experience it chiefly in the way of flight and avoidance.

It is interesting to preface Heidegger's account of anxiety with the description given by Kierkegaard, who was also deeply interested in this phenomenon:

> 'One may liken dread to dizziness. He whose eye chances to look down into the yawning abyss becomes dizzy . . . Thus dread is the dizziness of freedom, which occurs when freedom gazes down into its own possibility.'[31]

Thus for Kierkegaard anxiety is primarily associated with freedom—though admittedly with freedom conditioned by finitude. In anxiety man is confronted with his possibility and his responsibility. In Heidegger's analysis of anxiety, the emphasis has shifted somewhat. This shift is from the possibility to the facticity of human existence, which he regards as the primary disclosure of anxiety. It discloses man as 'being-there', possibility thrown into the world. There would be no flight from freedom if freedom were unlimited, but freedom is always tied down and circumscribed by the alien being of the world. In the mood of anxiety man is disclosed to himself as responsible for an existence of which he can never be the master.

Heidegger's phenomenological analysis of anxiety is developed along the lines of his analysis of fear, from which anxiety or dread is distinguished at each step. The object of fear, it will be recalled, was always something within the world. But the flight to which anxiety gives rise is not a flight from anything in the world—on the contrary it takes the form of a flight to precisely that which is within the world, that is, man allays his anxiety by losing himself in the world. The object of anxiety (we are speaking, of course, of ontological anxiety or dread, not of actual concrete anxieties in the popular sense) is wholly undefined—it is nothing in particular, nothing within the world. And whereas the object of fear has always a particular direction and location, that

[31] *The Concept of Dread*, O.U.P., p. 55.

which is dreaded, being nothing within the world, is nowhere. It cannot approach from any direction because it is already there—so near as to stifle the breath, and yet nowhere. That before which ontological anxiety is experienced is therefore nothing, and nowhere within the world. It must, therefore, be something standing apart from the world which confronts man in anxiety. It is, claims Heidegger, his own being-in-the-world which is disclosed—the self with its freedom bound up with the world, possibility thrown into the world. Anxiety, therefore, discloses to man that he is not at home (*nicht zu Hause*) in the world. We are, in the New Testament phrase, 'strangers and pilgrims on the earth'.[32] This contrasts with what was said before about the inauthentic existence which is at home in the world and seeks contentment and security in the world.[33] It explains also the flight from the disclosure of anxiety which shatters that illusory contentment, and arouses in man an uneasiness which preoccupation with the world and its concerns never fully removes. Here the teaching of existentialism appears to approach to that of the New Testament. Man's being is such that he cannot find contentment in the world, and even when he is lulled into a false sense of security, a fundamental uneasiness, which we have called for want of a better expression the mood of anxiety, arises out of the very constitution of his being and breaks in to disclose to him that he is not at home, that the world is uncanny (*unheimlich*), and can be hostile when man surrenders himself to it.

'It is no accident,' remarks Heidegger, 'that the phenomena of anxiety and fear—which are generally left undistinguished from one another—have come within the orbit of Christian theology, both ontically and, though within narrow limits, ontologically. That has happened whenever the anthropological problem of the being of man in relation to God gained a precedence, and guided the treatment of phenomena such as faith, sin, love and repentance.'[34] And he instances Augustine, Luther and Kierkegaard in support of his statement. Why should Heidegger say that it is 'no accident' that

[32] Heb. 11.13.   [33] *Supra*, p. 50.   [34] *S. u. Z.*, p. 190, note.

the phenomenon of ontological anxiety has been chiefly studied by Christian theologians? Although Heidegger does not explicitly say so, we contend that at this point the existential analytic has brought us to the threshold of religion, and that the concept of anxiety demands a religious interpretation—and with it the whole concept of human existence. For in this fundamental malaise, which springs from man's very being, there is disclosed not only the self and the world, but also God. The disclosure does not indeed yield the explicit knowledge of God, but directs man to God as the ground of his being, in a way which will shortly be more fully described. For what is this anxiety or dread, this basic malaise, this uneasy restlessness, this feeling of not being at home in the world, this disclosure which shatters the illusory contentment and security of everyday existence, but the *cor inquietum* of Christian experience? Augustine's famous dictum, 'Thou hast formed us for thyself, and our hearts are restless till they find rest in thee,'[35] might be interpreted as meaning that, confronted with the disclosure of that anxiety which relates to nothing in the world but arises from his own being, man has an alternative to that flight into an inauthentic existence of surrender to the world—namely, recourse to God, who is the ground of being, Creator of both man and the world.

But before we expand this point, let us return for a moment to the question of the relation of Heidegger's existentialist philosophy to religion. The charge against Bultmann is not only that his theological thinking is influenced by a human philosophy, which, in the eyes of some, would be grave enough, but further, that the particular philosophy which has exerted an influence on his thought is an atheistic and pessimistic philosophy. But is it true to say that Heidegger's philosophy is atheistic? He himself says that it is not, and is said to have defined his position as that 'he does not deny the existence of God, but affirms his absence'.[36] At first sight this cryptic statement might not seem to carry us very far

---

[35] *Confessions* I, 1.
[36] Quoted by Troisfontaines, *Existentialism and Christian Thought*, Dacre, p. 48.

in the direction of a religious philosophy, or even of a philosophy which could be expected to throw any light on the interpretation of religious faith. It depends, however, upon how we understand Heidegger's assertion of the absence of God. This appears to me to be part of Heidegger's revolt against convention and tradition. God may have been in the past in the sense that he may have been significant for man's existence. That is to say, there may have been a genuine *existentiell* knowledge of God, but, Heidegger thinks, that original knowledge has been so overlaid, trivialized and stultified by the deadening hand of tradition and dogmatism that God is now absent. So it has happened with the quest for being in philosophy: 'The dominance of tradition makes what it "hands down" inaccessible and more than ever concealed. What is handed down is taken as self-evident, and the way to the original sources is lost.'[37] If this interpretation is correct—and admittedly it is a pretty free and very tentative construction of Heidegger's cryptic utterance[38]—then his affirmation of the absence of God would be very much like Nietzsche's assertion that God is dead.[39] Mounier interprets this as meaning that Nietzsche proclaimed the death of God 'to the men who, even after having been responsible for it, dared not accept it as a fact.'[40] There are obvious resemblances as well as differences between Heidegger and Nietzsche. But just as Zarathustra, having broken the old tables of the law, proceeds to create new ones, so it might be claimed that Heidegger, having affirmed the absence of God, proceeds to look for him afresh. He speaks somewhat contemptuously of 'the remnants of Christian theology which have not yet been expelled from philosophical

---

[37] *S. u. Z.*, p. 21.
[38] Dr E. L. Allen has drawn my attention to Heidegger's interesting essay, 'Nietzsches Wort, "Gott ist tot" ', published in *Holzwege*, 1950. This essay confirms the two main points made here—the distinction between the affirmation of God's absence and the denial of him, and the comparison with Nietzsche which follows—but gives a much fuller discussion of the points involved, and to this the interested reader is referred.
[39] *Thus Spake Zarathustra*, p. 5.
[40] *Existentialist Philosophies*, Rockliff, p. 5.

thought',[41] yet his own return to philosophy's original search for being is also a return to the quest for God. Here we are on firmer ground. Blackham says of Heidegger: 'His philosophy takes shape as the historical quest for being, and is seen to be essentially religious.'[42] Copleston concurs: 'His philosophy is, in a sense, a seeking for God.'[43]

Admittedly this is scanty evidence that *Sein und Zeit* forms a suitable prolegomenon to the study of the theology of the New Testament. We have at most demonstrated a religious tendency, but no more than a tendency, in a philosophy which is, generally speaking, non-theistic and non-Christian. Nor will it suffice to say, as Copleston does, that the problem of God is not raised on the plane of the phenomenological analysis of man, and explain the 'absence of God' from Heidegger's philosophy as a mere circumstance attendant on his method. We are seeking to show now in connection with the concept of dread or anxiety that the problem of God is raised on the plane of the phenomenological analysis of man, even if the answer is not supplied there, and we shall seek to show again in connection with the transition to an authentic existence that the problem of God is raised once more, and that because Heidegger fails to come to grips with it his philosophy is exposed at that point to a very serious line of criticism. We must not make too much of religious tendencies in Heidegger's thought, just as we must not label it as atheistic. The religious tendencies are undoubtedly there, but I cannot find that they ever take any very definite shape.

What, then, are we to say of Bultmann's preoccupation with this philosophy? If we have shown that it is not actually atheistic, we have also given warning that it is not to be too lightly hailed as a religious philosophy, which would seem to be an essential condition of its being usefully employed in the interpretation of New Testament thought. A way out of the difficulty may, however, be found by distinguishing Heidegger the existentialist from Heidegger the ontologist. We saw already that Heidegger's investigation into the being of man

[41] *S. u. Z.*, p. 230.   [42] *Six Existentialist Thinkers*, Routledge, p. 103.
[43] *Existentialism and Modern Man*, Blackfriars, p. 18.

was intended to be the prelude to an investigation into the problem of being in general.[44] On the basis of the results of the existential analytic he was to have undertaken what he called a 'destruction' of the history of ontology, though this would at the same time have been the construction of a new philosophy of being.[45] Although this ambitious programme has not been formally carried out, there are pointers which suggest the direction of Heidegger's thought in its quest for being in the widest sense. Now Bultmann's concern is with Heidegger the existentialist, for, as we saw, the philosophy which is claimed to have a special relation to theology is 'that philosophical work which endeavours to develop in suitable concepts the understanding of existence which is given with existence'.[46] The existential analytic, which is simply the phenomenological description of man's own understanding of his being, has in itself nothing repugnant to religion—on the contrary, we are contending that it leads to religion. It is another question altogether what general ontology may be built upon the existential foundation, and if Heidegger rejects a religious interpretation and tends towards a non-theistic philosophy of being, that does not in any way alter the possible value of the existential analytic to the theologian, or argue against Bultmann's use of it.

The bifurcation between the theistic and the non-theistic interpretations of being, so far as these are built upon the existential analytic, first appears in connection with the concept of ontological anxiety. To explain how this bifurcation comes about, we may say that when man's existence is disclosed to himself in the mood of ontological anxiety as possibility bound up with the world, there are two possible ways in which he can interpret his situation. He can accept that he is thrown into an ocean of being, alien and even hostile to himself, in which he must exist; or he can seek a ground of being, which means simply a Creator who is author both of man's being and of the being of nature. Suffice to say for the moment that Heidegger appears to me to stop at the first possible interpretation. For him anxiety discloses the sea of

[44] *Supra*, p. 29 f.   [45] *S. u. Z.*, p. 19 ff.   [46] *Supra*, p. 10.

what is (*das Seiende*), into which man is thrown as isolated possibility. This is what he calls the facticity of man's existence, and is a genuine phenomenon which will require to be discussed later. But to concentrate on man's being thrown into this ocean of being, as if that were the only possible interpretation, gives a one-sided picture and leads, in fact, to that pessimism and nihilism which, not altogether unfairly, can be regarded as the logical consequences of Heidegger's philosophy. Our contention is that dread or anxiety not only discloses man cast on a sea of being, but also the ground of being; and that the analysis of anxiety as an ontological phenomenon remains incomplete unless we take into account this other possible interpretation implied in the disclosure. We said that in anxiety man is disclosed as responsible for an existence of which he is not the master. But equally original with, and implied in, the disclosure to man in anxiety of his own being as possibility thrown into the ocean of what is, is the disclosure of the possibility of a Being who is not thrown into the sea of what is, because he is himself the ground of what is, being itself, beyond both the *Vorhandenheit* of inanimate things and the *Existenz* of man, both of which are contingent and conditioned. In the language of an older philosophy, the idea of God is innate— that is to say, it is already given with man's understanding of his own existence. Schleiermacher's feeling of dependence, which he regarded as fundamental to religion, belongs here, though we should prefer to speak of a feeling of creatureliness —remembering, too, that this feeling is not bare feeling, but has its own implicit understanding. In anxiety man is disclosed to himself in his specific creatureliness, and it is anxiety, therefore, which makes possible the quest for God, the ground of being, which man can find neither in himself nor in the world. Jeremiah likened the quest for God to the instinct which mysteriously but unfailingly guides the migratory birds to their home in the proper season,[47] and the aptness of this comparison arises from its suggestion that the quest for God is not an accident or a luxury or an abnormality,

[47] Jer. 8.7.

75

but arises from the very constitution of man's being—which it does, if our interpretation of the phenomenon of anxiety is correct. 'It is the instinct of the human soul for the divine, an instinct which, unless perverted by evil habit'—in existentialist terminology, we would say 'by flight into concern with the world'—'guides it unerringly to its true home in God.'[48] Thus anxiety discloses to man with his own being the possibility of God, and gives rise to his search for God— the very motive behind Heidegger's own philosophy, if we may believe Blackham and Copleston.

It is, however, a commonplace of religious experience that God is not found by searching, and that faith, as a way of being, is man's response to God's revelation of himself. Anxiety is a condition of the knowledge of God, just as complacency prevents that knowledge, and in lighting up man's 'being-there' it discloses the possibility of the ground of his being, that is, his Creator, but it does not in itself yield an explicit knowledge of God. It opens the door to religion, and even pushes man through the door, but it is not yet religion. Anxiety or dread, as we have considered it, is still a formal ontological or existential structure, a bare horizon of possibility, which has to be made concrete in some ontical or *existentiell* experience before religion proper emerges.

Such an *existentiell* possibility is the experience of religious awe. This may be regarded as rooted in ontological anxiety, and there are obvious similarities—'creature feeling,' for instance, is mentioned by Otto as a primary characteristic of the experience of the numinous in awe. The distinction between the broad existential concept of anxiety or dread and the special religious concept of awe appears to me to be that whereas in anxiety the primary disclosure is of man's own being, while the possibility of God is lit up on the periphery, as it were, in awe the positions have changed, God's revelation of himself is central, while the being of man is now disclosed on the periphery.

It is worth noting that Otto's treatment of his subject[49]

[48] Skinner, *Prophecy and Religion*, C.U.P., p. 121.
[49] *The Idea of the Holy*, O.U.P., p. 8 ff.

approximates to Heidegger's methods in at least two important particulars. His approach is existential—he proposes to explore the numinous through the affective states of man's religious experience in which the numinous is encountered. His method is phenomenological, and consists in the detailed analysis of man's experience of the numinous. Let us take his phenomenological analysis into the elements *mysterium tremendum fascinans* as a basis for discussion.

The divine being is *mysterium* because it is wholly other. That is to say, it is not explicable in terms of everyday experience. The categories under which nature (*Vorhandenheit*) is understood are not applicable here. The existentials under which the being of man (*Existenz*) is understood may have a limited application by analogy, but are not exhaustive And since these are the only kinds of concepts that we have, we understand why, in speaking of God, we must always have recourse to symbolical and mythical language. A third kind of category—for which, so far as I am aware, neither philosophers nor theologians have yet invented a name—would be necessary for the description of God, the ground of being beyond both *Vorhandenheit* and *Existenz*. Presumably the numinous is such a category. Here, too, a further word must be said about the expression 'ground of being'. Ground cannot mean cause, which is a category of the *vorhanden*. It stands for the creative element in God, disclosed in experiences of the kind described above, though it is not explicitly conceived since it belongs to the *mysterium* of divine being, and can, therefore, only be spoken of by analogy as ground or cause. The element of *tremendum* brings us back to dread. It is man's awareness of his own finitude, not this time in the ocean of what is, but before the ground of being, God, in the encounter with whom man understands that he is 'but dust and ashes'.[50] The element of *fascinans* appears to be the other side of the phenomenon noted already in connection with the analysis of anxiety. Man was disclosed as 'not at home' in the world, hence his uneasy restlessness which finds expression in the quest for God. Now in the analysis of awe, God is

[50] Gen. 18.27.

77

revealed as *fascinans*, drawing man to himself, giving direction to his quest and meeting him in his search.

Let us now pause to consider what point we have reached. First, attention was drawn to the ontological significance of affective states, which Heidegger denotes by the term *Befindlichkeiten*. These, he claims, are moods, not purely feeling but having their own understanding, so that they disclose man to himself. One of these was selected as the *Grundbefindlichkeit*, namely, anxiety or dread, which yields a pre-eminent disclosure of the being of man. It isolates him from his concern with the world and discloses his 'being-there'. This, it was contended, opens up man's restless quest for God. Finally, within the existential possibility of anxiety we came to the concrete experience of religious awe in which man is set before God, whom he apprehends as the numinous. This is that existential knowledge of God of which we spoke before in connection with the doctrine of creation. We do not infer the Creator from the creation by argument (for, if we did so, we would reach the objectified God of metaphysics, not the holy and living God of religion and theology). But in ontological anxiety there is disclosed to man directly with his own finite being the possibility of the ground of his being, namely, God, and the possibility is actualized in God's revelation of himself in religion.

Corresponding roughly to the broad existential concept of *Befindlichkeit* we find one of Saint Paul's anthropological concepts, namely, καρδία. This term occurs very frequently in the Pauline writings, and again there is variety of usage. Often it seems to stand for the whole self, as willing, understanding and doing, and therefore this concept is hard to distinguish from νοῦς. Bultmann, however, draws a distinction which throws light on the characteristic use of καρδία. In this concept, he maintains, the element of knowing, so important for νοῦς, is not stressed, but rather the elements of feeling.[51] In the New Testament, of course, there is no sharp distinction between understanding and feeling, and that is true to life. Understanding has its moods, and moods have

[51] *Th. des NT*, p. 218.

their own understanding, as we noted already. But Bultmann's distinction seems to be justified, for καρδία is used characteristically in connection with such affective states as love, pain, penitence and so on.[52] In some passages καρδία approaches the specific sense of the *Grundbefindlichkeit* and is connected explicitly with the knowledge of God, notably, for instance, when it is said that 'God, who commanded the light to shine out of darkness, hath shined in our hearts, to give the light of the knowledge of the glory of God in the face of Jesus Christ.'[53] But in the natural man who has turned away from God to the world, the light of the heart that might direct him to God is darkened: 'their foolish heart was darkened'.[54] It would, of course, be absurd to claim that there is any rigid parallel between καρδία and either *Befindlichkeit* or *Angst*, but, on the other hand, these existential concepts do help us to determine the place of καρδία in the Pauline anthropology.

The connection of the ontological interpretation of affective states with the knowledge of God is, however, implied in other Pauline passages. Saint Paul himself claimed to have extraordinary and even ecstatic religious experiences. These must have been accompanied by profound emotional moods, and it is significant that the apostle explicitly connects them with revelation (ἀποκάλυψις) of God.[55] This is true of his own account of his conversion experience as he described it in the Epistle to the Galatians.[56] Commentators are agreed that the period before Saint Paul's conversion must have been one of inner conflict and doubt, and it would not be unfair to say that at that time he must have been in the mood of anxiety. Yet this anxiety was the beginning of a new understanding of himself, in Bultmann's phrase, and made it possible for God's revelation—as he calls it himself—to reach him. This confirms the view of ontological anxiety set out in the preceding pages. In the mood of anxiety which isolates him from the world, so that he no longer feels at home, man begins to question his own

---

[52] E.g., II Cor. 8.16; Rom. 9.2; 2.5. [53] II Cor. 4.6.
[54] Rom. 1.21. [55] Gal. 1.12; II Cor. 12.1. [56] Gal. 1.11-17.

understanding of himself. His questioning may lead him to despair, as in the philosophies of Heidegger and Sartre, or it may lead him to the quest for God and so bring him to the encounter with God in faith.

The concept of anxiety or dread makes its appearance also in the Johannine writings, though implicitly rather than explicitly. When Jesus claimed to be the light of the world, the good shepherd, the true vine,[57] it is assumed in each case that man is looking for light for his way, a shepherd of souls, a ground of being. 'He needs,' says Bultmann, 'an understanding of himself in his world ... consciously or unconsciously, he is agitated (bewegt) by this question.'[58] Admittedly, man often follows a false light or a false shepherd. He flees into the illusory security of the world to allay his anxiety. Yet again this very flight is evidence of his fundamental malaise, which everyday concern with the world can never quite extinguish because it belongs to the being of man himself.

Incidentally, Bultmann has very skilfully shown how the Jews sought to set aside the uneasiness (Störung) which our Lord aroused in them. They appealed to their law, their history, their honour (the familiar world in which they felt at home), and they raised against Jesus trivial objections, such as his Galilean origins.[59] This recalls an earlier part of the discussion[60] in which we complained that Bultmann himself had stripped our Lord of the numinous character which the Gospels ascribe to him, and represented the historical Jesus as simply a teacher of practical philosophy. But here he is surely right in pointing out that it must have been a characteristic of the historic Jesus to disturb men— to make them question their self-understanding in the mood of anxiety. This is, indeed, what we would expect of Jesus as the revelation of God. The Jews sought to explain away this feature in the person of Jesus, so as to quieten the feeling he had aroused and restore their sense of security in their way of life. No doubt with a different motive, much modern

[57] John 8.12; 10.11; 15.1.
[59] John 7.42. Cf. *Th. des NT*, pp. 375-379.
[58] *Th. des NT*, p. 373.
[60] *Supra*, p. 22 ff.

criticism has been equally active in explaining away the numinous elements in the personality of the historic Jesus. Recognition of the importance for religion and theology of the concept of ontological anxiety might give a more balanced picture of the actual Jesus, who must have stirred such anxiety, but Bultmann does not follow up this line and remains content with a very attenuated picture of the historic Jesus.

IV

THE THREAT TO EXISTENCE

12. *Facticity*

THE term 'facticity' (*Faktizität*) has been already encountered, but it has not so far been formally defined, nor has its
place in the existential analytic been indicated. This term
also stands for a way of being—the way of being in which I
exist as a fact. That does not mean a fact of nature (*vorhanden*)
or a purely objective fact, which I never am, but a fact in
the sense that 'I am and have to be'.[1] Even if my whence and
whither remain hidden, the stark fact that 'I exist' shows itself,
that is to say, is a phenomenon which the existential analytic
must seek to describe. I am there, I am in the world—that is
a fact, even if it is a mystery how or why or to what end.
Facticity, too, is part of the disclosure of dread or ontological
anxiety, but it is the other aspect—the one which, we
suggested, becomes dominant in Heidegger's quest for
being, and is at the root of his pessimism. Yet, even on a
religious interpretation of man's existence, facticity remains
as a phenomenon to be taken into account. If man is disclosed in his creaturely relation to the ground of being, he is
also disclosed in the ocean of what is, isolated possibility
thrown into the world.

The notion of facticity was already present in the preliminary sketch of the concept of existence. It was stated
then that a fundamental character of existence is that it is
always mine (*Jemeinigkeit*). However much my dispositions,
abilities, circumstances and so on resembled those of another
person—suppose even that they were identical and indistinguishable, if that were possible—there would still be the
unbridgeable gap between an existence that is his and an

[1] *S. u. Z.*, p. 134.

existence that is mine. That I am myself and no one else is the unaccountable fact at the bottom of this structure of facticity in existence. That this fact is of a different order from facts of nature also follows from the initial concept of existence from which we set out. I can never be purely an object to myself, even in my facticity. I can try to objectify myself, I can call to my assistance psychology, statistics, and whatever methods of observation are calculated to yield the most objective results obtainable, but I can never be quite detached because I have that relation to myself as existing in virtue of which I am at once subject and object, or—if such a way of speaking is preferred—I transcend the subject-object relationship. Hence my existence is never a fact to me as the Forth Bridge is a fact—it is always my own. Yet it is a fact in the sense explained above—that I am and have to be myself in my world.

Facticity is characterized not only by the stark individuality (*Jemeinigkeit*) of my existence but also by what Heidegger calls in somewhat uncouth language 'thrownness' (*Geworfenheit*). 'An entity of the character of *Dasein* is there, in the sense that, whether explicitly or not, he finds himself thrown (into existence).'[2] According to Troisfontaines, the idea of thrownness came to Heidegger when he was serving in the trenches during the First World War. It is that outside our control which enters into the structure of our existence to circumscribe and narrow down our possibilities. I am responsible for my existence and I can choose between my possibilities, but already with my existence and its possibilities there is given my facticity, for which I am not responsible and which I have not chosen—namely, that I have to be myself in my world. Plato was aware of this problem, and in the myth which he tells of pre-existent souls choosing their lots before they enter the world, sought to reconcile the elements of freedom and facticity in human existence.[3] The point is that I never begin from scratch, so to speak, I am always already thrown into a situation, given over to my being.

[2] *S. u. Z.*, p. 135.   [3] *Republic*, 618 ff.

Man's possibilities are, therefore, to a considerable extent determined by his facticity, and may be frustrated by it. He has to live out his existence in his world, and it is no dream-world, for however much he may seek to conceal it from himself, he is ultimately not at home. We can see now why Heidegger claimed that the ontological disclosures of scientific thinking fall far short of the original disclosures of mood. 'Pure theory,' he says, 'even if it penetrated to the innermost heart of objective being, could never discover the menacing.'[4] Yet to me as existing it is more important to know that the environment contains a threat to my existence than to know the abstract theory of its structure and existence, just as it was more important for the farmer to know the significance of the south wind for his agricultural projects than to know its objective properties as a stream of air with a given geographical direction. With facticity there is disclosed the standing threat to human existence, contained in existence itself as being-in-the-world. Man must live along-side an entity, the being of which is alien to his own being. It has no meaning or sense in itself, apart from what man's understanding projects upon it in constructing his world—though, of course, it is a fair question whether man could understand or use something entirely alien, since that would seem to be unintelligible and unusable. This is precisely the point where Christian thought, with its doctrine of creation, diverges from the thought of Heidegger, as we shall see in a moment. But man in his world is always under the threat of being engulfed and lost in his world, so that he loses his authentic being.

If man in the ocean of what is, possibility entangled in facticity, were the whole picture, the only logical outcome would seem to be that heroism of despair, the determination to be myself within and in spite of the limitations of a miserable existence, which we associate with Heidegger and Sartre, and with the atheistic type of existentialism in general. But on the other hand, if anxiety discloses the possibility of a ground of being, being itself, beyond the con-

4 *S. u. Z.*, p. 138.

tingency of both *Vorhandenheit* and *Existenz*, that is, divine
Being, man's finitude may be interpreted as creatureliness.
And further, if this bare possibility is made concrete and
actualized in God's revelation of himself in religious faith, the
absolute dualism of *Vorhandenheit* and *Existenz* disappears, and
becomes a relative dualism. God is the Lord of all being,
Creator of man and nature alike, so that although man
differs from nature in his being, he has a common origin
with it in God, the ground of all being. The picture is only
made complete when God, the ground of being, is seen over
against man as existing in the ocean of all that is. And it may
be argued that if the dualism of man and nature were
absolute (as it seems to be in Heidegger) and these two ways
of being quite alien to one another, the construction of an
instrumental world, and the projection of meaning upon
what is, would be impossible. Its possibility becomes intelligible in the light of the biblical doctrine of creation, which
shows us man and nature alike deriving their being from the
Creator God.

There are elements of dualism both in existentialism and
in New Testament thought. In existentialism we have already
noted the contrasted concepts of authenticity and inauthenticity, *Existenz* and *Vorhandenheit*, possibility and facticity. In
biblical thought we have noted the contrast between man
and nature; the Johannine opposition of light and darkness,
truth and falsehood, and so on; and the double concept of
the κτίσις as at once the creation of God for man and a
possible threat to man—a view with obvious correspondences
to the existentialist concept of the world.[5] Attempting some
analysis of these contrasts, we find: (*a*) the dualism of man
and nature, *Existenz* and *Vorhandenheit*; (*b*) the dualism in
man himself, possibility and facticity, the breath of life and
the dust of the ground; (*c*) the dualism within man's possibility, to exist authentically or inauthentically, to have his
being in light or in darkness; (*d*) the dualism or rather
ambiguity in the concept of the world in both Christian and
existentialist thought.

[5] On these points, *supra*, pp. 18-19, 46-47, 50-51.

All these contrasts, however, appear to be reducible to that between man and nature. The ambiguity of the world arises from man's attitude to it, this in turn springs from his dual possibilities, and these originate from his being-in-the-world, so that the fundamental dualism seems to be man and world, or man and nature, or *Existenz* and *Vorhandenheit*.

Now in the absence of God, to use Heidegger's expression, this dualism of *Existenz* and *Vorhandenheit* appears to be absolute and ultimate. It finds expression in another description which Heidegger gives of facticity, as man's imprisonment within his destiny with the alien being of the world.[6] The use of the term 'imprisonment' in this connection will immediately suggest to the student of the New Testament a comparison with Gnosticism. Gnosticism in the first century and existentialism in the present century have both exerted an attraction on the Christian apologist, and for very much the same reason, namely, that both distinguish the being of man from the being of the world, and deny that man can be understood as simply a part of the world. Bultmann points out that 'in the Gnosis as in Christianity there came to consciousness the fundamental difference between the being of man and the being of nature, and thus the world became alien to the self, even a prison.'[7] Because of this point of contact, the New Testament writers sometimes found it convenient to employ Gnostic terminology for the presentation of their thought to Hellenistic minds. But the relation was a superficial one, and could not be pressed too far. Christianity and Gnosticism were agreed that man and nature differ in their being, as against the classical attempt to assimilate man to the cosmos, but for Christianity the difference was relative, whereas for Gnosticism it was absolute. Christianity had a doctrine of creation and referred both man and nature to God as their author, while Gnosticism did not. Hence Gnosticism proved to be a dangerous fellow-traveller for Christianity, and the same will be true of existentialism if its dualism remains unqualified. Without belief in a Creator God, Heidegger cannot bring together

[6] *S. u. Z.*, p. 52.   [7] *Th. des NT*, p. 164.

Existenz and *Vorhandenheit*, therefore the opposition of possibility and facticity remains unresolved, and the practical outcome is heroic despair. Admittedly his aim is to discover the totality of being, embracing both *Existenz* and *Vorhandenheit*, and that, we say, is really a seeking for God. But failing the accomplishment of his aim, the cleavage between the two ways of being remains absolute. Man's possibility in the grip of facticity is hopeless, and the estimate of Heidegger's thought as a philosophy of despair seems just.

For religious thought facticity remains, and so does a relative dualism—'The Lord God formed man of the dust of the ground' (facticity), 'and breathed into his nostrils the breath of life' (possibility)[8]—for we take it that these contrasted elements are to be interpreted existentially as ways of being, and not as substances, such as soul-substance and body-substance. But the difference here is that the dualism in the being of man is set against the unitary ground of his being, that is, God. This does not in itself solve the problem of facticity, or make it cease to be a problem. The Book of Job and the Psalms show the urgency of the problem of facticity for religious minds, and that it remains an impenetrable mystery. Nevertheless, the problem is at least eased somewhat. Facticity no longer leads to pessimism, for in the light of faith in a Creator God, the author both of man and nature, faith in his providence becomes possible. That possibility is only brought to concretion within the context of the Christian revelation, but it is already present as possibility with the disclosure of a ground of being. And while it is not arrived at by reasoning, it is supported by the argument that the world as a workshop is only possible because nature, like man himself, is the creature of God, to whom man may say of himself: 'Thou madest him to have dominion over the works of thy hands; thou hast put all things under his feet.'[9] Yet, at the same time, creation and providence remain mysterious, for the reason already stated, that the categories of thought under which man understands nature and his own existence must necessarily fail to

[8] Gen. 2.7.   [9] Ps. 8.6.

comprehend the ground of being which lies beyond them both.

Let us now illustrate these points with reference to the New Testament. Saint Paul is well aware of the problem of facticity, of the resistance and standing threat to the 'inward man' (understanding possibility) which arises from his own constitution as being-in-the-world. 'For I delight in the law of God after the inward man: but I see another law in my members, warring against the law of my mind, and bringing me into captivity to the law of sin which is in my members.[10] Here, admittedly, the apostle is speaking of sin, but sin is made possible and there is the standing temptation to sin because he is in the world, because his being is constituted not only by the 'inward man' but also by the 'members'. Presumably in the days of his zealous legalism Saint Paul found no solution to his problem, for the law itself was a flight from surrender to God and an attempt to find security in something that really belongs to the world.[11] But with his discovery of the God of grace (and we shall see later that Bultmann interprets the New Testament concept of grace as something very like providence) Saint Paul found a ground of hope. 'We know that all things work together for good to them that love God . . . If God be for us, who can be against us?'[12] That is not to say that the problem of man's facticity had become as clear as daylight. It was still a mystery, but no longer a hopeless mystery. He was 'perplexed but not in despair . . . cast down but not destroyed'[13]—and the occurrence here of the 'thrown' metaphor, reminiscent of Heidegger's *Geworfenheit*, is rather interesting. The threat to man's existence as possibility conditioned by facticity, a self entangled in a world, is not minimized. Even the Christian believer is still menaced in his being. 'So long as he lives in the flesh,' says Bultmann, 'his being is one that is permanently threatened and beset by trials.'[14] Saint Paul himself gives expression to the possibility that 'when I have preached to others, I myself should be a castaway'—again the metaphor

---

[10] Rom. 7.22-23.   [11] *Supra*, p. 68.   [12] Rom, 8.28, 31.
[13] II Cor. 4.8-9.   [14] *Th. des NT*, p. 317.

of being thrown into an abyss.[15] Yet while the threat is faced, there is found a ground of hope that is lacking in Heidegger's philosophy. Man and the world belong alike to God, so that the opposition between them is not absolute. Heidegger offers the alternatives of being lost in the world through surrender to its alien being which surrounds us, or of resolving to be myself in the narrow limits open to me in an existence of which I can never be the master. The New Testament is well aware of the first of these alternatives, but for the second it substitutes the possibility of being myself by the grace of God who has mastery of all being. At present, however, our concern is with the inauthentic mode of existence, and we must now consider how the threat to existence involved in facticity develops.

13. *Depersonalization*

The world of work and practical concern is a common world (*Mitwelt*). The instrument which I use not only implies the total instrumental system, as we already saw, but also the existence of other persons to whom these instruments are to hand in their concern as they are to me in mine. Generally, indeed, the instrument which I use is the result of the work of someone else, and the work which I do with it is appointed for yet another person. The book in my hand, for instance, was written by A, printed and bound by B, published by C, bought from D, and I am now reading it so that I can say something about its contents to E—and so we could continue indefinitely. Thus 'being-in-the-world' implies 'being-with-others' (*Mitsein*).[16]

It follows, therefore, that for Heidegger community belongs to being-in-the-world, which man always is. It is not something added on to individual existence, as, for instance, by a 'social contract', but something which necessarily belongs to existence. It would still be true, he claims, that I am 'being-with-others', even if no others are present or perceptible, supposing I were a hermit or a shipwrecked mariner.

[15] I Cor. 9.27. [16] Cf. *S. u. Z.*, p. 117 ff.

This is worth observing, because although Heidegger, like the existentialists in general, has strong individualist tendencies, his individualism is quite different from the individualism of eighteenth-century thinkers, of whom Rousseau will serve as an example. Heidegger's individualism appears to me to be accidental rather than essential to his philosophy, which clearly recognizes 'being-with-others' as a necessary way of being of the individual, a basic existential. Yet the concept of 'being-with-others' is a side of his philosophy which is left curiously undeveloped, and we shall later have cause to ask whether this bias of Heidegger towards individualism does not reflect itself in Bultmann's thought also.

Although other persons are met out of the world with which I am concerned, they do not belong to the world any more than I do. They have the character of 'being-there-with-me'. (*Mitdasein*). They are, therefore, not objects within the world, but co-existents with me. Thus it follows that I am never related to a person as I am to a thing. A thing is to me an instrument, and my relation to it is practical concern (*Besorgen*). But my relation to a person is personal concern (*Fürsorge*)—a broad term which Heidegger uses to cover all kinds of personal relationships. A person is never a mere object. Here Heidegger is distinguishing between the 'I-it' and the 'I-thou' relationships, yet once again, beyond a formal definition, the theme is left largely unexplored.

'Being-with-others' has the two fundamental possibilities that we have learned to expect in Heidegger—it can be authentic or inauthentic. In the authentic mode it helps the other to his freedom, to the attainment of his true self. In the inauthentic mode it makes possible dominance and the corresponding dependence, and it depersonalizes, destroying rather than liberating the true being of man. It does so because, just as I can mistakenly regard myself as an object belonging to the world, so I can regard another person in that way, and treat him impersonally. It is with this inauthentic mode of 'being-with-others' that we are concerned for the present, and to it Heidegger has given full consideration.[17]

[17] *S. u. Z.*, p. 126 ff.

In this inauthentic way of being-with-others, I am subject to others. They have, so to speak, taken away my being, so that I am no longer myself. Yet when I ask who it is that has thus acquired dominance over me, and makes my decisions for me, it turns out to be no one in particular. It is the neuter '*das Man*' in Heidegger's terminology, the German impersonal pronoun denoting an indefinite subject of action. We might translate it into English as 'people' or 'the public' (the expression used by Kierkegaard for the same phenomenon), though perhaps these terms scarcely do justice to the sheer impersonality of the neuter '*das Man*'.

For the most part, Heidegger contends, a man is not himself but others, in the sense of being part of the public. He enjoys what the public enjoys, and he finds shocking what the public finds shocking. He reads and sees and judges as the public does, all become uniformly alike, and thus men 'unfold their own dictatorship'.[18] Yet the dictator is no one in particular, but the amorphous depersonalized mass to which all are subject.

We must briefly review the principal characteristics of this depersonalized way of being, as they are mentioned in Heidegger's phenomenological analysis. There is 'everyday-ness' (*Alltäglichkeit*). We have already frequently met the expression 'everyday existence'. This is a technical term with Heidegger. It stands for a way of being dominated by unthinking habit, a mechanical following of the ways laid down for us in an established order. Then there is 'average-ness', or mediocrity (*Durchschnittlichkeit*), which comes about as the result of a levelling tendency (*Einebnung*) present in the use by all of facilities which make all alike—filling up forms, queueing for transport or entertainment are familiar examples. 'Every supremacy is silently suppressed, every original thought is glossed over as well known, every triumph is vulgarized, every mystery loses its power.'[19] Publicity (*Öffentlichkeit*) is another related characteristic of the depersonalized way of being. Whereas dread isolates the individual in his facticity and responsibility, in publicity he can forget

18 *S. u. Z.*, p. 126.   19 *S. u. Z.*, p. 127.

himself and his responsibility, and so allay his anxiety, by identifying himself with the indeterminate impersonal multitude. Talking (*Gerede*) is the everyday way of speaking which, instead of disclosing anything as it really is, rather makes it become what the public says that it is.[20] Corresponding to this baseless talking there is a scribbling (*Geschriebe*) or popular literature which passes for writing. This scribbling really obscures the truth, but it becomes popular and authoritative because it tells people what they want to hear. Finally there is curiosity (*Neugier*). This is the desire to enter into experiences without taking the resolve to have them for one's self. The cinema affords imaginative entry into the gay luxurious world of Hollywood; the 'thriller' gives the reader the excitement of sharing in the deeds of daring of the hero, without needing to leave his fireside; the sensational type of Sunday newspaper makes possible vicarious indulgence in crime and adultery, even if the reader professes (and himself believes) that he is horrified by the stories which it reports.

These artificial devices prevent an authentic 'being-with-others', and pervert it into the public, the depersonalized way of being that characterizes man in the mass. The ontological significance of the concept of the public is that it again shows us man's flight from his responsibility. In escaping into the public, man avoids being pressed to the point of decision. Because what the public does is done by no one in particular, the public relieves the individual of his accountability. The everyday self is called by Heidegger the 'public self' (*Manselbst*), and he distinguishes it from the authentic self. This public self is lost, in the sense of being scattered through the public, frittered away in the trivialities of talk, curiosity and the rest, and in this inauthentic being-with-others man conceals from himself the challenge of his existence.

The public is a universal way of being for man. The individual can never completely loose himself from its dominance, even if he were to attempt it. The authentic self is therefore

20 Cf. *S. u. Z.*, p. 167 ff.

not a breakaway from the public, but an existential modification of the public, the public being considered as one of man's fundamental ways of being, that is, an existential.[21] This means that the individual must be himself within and in spite of the public. He need not take the public as his hero, yet he can no more get away from it altogether than he can get away from the world. The concept of the public is therefore related to facticity also. Just as man is always already thrown into a world which limits his possibilities, so he is also thrown into a public, a social environment, which necessarily circumscribes his possibilities, even if he is able to resist falling under its complete domination. It remains the all-powerful but impersonal (and that means here sub-personal) tyrant, yet the irony of the situation is that man himself has created its power in his stampede from the ultimate issues of his existence into the illusory security of an inauthentic collectivism.

Man is always and everywhere more or less depersonalized. Yet it might be said that depersonalization is especially characteristic of the modern era. As such, it has received detailed attention from another philosopher of existentialist tendencies, namely, Jaspers, in his study of the present situation of mankind.

'The inevitable mass-effect,' he says, 'is intensified today by the complicated articulations of a modern economic society. The rule of the masses affects the activities and habits of the individual. It has become obligatory to fulfil a function which shall in some way be regarded as useful to the masses. The masses and their apparatus are the object of our most vital interest. The masses are our masters; and for everyone who looks facts in the face his existence has become dependent on them, so that the thought of them must control his doings, his cares and his duties. Even an articulated mass always tends to become unspiritual and inhuman. It is life without existence, superstition without faith. It may stamp all

[21] *S. u. Z.,* p. 130.

flat; it is disinclined to tolerate independence and greatness, but prone to constrain people to become as automatic as ants.'[22]

The factors which have accentuated depersonalization in the modern world are well known. Industrialization condemns multitudes to mechanical tasks, and herds them together in over-grown cities; press, radio, television and advertising mould what is called public opinion, and relieve the individual of the necessity of thinking and deciding for himself; commercialized sport and entertainment have a deadly uniformity the world over. And depersonalization has perhaps reached its pitch in modern warfare, in which the individual has almost ceased to count.

It would be tedious to enlarge upon these themes, since they have become themselves the well-worn and, one may almost say, trivialized topics for contemporary statesmen, journalists, churchmen and philosophers. They have themselves been turned into platitudes that have lost their power, exactly as Heidegger says—'every original thought is glossed over (by the public) as well known.' Thus the public has already gone far to depersonalize and rob of their sting even pronouncements on the very menace of depersonalization. They have become so familiarized and vulgarized that we can now hear them without uneasiness. Has not this been the fate of existentialism itself? 'The very last thing in absurdity during this century,' says Mounier, 'must have been the craze for existentialism, the degeneration into idle daily gossiping of a philosophy whose whole purpose is to drag us away from our idle gossiping.'[23] But *das Man* is stronger than the philosopher.

Depersonalization, it is worth remembering, has proceeded almost as far in the western democracies as it has in the countries which have fallen under dictatorship. The factors contributing to depersonalization are universal in their distribution through the civilized world. Totalitarianism—if by that is meant the omnicompetence of the state—is in theory possible within a democracy as well as under a dictatorship. It has often been pointed out that the ideal of the welfare state, however laudable and desirable in many ways, seems to be one that must be purchased at the price of progressive depersonalization. The twentieth century has been called the age of the common man, but it is open to question whether this means a recognition of the rights and dignity of every man, or a levelling of all men to the average uniformity of mass existence.

It is against this background of modern depersonalization that Heidegger's individualism must be understood, and this explains our suggestion that it is accidental rather than essential to his philosophy. Heidegger himself deserted the haunts of the public to study the poems of Hölderlin in the solitude of the Black Forest. That is the typical reaction of existentialism against the dominance of the impersonal public. As an attempt to rescue and restore individual existence and responsibility, it is so far good. But it seems to stop there, and leaves undeveloped the concept of an authentic being-with-others, though this, as we saw, on Heidegger's own analysis necessarily belongs to the authentic being of the individual, which would be incomplete without it. On the other hand, Christianity, while agreeing with the existentialist philosophy in recalling man from collective irresponsibility to the point of individual decision, goes further than a mere individualism and in the Church holds out to men the possibility of an authentic being-with-others in which individual freedom can alone be made complete. An extravagant individualism can be as irresponsible as an impersonal collectivism.

Such exaggerated individualism characterizes existentialist philosophy in general, but this is an accidental consequence of the violence of its reaction against the pressure of contemporary collectivism. The concept of an authentic being-with-others has its place in existentialist thought, although it has not been significantly worked out as yet. It frequently happens that the existentialist artist breaks with artistic conventions, the existentialist philosopher rejects the accepted moral code, the Christian existentialist finds no use for the organized Church. All of these appear to make the mistake of throwing out the baby with the bath-water. They are right in so far as they seek to emancipate the individual personality from something that is dead, mechanical and impersonal, but wrong in so far as they remain on the level of mere individualism.

Heidegger's concept of *das Man* does fairly describe a way of being in which the individual loses himself and becomes depersonalized, but it would surely be quite wrong to conclude that all tradition, custom and habit belong to this way of being and are therefore inauthentic. Even the everyday utterances of conscience, as we shall see later, are regarded by Heidegger as nothing but the voice of *das Man* —they express the public code of conduct. But there can be a living tradition as well as a dead tradition—and the Christian must certainly believe so, since tradition is essential to the Church. A tradition would be dead where it was mechanically and unthinkingly taken over, but it is alive where each new generation consciously decides to receive it. Our Lord did not attack the religious traditions of the Jews as such, but only because they were mechanical traditions without authentic obedience.

But even the unthinking habit of 'everydayness', in which there is no conscious decision, is not always to be dismissed as worthless. The late Lord Lindsay gives a good illustration of the place of moral habit in life.[24] Supposing I were a person specially prone to the temptation to get drunk, there would be no virtue in going through a moral struggle and making a fresh *existentiell* decision every time I had to pass a public house. That would be nothing but a waste of time —and a very serious waste of time in some of our cities where there are places of refreshment situated at short intervals along the street. It is much better that I should form the habit of walking past without giving the matter a thought. Aristotle, indeed, went so far as to teach that 'moral virtue comes about as a result of habit.'[25] It is by doing good

[24] In his introduction to Mill's *Essay on Liberty.*   [25] *Ethica Nicomachea,* 1103a.

actions that a man becomes good, that is, forms good habits. But in that case individual decision, free from the influence of tradition, custom and habit, cannot have the exaggerated place which the existentialist tends to assign to it.

With these qualifications, however, we recognize the broad truth contained in the concept of *das Man*. The social unit can and always more or less does become collectivism rather than community, inhuman and depersonalized, more stupid and more immoral than the individual. *Das Man* is an existential, a possible way of man's being, which means that it is man himself who creates the tyranny of the public. He surrenders his individual being to its domination in order to get away from his individual responsibility and so lull his anxiety. He is always more or less under its dominance, and especially in the modern era. But this is not a genuine being-with-others, it is 'a strained and ambiguous adaptation of one to the other', 'enmity under the mask of friendship', 'the secret persistence of envy'.[26]

No doubt the earliest biblical religion was in the main collective in its character. But if Eichrodt is right, the significance of the prophetic revival in Israel lay in the summons—or possibly the recall—to individual responsibility before God.[27] One aspect of the teaching of Jesus may be regarded as a renewal of the prophetic summons under new conditions, a protest against formal traditional observance coupled with a demand for 'genuine radical obedience'[28] —and that implies understanding and consent on the part of the individual who obeys. The New Testament writers, therefore, already had before them the protests of our Lord and of the Hebrew prophets against the dangers of a collectivism which sheds man of his responsibility.

In the New Testament theology proper, we find this depersonalized collective existence exhibited in the concept of the κόσμος which is common to both the Pauline and the Johannine writings. We have already noted that in the Fourth Gospel the κόσμος may mean simply the created

26 Cf. *S. u. Z.*, p. 175, and Jaspers, *op. cit.*, p. 42.
27 *Supra*, p. 19.   28 *Th. des NT*, pp. 10-12.

world,[29] and the same is true of a few passages in Saint Paul's epistles,[30] though he generally uses the term κτίσις in this sense. For neither of them, however, does κόσμος mean, as it did for the Greeks, the rationally ordered universe in which God, man and nature have all their place. The idea is quite foreign to biblical thought, in which God stands outside the world as its Creator, and in which also man is discontinuous in his being with nature.

In the typical New Testament usage, κόσμος is 'not a cosmological but a historical concept'—and that means an existential concept, a way of man's being.[31] It is the sphere of human relations, men in their totality. That God shall 'judge the world', or that sin has 'entered into the world', or that there is a 'wisdom of the world' are statements only intelligible if the world is understood in an anthropological or existential sense.[32] The same is true of the Johannine usage, for instance in passages which speak of the hatred of the world for Christ's disciples.[33] There is an opposition between the world, understood as the human sphere, the totality of mankind on the one hand, and the sphere of God on the other. It is conceived as under the domination of 'the prince of this world' or 'the god of this world (αἰών)', who is the enemy of God.[34] The world dominates and rules over the individuals who constitute it. 'The spirit of the world' lies over men.[35] 'This spirit,' says Bultmann, 'expressed in modern speech, is the atmosphere to whose compelling influence each one contributes, and, at the same time, under whose influence he lies.'[36] The relation of the Christian to the world is that while he has overcome the world and been freed from its tyranny, he remains in the world so long as he exists on earth, continually exposed to its threat.[37]

How is the κόσμος related to *das Man*? Bultmann's interpretation of this New Testament concept has very obvious points of contact with Heidegger's existential analysis. But

---

29 *Supra*, p. 52.   30 E.g., Rom. 1.20.   31 *Th. des NT*, p. 250 ff.
32 Rom. 3.6; 5.12; I Cor. 1.20.   33 John 15.18; 17.14.
34 John 12.31; II Cor. 4.4.   35 I Cor. 2.12.
36 *Th. des NT*, p. 253.   37 I Cor. 3.21-22; John 17.11.

the New Testament concept of the world as a kind of organized rebellion against God is infinitely grander and more terrifying than the concept of the tyranny of the public in existentialism. That is because the world is a concrete ontical phenomenon met in actual moral and religious experience, whereas *das Man* is a formal existential-onto-logical concept. Yet it is this ontological concept which makes clear the meaning of the ontical concept, and relates it to the whole structure of man's being. Only because man has in the structure of his being the possibility of an inauthentic being-with-others, as set out in the existential analytic, can there be this tyrannizing solidarity of human sinfulness which the New Testament calls the world. The world is the most terrifying manifestation and concretion of that possibility of man's existence which Heidegger calls *das Man*. It is along such lines that Bultmann has conducted his existential exegesis of the κόσμος. The κόσμος is not a place or a substance or an environment, but a way of man's being in which, in his flight from his individual responsibility, he loses his true self. Into this world all men are 'thrown', so that it is a factor in the facticity of human existence. It is in the world and in spite of the world (to adapt Heidegger's phrase about *das Man*) that men must decide for God and live the Christian life. This account of the κόσμος appears to be intelligible, convincing and loyal to the New Testament.

But what of the New Testament idea that the κόσμος is under the dominion of hostile powers? An existential exegesis will find no room for demonic forces in the world. The question, however, is what the New Testament writers really believed about such demonic forces. They sometimes used mythological language about the rulers of this world, but they certainly did not accept the Gnostic dualism of a demonic world of darkness over against the divine world of light. When Saint Paul speaks of the entry of sin into the world, he attributes it not to powers of darkness but to Adam.[38] Hence Bultmann seems to be justified in his conclusion that the authentic view of the New Testament is that

[38] Rom. 5.12.

it is man himself who has given to the κόσμος its hostile demonic character, just as we saw in the case of the κτίσις.[39] 'Its power is derived at bottom from man himself,' says Bultmann, or, in Heidegger's language, 'man has unfolded his own dictatorship'. The natural man has decided for the world rather than for God, and in that act of decision he has given it its hostile character.

While the New Testament recalls the individual from the world to a decision for God, it does not rest there, but sets over against the false community of the world the authentic community of the Church, the ἐκκλησία which is called out of the world. We asked already whether Bultmann is not perhaps unduly influenced by existentialist individualism, and so fails to do justice to the New Testament conception of fellowship. Here we may see another instance of the selective influence of existentialism in his thought. Alternatively it could be argued, of course, that this is simply the Lutheran influence in Bultmann's thought, perhaps reinforced by the existentialist tendency to individualism, since the prevailing German tradition in the Church has in general concentrated on individual piety to the neglect of Christian community.

This, however, takes us beyond the limits of the present part of the inquiry, which is into man's inauthentic way of being, and the question of the Church must be reserved until later. We now pass to a broad existential concept which gathers up some of those that we have already met.

14. *Fallenness*

We now summarize briefly the position so far reached in our survey of the analysis of existence. Human existence has been exhibited as possibility conditioned by facticity. But man flees from the disclosure to himself in anxiety of his 'being-there'. On the one hand he identifies himself with the world and becomes absorbed in 'worldly' concern; on the other hand he sheds his responsibility in the depersonalized

[39] *Supra*, p. 51.

collective way of being which we called the public. In his everyday talking he conceals from himself the challenge of his existence. In curiosity he substitutes the imaginary for the real. These characteristics are brought together in Heidegger's concept of fallenness (*Verfallenheit*).[40] This is a fundamental way of everyday being, and with it, he says, we reach a sharper definition of what he means by inauthenticity as a basic possibility of existence.

Man's fallenness has a twofold aspect. It is first a fall into the world, out of which he tries to understand himself. He relates his possibilities exclusively to things, absorbs himself in concern with them, and finds himself at home (*vertraut*) among them, thereby obliterating his awareness of the gulf which separates his being from the being of the world, and concealing from himself that he is not at home. This appears to be primarily the flight from facticity. Brunner has argued that it is not technology which has produced the problems of modern civilization, but rather modern civilization which has created for itself the problem of an uncontrolled technology.[41] Man's intense preoccupation with the world of things, he believes, is simply the expression of his delusion that he can solve the problems of his existence by the mastery of things, or, expressed in biblical language, his reaction to the temptation, 'Ye shall be as gods'.[42] Presumably for the gods the limitations of facticity are removed and possibility is unhindered, hence we suggest that this preoccupation with things is the flight from facticity.

Fallenness is secondly a fall into collectivism, in which the individual surrenders his will to the depersonalized mass, and follows the crowd. This appears to be primarily the flight from possibility, so far as that means responsibility. As belonging to the public, the individual need not think or decide for himself, nor need he have any qualms of conscience, for what everybody does must be right. In the modern world with its vast technical apparatus, in serving which men themselves become instruments, factory 'hands',

[40] Cf. *S. u. Z.*, p. 175 ff.
[41] *Christianity & Civilization*, Nisbet, vol. 2, Lect. 1.   [42] Gen. 3.5.

these two aspects of fallenness are, of course, very closely combined.

Complementary to these two positive aspects of fallenness is a negative one. Man is fallen away from himself (*abgefallen*), he has lost the authentic power to be himself (*Selbstseinkönnen*). His true self is lost and scattered in the world—that is to say, in the instrumental world of things and in the depersonalized world of the public. To use another metaphor of Heidegger, man is uprooted (*entwurzelt*).[43]

Heidegger's phenomenological analysis of fallenness yields three important structures. The first is temptation (*Versuchung*). We saw already that man's existence is permanently threatened in virtue of his facticity. So long as he exists, he is alongside the world which invites him to surrender to its alien being. But Heidegger here goes further. Man wants to surrender to the world. He tempts himself. He flees from himself and desires to fall into the world. In his everyday talking and curiosity, says Heidegger, he prepares for himself the permanent temptation to fallenness. The second structure is contentment (*Beruhigung*). As fallen, man is delivered from the restlessness engendered by dread. In his concern with things and his solidarity with the public, he is no longer disturbed by the ultimate issues of existence—unless, of course, his security is taken away from him for some reason or other, and then the mood of anxiety breaks in to shatter this contentment. The contentment is illusory, and we shall return to its illusory nature later. Finally there is the structure of alienation (*Entfremdung*). As fallen, man is cut off from his true self and from his authentic possibilities. The deeper his fall into the world, the further he is from himself. And further, like a stone falling with increasing velocity, man must become more and more entangled in the world. His contentment does not bring rest, for he must drive himself further into the world and so further from himself.

It must be clearly understood that Heidegger here is dealing with a purely ontological concept. We must, therefore, beware of any facile identification of fallenness with

[43] *S. u. Z.*, p. 177.

the ethico-religious concept of the fall of man familiar in Christian theology. Fallenness, in Heidegger's sense of the term, is not a general property of man, as, let us say, rotundity is of a ball. It is an existential, a pure possibility which is open to man in virtue of his ontological structure. Heidegger himself is quite explicit on this point. He says that he is making no ontical pronouncement on the corruption of human nature.[44] He claims that he has said nothing to indicate whether, ontically, man is in a state of corruption or in a state of innocence or in a state of grace. All that has been said is that man is so constituted that fallenness, in the sense of that term which has been explained, is a possibility for him. It is another question whether the possibility is actualized.

Yet there is a connection between the purely ontological concept of fallenness and the ethico-religious concept of a fallen humanity. So far as the latter claims to be an actual description of man's condition, it already assumes the ontological concept of fallenness, that is to say, it assumes that man is so constituted in his being that fallenness is a possibility for him. What the theologian understands by fallenness is a concrete *existentiell* situation. This understanding is to be validated and clarified by relating it to man's ontological structure, and by showing that it does lie within the horizons of what is genuinely possible for man. But these horizons are delineated by the existential analytic, which reveals, among other phenomena, this existential concept of fallenness. Hence Heidegger's claim that for the proper understanding of the ethico-religious concept of the fall, the theologian must consider it in relation to its ground in the ontological concept of fallenness.[45] But the elucidation of the ontological concept is not itself the work of theology, but of the pre-theological inquiry into the ontological assumptions of all theology—in other words, it is the work of what Heidegger calls the existential analytic or (which is the same thing) what Bultmann more fully describes as 'the philosophical work which endeavours to develop in suitable

[44] *S. u. Z.*, p. 179.   [45] *S. u. Z.*, p. 180.

concepts the understanding of existence which is given with human existence.'[46]

We must now see how Bultmann follows the method which he has himself prescribed in connection with the concept of fallenness, and we do so by considering his treatment of two important New Testament concepts—σάρξ and ἁμαρτία. In his exposition of these the influence of Heidegger's existentialism is clearly discernible.

Bultmann begins with a very clear statement of his position.[47] Evil is a falling away of man from himself, a mistaken orientation of himself away from his authentic being. But this is at the same time sin, rebellion against God, who as Creator gave to man his being. To attain or to lose his authentic being is equivalent on man's part to recognizing or denying God as his Creator. To deny the Creator means, however, to turn to the creation. Man lives for and from the world. Man is thus fallen away from the authentic being that God has given him into the world, in concern with which he seeks to live by his own power without God. This is the essence of sin.

So far this looks very much like a theological version of Heidegger's concept of fallenness. Bultmann concedes that we will not find these views so clearly and summarily formulated in the New Testament, but nevertheless, he maintains, they represent the understanding of man's fallen condition implicit in the Pauline epistles, and here made explicit in the light of our understanding of man's existential constitution. The justification for his interpretation is to be sought both in the anthropological concepts already discussed, and in the elucidation of the two concepts of σάρξ and ἁμαρτία, to the consideration of which he now proceeds.

As with σῶμα and καρδία, he points out that the term σάρξ, the flesh, shows a variety of usage in the New Testament.[48] It seems to mean simply man's physical body, in passages like those in which Saint Paul speaks of the 'infirmity of the flesh' or of a 'thorn in the flesh'.[49] In a wider sense, and following the Old Testament usage, σάρξ, sometimes coupled

[46] Supra, p. 10.
[48] Th. des NT, p. 229 ff.
[47] Th. des NT, p. 228.
[49] Gal. 4.13; II Cor. 12.7.

with αἷμα, can stand for mankind, with reference to man's finite creatureliness, and implying perhaps a contrast with the being of God, as, for instance, when Saint Paul says that after his conversion he went into Arabia, and 'conferred not with flesh and blood'.[50] From this it is only a step to a still wider sense in which σάρξ comes to mean the sphere of the natural in which man's transient earthly existence as flesh and blood is set. Thus it can be said of believers that they 'are not in the flesh',[51] which does not mean that they are no longer on earth, but that they are no longer founding their lives on the natural and the creaturely. In this sense σάρξ obviously approximates to κόσμος, the meaning of which was already discussed.

The specifically bad sense of σάρξ has not yet clearly emerged. Bultmann brings it out by a comparison of the expressions ἐν σαρκί and κατὰ σάρκα. 'The life which I now live in the flesh'[52] is an expression which passes no ethical judgment. It means simply that so long as I exist, I exist in the sphere of the natural and the earthly. Within this sphere man moves, 'it delimits his horizon, the possibilities of his activity and suffering'.[53] Thus ἐν σαρκί simply recognizes man's facticity as existing in a world in which he is not at home and in which his possibilities are circumscribed. The threat to his existence is already given with his facticity, but it is still only a threat.

But when Saint Paul says that men 'are after the flesh' (κατὰ σάρκα) or 'purpose after the flesh' or 'walk after the flesh'[54] then in the characteristic use of this expression (for there are exceptions, as Bultmann recognizes) it is implied that what is done is not simply within the sphere of the natural, but that in addition it is evil or sinful. Where has the transition to this new meaning taken place? It lies in this, that whereas to be ἐν σαρκί means usually no more than to exist in the earthly environment, to be κατὰ σάρκα means that man has already decided for the earthly and the natural, and has rejected God, and with God his own

[50] Gal. 1.16.   [51] Rom. 8.9.   [52] Gal. 2.20.
[53] *Th. des NT*, p. 231.   [54] Rom. 8.5; II Cor. 1.17; 10.2.

authentic being. He is not only in the world, he has fallen into the world.

The flesh is to be understood as a way of being, not a substance. Thus to say that 'in my flesh dwelleth no good thing'[55] is no Gnostic disparagement of the body or recognition of an inherently evil matter. What God has created is good, but when man decides for the creation rather than for the Creator, he makes it evil. There is no good thing in the flesh in the sense that man cannot found his life upon it, and if he attempts to do so, it becomes evil. But this evil is not external to man, but derives from him as existing possibility. Just as with the κόσμος, Saint Paul sometimes speaks of the σάρξ almost as if personified, a kind of demonic master ·to whom, for instance, man may be a debtor.[56] But it is man himself who has given to the σάρξ its tyrannical power.

Bultmann's existential treatment of the concept of σάρξ enables him to explain how Saint Paul brings together as manifestations of the life according to the flesh such diverse human activities as the sensuality of the pagans, Jewish legalism and Gentile philosophy. It would be a gross misunderstanding to associate the σάρξ primarily with what we call 'sins of the flesh'. For Saint Paul the righteousness of the Jews and the wisdom of this world, however on the surface they differ from sins of sensuality, are equally a manifestation of 'confidence in the flesh'. They represent a falling away from God and a turning to the creature and the man-made.

In a way which yields results not unlike those of Heidegger's phenomenological analysis of fallenness, Bultmann now proceeds to indicate some of the principal characteristics of the life after the flesh as these are found in the Pauline epistles. It is a life of desiring (ἐπιθυμεῖν). Fallen man is driven restlessly on by 'the lust of the flesh',[57] becoming more entangled in the creation and further removed from the Creator. Yet along with this goes an illusory contentment which finds expression in the boasting (καυχᾶσθαι) of men who fancy that they have mastered the problems of their existence by their own creaturely devices. The Jews boast

[55] Rom. 7.18.　　　[56] Rom. 8.12.　　　[57] E.g., Gal. 5.16.

of their righteousness, the Greeks of their wisdom, and both, by this confidence in the flesh, show their misunderstanding of the human situation.[58] Two further characteristics of the life after the flesh have been noted already—fear and enslavement.

When we read Bultmann's very carefully documented analysis of the Pauline concept of σάρξ, it may occur to us that he has said very little that is new. It is true that the different meanings that he has indicated can mostly be found in earlier commentators,[59] but what appears to be original in this part of Bultmann's work is the way in which these different meanings for the flesh are brought together in the light of his concept of existence—and particularly the neutral meaning of σάρξ as the natural, and the bad meaning of σάρξ as the sinful. The distinction does not lie in anything outside man himself, but in man's *existentiell* decision for the creaturely rather than for the Creator, which makes the natural evil. And further, in the light of the same concept of existence, the connection of σάρξ with σῶμα, νοῦς, καρδία, κτίσις and κόσμος is made clear. Bultmann is here doing the proper work of the systematic theologian in exhibiting the Christian understanding of man in a closely connected and coherent system of thought. He is not content to show us isolated aspects of man from the New Testament teaching, but has built up the various concepts into a unified and systematic anthropology. But he has only been able to do this because of his ontological understanding of man. Admittedly he appears to have derived this understanding from Heidegger's existential analytic. But what can it be said that he has imported into his interpretation of the New Testament teaching except a remarkable degree of clarity and consistency? As Bultmann himself claims, the philosophy of existence does not prejudice the content of the answer which theology seeks from the exegesis of the sacred texts, but it 'opens our eyes' to the meaning of the text. The *Begrifflichkeit* of existence, as that has been analysed and explained in the

58 Rom. 2.17 ff.; I Cor. 1.19-31.
59 Cf., e.g. Burton, *Galatians, I.C.C.*, T. & T. Clark, p. 492 ff.

preceding pages, has provided Bultmann with a groundwork in the light of which he has gathered together the isolated concepts of New Testament thought and exhibited their structural relationships. Bultmann's exposition seems to stand up to Tillich's criterion, quoted earlier[60]—'the test of a phenomenological description is that the picture given by it is convincing, that it can be seen by anyone who is willing to look in the same direction, that the description illuminates other related ideas, and that it makes the reality which these ideas are supposed to reflect understandable.'

And further, although Bultmann has followed fairly closely the pattern of Heidegger's existential analytic, and has borrowed much of Heidegger's terminology, let us remind ourselves again that the leading ideas of the philosophy of existence are not peculiar to the twentieth century, but represent a rediscovery, in reaction to the extreme objectivism of modern thought, of truths that first appeared long ago in the history of philosophy. Some of these truths—and the most important of them—were familiar to the biblical writers, and for that reason we were able to draw attention to several points of affinity between existentialism and biblical thought. Hence in spite of Bultmann's employment of modern existentialist terms—such as ontological and ontical, existential and *existentiell*—it must not, therefore, be inferred that the systematic anthropology which he has constructed from the Pauline concepts would be foreign to the mind of Saint Paul himself. It was not Saint Paul's business to set forth a formal ontology, yet there must have been some understanding of the being of man underlying his thought, and Bultmann would claim that that understanding implicit in the Pauline writings is something very like the concept of existence as that has been analysed by Heidegger and other thinkers of his school. And it must be confessed that Bultmann's remarkable success in gathering into a unity the various Pauline concepts and the different meanings within each concept argues strongly in his favour, for it is hard to see how he could have discovered and exhibited this unity,

[60] *Supra*, pp. 35-36.

dependent on the central concept of existence, unless it was already there in the mind of the apostolic writer.

We have not yet examined the phenomenon of alienation, which, as we saw, belongs to Heidegger's concept of fallenness. With this theme we come to the very important Christian concept of sin (ἁμαρτία), which implies not only moral evil but alienation from God. In the absence of God from Heidegger's philosophy, no genuine concept of sin is therefore possible for him. The alienation of a fallen existence is alienation from the authentic self, not from God. Is sin, therefore, a concept which we cannot integrate with the others, or link up with the concept of existence? By no means. It is clear that Saint Paul also understands sin as alienation from the authentic self: 'It is no more I that do it, but sin that dwelleth in me.'[61] The authentic self is lost, and the inauthentic or sinful self—here expressed simply as 'sin'— has taken control. This 'strife between ego and ego', as Bultmann calls it,[62] is only possible because man exists in Heidegger's sense of having a relation to himself, because he is σῶμα as Bultmann understands that term. But what, then, becomes of the notion of alienation from God, which is quite essential to the Christian concept of sin? That is simply answered. So far as man is fallen away from his true self, he is fallen away from the being which the Creator has given him. He is, therefore, denying God and rebelling against God, whose command is life—that is, the authentic existence for which man was created.[63] Alienation from God follows from alienation from the authentic self. 'The carnal mind'— that is to say, precisely this fallen understanding of the self— 'is enmity against God.'[64]

Sin in the New Testament is an ontical conception—it describes not only a possibility for man but his actual condition. 'All have sinned, and come short of the glory of God.'[65] What is the ground for this belief in the universality of sin? Saint Paul, as we saw already, traces the origin of sin not as the Gnostics did, to matter or demonic agency, but to man

[61] Rom. 7.17.   [62] *Th. des NT*, p. 241.   [63] Rom. 7.10.
[64] Rom. 8.7.   [65] Rom. 3.23.

himself, more precisely, to Adam.[66] He seems to argue there for a hereditary or original sin. Bultmann is unwilling to accept this, since it seems to him to cut away the ground of responsibility. He suggests—while freely admitting that his interpretation is here a very tentative one—that Saint Paul may mean that as Christ opens to man the possibility of life, so Adam opens the possibility of sin and death. This, however, seems a very strained and inadequate interpretation, since surely the possibility was there, as possibility, even before Adam realized it, and the whole point of Saint Paul's teaching is that now it is more than possibility, it is fact. Even Heidegger in his teaching that man tempts himself and prepares for his own fall seems to do more justice to the seemingly innate tendency of man to prefer the evil to the good. Bultmann, however, immediately goes on to another argument, not found explicitly in Saint Paul, but derived from his concept of the κόσμος as that has been already explained. Every individual is born into a falsely oriented humanity. He understands himself in the light of this, and becomes partly responsible for it. Whether this can be accepted as an adequate account of original sin is open to question, but it may be said that all theologians who are not content with contradicting themselves have their difficulties in doing justice both to the evil tendency in man which makes him prefer darkness to light, and to the responsibility which must be his if he is accountable for his existence.

For the sake of completeness, we must look also at the Johannine writings, which Bultmann seeks to interpret from the same existential point of view. The term σάρξ as Saint Paul develops it is practically absent. When the word does occur it usually has the neutral sense of the natural and this-worldly, as in the concept of the Word made flesh to express the thought of God's coming into this world in Christ.[67] It follows then that sin is not, as with Saint Paul, associated with the flesh. It is, as is well known, related rather to unbelief. The Holy Spirit will reprove the world of sin 'because they believe not in me.'[68] But we saw already that

[66] Rom. 5.12-19.   [67] John 1.14.   [68] John 16.9.

belief or knowledge, as the term is understood in the Fourth Gospel, is not to be taken in any narrow intellectual sense, but touches on the whole of existence.[69] Thus unbelief is the rejection of the Word, a preferring of darkness to light, a decision for the world rather than for God. On the other hand, the Pauline concept of the flesh does not denote primarily the sins of sensuality, but again a trust in the natural and this-worldly as against God. Allowing, therefore, for the different terminology, the fundamental understanding of sin in the Johannine writings is capable of being explained in a way very close to that which we have seen applied to the Pauline writings.

We have now traced the threat to human existence from its origin in human facticity, through its realization in preoccupation with the world and depersonalization in the crowd to its full concretion in the fallen life of sin. This is everyday inauthentic existence, in Heidegger's terminology, or the life of the natural man, in the more familiar language of the New Testament. We have now to ask what is the significance of this way of being which has been sketched out. Has it any value? Is it an illusion? And, of course, even as an illusion, it might have value if that illusion were intended to defend man against a reality too terrifying to be accepted. We must also ask what is the alternative, and whether there is more than one alternative to the inauthentic existence described. But first we turn to the question of significance.

[69] *Supra*, p. 66.

V

THE SIGNIFICANCE OF
EXISTENCE

15. *Care*

ARE we now in a position to estimate the significance of human existence, as it has been analysed in the various existential concepts? Is there some single concept that will show us the meaning of existence as a whole? And with this question goes also the question of value—really the question whether life is worth living, or whether it is a burden that no one would desire for himself. Let us first be clear that we are not yet in a position to answer the question fully—even supposing that it could be answered fully. What we have examined so far is (*a*) the basic ontological structure of all human existence and (*b*) the ontological structure (together with some of its ontical manifestations) of that fundamental possibility of human existence which Heidegger calls the inauthentic mode of existence. The present synthesis, therefore, cannot claim to be a complete interpretation of the meaning of existence, since we have confined ourselves chiefly to the inauthentic way of being, and we can only see the whole picture after we have examined what is meant by the concept of an authentic possibility of existence.[1] The concept which Heidegger advances as an interpretation of the being of man, so far as that has been already described in inauthentic everyday existence, is care.

This comprehensive concept unifies three of the fundamental characters of existence. The first is possibility. Man is always ahead of himself, incomplete in his being. He stands

[1] Cf. *S. u. Z.*, p. 192 ff.

before a 'not yet', he projects possibility. The second is facticity. Man exists as a fact, and his possibility is always tied down to his facticity. He is thrown into a situation, and his possibility is related to that situation. The third is fallenness. Man is fallen into the world in his practical concern with it. He is not only thrown into it, he has himself chosen it and surrendered himself to it. These three structures of the being of man—being ahead of himself, being already in the world, being concerned with the world as his home—together constitute care (*Sorge*). By this Heidegger insists once more that we are to understand a purely ontological concept. It is not to be confused with ontical anxiety, but on the other hand it makes such anxiety possible for man— it is that structure of his being in virtue of which 'he looks before and after' and at the same time is concerned with his world.

Is it merely by accident that at this critical juncture of his work, when he is concerned to put forward a comprehensive concept that will interpret the meaning of man's everyday existence, Heidegger has resort to a myth? Or is this a tacit acknowledgment that in the communication of the kind of knowledge which we call existential, the myth has its own indispensable function? Heidegger's ostensible reason for introducing his myth is to relate the result of his analytic to traditional and so-called common-sense understandings of the being of man. After all, the existential analytic was supposed to exhibit the understanding of existence which is already given with existence. As existing, man is disclosed to himself, and the work of the analytic is simply to make explicit that which is already somehow understood. But actually Heidegger's argument has introduced many ideas which are quite unfamiliar to common sense, and even to traditional philosophy, and he apologizes himself for the difficulties of his terminology in seeking to express his existential philosophy.[2] But now he pauses to make the claim that his interpretation of the being of man is an old one, and that it is faithful to the pre-ontological common-sense understanding

[2] *S. u. Z.*, pp. 38-39.

which man has of his own being, which the philosopher has merely analysed and set out in a systematic *Begrifflichkeit*.

The Latin myth, which is attributed to Hyginus, the reputed compiler of a handbook of mythology from Greek sources in the second century of our era,[3] is worth quoting:

> 'When Care once crossed a river, she saw some clay, and with thought she took a piece and began to shape it. While she was deliberating what she had made, Jupiter came along. Care asked him to confer spirit on the piece of clay she had shaped. This Jupiter gladly granted. But when she wished to bestow her name on the creature, Jupiter forbade her, and demanded that his own name must be given to him. While Care and Jupiter quarrelled over the name, Earth arose also and desired that her name be conferred on the creature, since she had given him a piece of her body. The disputants asked Saturn to be their arbiter. Saturn communicated to them the following decision, which seemed just: "Thou, Jupiter, since thou gavest the spirit, shalt take it at his death, and thou, Earth, since thou gavest the body, shall take it. But because Care first formed the nature of this creature, she shall possess him as long as he lives. And because there is a dispute over the name, he shall be called *Homo*, because he is made of earth (*humus*)." '

The importance of this myth, in Heidegger's view, is not only that it perceives care to be that which belongs to man's temporal existence as its distinctive character, but also that it connects care with the common view of the constitution of man as spirit and body. But whereas spirit and body are mistakenly understood as substances, they are to be properly understood as possibility and facticity, two of the constitutive elements of care—as, indeed, we suggested in connection with the Genesis account of man's creation out of the breath of life and the dust of the ground.[4] This raises the further question how far Heidegger's myth is comparable to the Old Testament story. We must note two very significant

[3] Cf. *Oxford Classical Dictionary*, p. 443. [4] *Supra*, p. 87.

differences. The first is the crude polytheism of the classical myth, which attributes the spirit to Jupiter and the body to Earth, a dualism which is reflected in Heidegger's own inability to bring together *Existenz* and *Vorhandenheit*. In contrast the Bible shows us the entire man as the work of the Creator God, who is the ground of his being both in his possibility and in his facticity. The second difference is that the Latin myth depicts man as already fallen. His origin is care, and fallenness is a necessary element in care. There is a distinct strain of pessimism in the view of man taught in this myth. The Bible, on the other hand, shows us man as created in the image of God before there was any mention of a fall. Man was not, therefore, created for a life of care but for an authentic existence, and so far as such an existence is withdrawn from fallenness, it is also withdrawn from care. 'Take no thought, saying, What shall we eat? or, What shall we drink? or, Wherewithal shall we be clothed?'[5] Jesus taught his disciples, thus recalling them from a life of care in which the self is scattered in a multiplicity of concerns to the life of faith in God.

Caring (μεριμνᾶν) is, as Bultmann points out, a characteristic of the fallen life in the Pauline teaching.[6] We should be careful to note, however, that the New Testament μεριμνᾶν is not Heidegger's ontological concept of care, but an actual or ontical concern for 'the things of the world',[7] through which concern man falls into the world and attempts to build his life on it rather than on God. This μεριμνᾶν is therefore nearer to what Heidegger calls practical concern (*Besorgen*) than to care as such (*Sorge*)—though Heidegger explicitly recognizes the close connection between the two concepts.[8] Since such caring belongs to the life after the flesh, Saint Paul's prayer is that the converts may be 'without carefulness'[9] and elsewhere he even bids the Christians 'be careful for nothing'.[10]

If the concept of care occupies so central a place in the existential analytic as the interpretation of the meaning of

[5] Matt. 6.31.   [6] *Th. des NT*, p. 237.   [7] I Cor. 7.33.
[8] *S. u. Z.*, p. 57.   [9] I Cor. 7.32.   [10] Phil. 4.6.

everyday existence, and if, as has been claimed, there is an affinity between the existentialist and the New Testament understandings of the being of man, then why, it may be asked, does this concept enter so slightly and so ambiguously into the New Testament teaching about man? That question, however, raises no serious difficulty for the main argument. It is to be answered by repeating something that has been said several times already, namely, that the New Testament writers are not concerned to expound an ontology as such. Their interest is not primarily existential but *existentiell*, that is to say, they are not trying to teach the philosophy of the good life but the living of the good life. Thus Saint Paul is rightly far more concerned with the ontical concept of sin than with any ontological concept, and has more to say about it. But it is the business of the theologian to go behind these ontical concepts to the underlying ontological assumptions, if he would rightly understand them and exhibit them in their connection together. That is the work of systematic theology. It is something like the ontological concept of care, the unity of possibility, facticity and fallenness in the being of man, which shows us how sin, as Saint Paul understood it, is possible for man, and which enables us to integrate most fully the many different concepts which Saint Paul employs to describe the life of man under sin.

In such a fallen existence, then, man bears a burden of care (a phrase not unfamiliar in Christian devotion), or rather, he is his own burden of care. Is this, then, the significance of man's everyday fallen existence?—for it was from the question of significance, it will be remembered, that we set out in this discussion of care. Or have we found that existence to be devoid of significance altogether? Before we can fully answer that question, we must turn to yet another phenomenon which seems to stultify even further the everyday existence of the natural man. This other phenomenon is death.

16. *Death*

Natural death is something of a mystery even to the physiologist. It is as yet by no means clear to biological science why the higher organisms should become senescent and eventually die. Here, however, we are not concerned with death as a natural happening, but with death as an existential phenomenon—and to Heidegger must go the credit of having drawn attention in recent times to this way, long neglected, of understanding death.

As a preliminary definition of death, we may say that it is loss of being.[11] Death is the end of man as 'being-there' or 'being-in-the-world'. Heidegger is careful to point out explicitly that this does not prejudge the question whether man has another being after death, whether he can be elsewhere or in another world. 'Only when death is fully grasped in its ontological character are we justified in asking what is after death.'[12] To begin with, we are approaching the problem of death purely as a phenomenon of human existence. Neither is Heidegger concerned with what he calls a metaphysic of death—how and why it came into the world, its significance as an evil, and so on. These questions also presuppose an ontological understanding of death, and until we have clarified that, we cannot hope to answer them—or even understand them properly.

But how can we hope to arrive at a full existential concept of death? Death as a natural phenomenon can be investigated by the normal methods of science. But death as an existential phenomenon must be investigated by the phenomenological method, that is to say, man's experience of death, this being considered to stand outside nature, is to be analysed. Clearly there is a difficulty here which did not arise with any of the other phenomena of existence. Death being by definition loss of his being, anyone who experiences death seems thereby to be robbed of the possibility of understanding and analysing it. He has ceased to be—at any rate in the sense of having the kind of being that we know in this world—therefore he has ceased to be disclosed to himself, and has no possibility of understanding what his death has been.

May information be obtained from considering the death of others? We observe them ceasing to exist, going out of the

[11] *S. u. Z.*, p. 237.   [12] *S. u. Z.*, pp. 247-248.

world. But the death of others is experienced as the loss sustained by those who remain behind, and not as the loss of being which the deceased himself has sustained. Nor can he any longer communicate with us to describe that loss of being. So it would seem that inquiry into the death of others, while it may teach us much about death considered as a natural phenomenon, can never disclose the existential concept of death. There is contained in this seemingly negative result, however, one positive character of death, namely, that it is always my own, since it cannot be experienced vicariously. It therefore shares one of the fundamental characters of existence—*Jemeinigkeit*. 'No one can die for another. He may give his life for another, but that does not in the slightest deliver the other from his own death.'[13] Death is untransferable and isolates the individual. He must die himself alone.

Is there any analogy which might throw light on death? We think of death as the end of man as being-in-the-world. This end is not something added on, so to speak; it belongs itself to the being of man. In that respect it might be compared to the ripeness of a fruit, which is not something added to the fruit in its immaturity, but means 'the fruit itself in a specific way of being'.[14] The analogy breaks down at that point, for whereas ripeness is the fulfilment of the fruit, the end may come for man when he is still immature or it may delay until he is broken down and exhausted with his fulfilment long past. But here again one positive result emerges. Death belongs to my possible ways of being— though in a unique kind of way, since it is the possibility of ceasing to be. It is already a possibility present in existing, so here again it shares a fundamental character of existence, and as a present possibility it is disclosed to me and can be analysed. Combining the two results, death appears as my own present untransferable possibility of being no longer in the world.

Heidegger clarifies this preliminary understanding of death as an existential phenomenon by referring it to his

[13] *S. u. Z.*, p. 240.　　　　　　　　[14] *S. u. Z.*, p. 243.

interpretation of the being of man as care. It will be remembered that care had a threefold structure—possibility, facticity and fallenness. Death belongs to man's possibility—it is, indeed, his most intimate and isolated possibility, always his own. We may note in passing that at this point Sartre disagrees with Heidegger. For him death is not a possibility but the cancellation of possibility. Yet this is not very different from what Heidegger expresses paradoxically by saying that death is 'the possibility of the impossibility of existence'.[15] And further, by possibility Heidegger does not mean simply a contingency that may happen to me, but a genuine possibility of existence which, as will be seen later, man may in a certain way choose for himself. Death always confronts me as my own isolated possibility.

This possibility of death is not accidental or occasional. It belongs to man's facticity. He is always already thrown into the possibility of death, as existing. His being, whether he is always conscious of it or not, is a 'being-unto-death' (Sein-zum-Tode). This possibility is therefore, on the one hand, certain—it is the one possibility of which we may be quite sure that it will be actualized. Yet at the same time it is, on the other hand, always indefinite, because as possibility it is already present, I am already thrown into it, and we never know when it will be realized. 'Man is always old enough to die.'

Fallenness is related to the flight from death. In his everyday inauthentic existence man avoids the thought of death, and conceals from himself its real significance. We are all familiar with symptoms of this flight from death. Some people have a horror of cemeteries, or even of going to see their friends in hospital. The very word death is avoided, and some euphemism substituted for it—'passing away', 'being at rest', and so on. Since fallen man is concerned with the world and has founded his life on it, to go out of the world means for him the shattering of his existence, and he does not wish to think of it. 'People die'—that much is recognized, but in this way death is depersonalized. The

[15] S. u. Z., p. 262.

impersonal way of speaking serves to conceal the real issue, which is that I die, and that my death is disclosed to me as a present possibility. In everyday talking of death it is generalized and reduced to a natural phenomenon, and thus it is robbed of its sting, and its significance for my existence is evaded. As Heidegger says, it is made to assume the character of escaping notice (*Unauffälligkeit*) which, as we saw,[16] belongs to that which is immediately to hand in the world.

It is obvious that for the interpretation of the biblical thought of death, it is the existential and not the natural phenomenon that is relevant. Death is understood in its significance for human existence, in relation to man's possibilities and projects over which hangs 'the shadow of death'. Death is not merely an observable happening, but a problem for man's existence. In the Psalms particularly there is 'a clear facing of the facts of life and death'[17]—and that by men who, like Heidegger in our time, had no assurance of any life to come. Man is bidden to return to destruction, to the dust from which he was formed, which seems to stultify his existence; no sooner does he flourish than he is cut down and withered; he may prolong his life for seventy or eighty years, yet the best of his days are labour and sorrow, and the inevitable end comes suddenly.[18] And these thoughts the psalmist relates to his own existence. Such a concept of death is existential, and might quite fairly be analysed as the concept of my own certain non-transferable and ever present possibility.

As well as this clear facing of the existential significance of death, we also find that note is taken in the Bible of the other side of the picture—fallen man's flight from death, and his avoidance of it in the understanding of his own existence. The best illustration of this is our Lord's own story of the rich man who proposed to build more commodious barns in which to store his expanding possessions, intending to live at his ease for many years.[19] Death overtook him before his plans were carried out. Absorbed in his concern with the

16 *Supra*, p. 48.
18 Ps. 90, vv. 3, 6, 10.
17 Oesterley, *The Psalms*, vol. II, p. 407.
19 Luke, 12.19.

world, he understood all his possibilities in terms of the
world, and overlooked his capital and nearest possibility—
that of his own death. Death can be overlooked, in spite of its
importance, precisely because man wants to overlook it. It is
depersonalized and objectified, the mystery and the imminent
threat are taken out of it, it becomes just a natural event in
the familiar world of events, and as such it is made to share
the character of escaping notice (*Unauffälligkeit*) which
belongs to the everyday understanding of the world and
which serves to mask the hostility of what is within the
world.

This biblical teaching on death does not accord to it the
exaggerated place which it holds in Heidegger's thought,
nor does it encourage the kind of preoccupation with death
which, as we shall see, Heidegger advocates. But there is
agreement in the call to face death squarely as an issue
touching my individual existence, and in the condemnation
of man's tendency to conceal from himself the ever present
possibility of his death. This traditional biblical understanding of death is already assumed in the New Testament
theology of death, but here the central problem is the relation
between death and sin. The connection of the two was, of
course, already familiar from the Old Testament, in which
death was conceived as a punishment for sin.[20] Saint Paul
also thinks of death in this way. Sinners are 'worthy of
death' in the judgment of God, death is 'the wages of sin'.[21]
There is, however, another line of thought in Saint Paul
which represents death as the necessary consequence of sin.
It is not simply a legal punishment, something added to sin
from outside, so to speak. It is conceived as the specific fruit
of a life after the flesh, arising necessarily from sin and with
sin. Thus Saint Paul can say that 'he that soweth to his
flesh shall of the flesh reap corruption', and, 'the sinful
cravings, which were by the law, did work in our members
to bring forth fruit unto death'.[22] Bultmann thinks that these
two lines of thought—death as punishment for sin, and death
as inherent consequence of sin—are left unreconciled in

[20] E.g., Gen. 3.19.   [21] Rom. 1.32; 6.23.   [22] Gal. 6.8; Rom. 7.5.

Saint Paul's teaching.[23] But it could be argued that the second is but an interpretation of the first, a deeper insight into the traditional belief that death is the punishment of sin. On this view death is already there as punishment with the sin itself. The punishment is contained in the sin, it is not something externally added. So Dante in his description of hell interprets the specific punishment of each sin as nothing other than the disintegration of personality which arises out of the sin itself.[24]

But whether the two lines of thought are reconciled or not, it seems clear that it was to the second that Saint Paul attached the chief importance. Because death is the fruit of sin, it follows that death is, in a sense, already present. He can say of sin not only that it has deceived him, but that it has already slain him.[25] And at this point we may widen the scope of the argument to take in the non-Pauline writings of the New Testament, for the understanding of death as the present consequence of sin appears to extend through almost the whole range of New Testament thought. In the first of the Johannine epistles we read that 'he that loveth not his brother abideth in death',[26] while in the Epistle to the Ephesians (which Bultmann does not accept as Saint Paul's) we find possibly the clearest formulation of all: 'dead in trespasses and sins'.[27]

This idea of the close connection between sin and death appears, therefore, to be of considerable importance for the understanding of New Testament thought, yet it is an extremely difficult one. Is it anything more than a figure of speech? We can understand what is meant by saying that the sinner is spiritually dead—that is a metaphor, and admittedly a very vague one, but it does suggest to the mind a condition into which men may fall. Yet leaving such figures aside, is it possible to show some genuine relation between sin and death, in virtue of which death could be understood as somehow the consequence and, as it were, the punishment of sin, and in the light of which death could be

[23] *Th. des NT*, p. 244.   [24] Cf., e.g., *Inferno*, cantos V, XXIII.
[25] Rom. 7.11.   [26] I John 3.14.   [27] Eph. 2.1.

understood as already somehow present in fallen human existence? We can, of course, understand that in particular cases there may be a connection between sin and death—excessive drinking, for instance, might lead to death. But that is a natural, indeed a causal connection, whereas we are looking for an existential connection. We are concerned not with death as a natural phenomenon but with death in its significance for existence. And, in any case, something much wider than such isolated cases as a man drinking himself to death was implicit in the New Testament thought of a connection between sin and death, and it is that wider connection which we must seek to explain.

We orient the discussion again to the existential analysis which, it was argued, has enabled Bultmann to show to a remarkable extent the interrelations of the various anthropological concepts of the New Testament. The fallen life was shown to be the scattering of the self in the multiplicity of worldly concerns. It is man's fall away from his true being, and it is therefore the loss of his being. In Bultmann's words, 'man "sold under sin"[28] has lost himself and is no longer at one with himself (*bei sich selbst*)'.[29] The aspect of sin brought out here is loss of being. But death, considered as an existential phenomenon, was also defined as loss of being.[30] So it is no mere metaphor to say that in the life of sin death is already present as the consequence—or rather, the concomitant—of sin, since both sin and death are characterized ontologically by loss of being. In his 'trespasses and sins' man is already in a condition of death in so far as he has sustained a loss of being.

With physical death, the loss of man's being as we know it in this world is complete. The body has ceased to belong to an existing *Dasein* and has become a mere thing—at first something still organic, but in course of time indistinguishable dust with nothing left to show that it ever existed and stood apart from the inanimate nature of which it has now become a part. As Heidegger remarks, death shows us 'a remarkable phenomenon of being, which may be defined as

[28] Rom. 7.14.   [29] *Th. des NT*, p. 244.   [30] *Supra*, p. 117.

the transition from man's way of being (*Existenz*) to the way
of being of a thing (*Vorhandenheit*). The end of the entity qua
Dasein is the beginning of the same entity qua *Vorhandenes*.'[31]
But that remarkable transition from the being of a man to the
being of a thing may be regarded in one sense as nothing
other than the fulfilment of the life of sin. Man in his fallen
existence has surrendered himself to the world, has identified
himself with it and projected his possibilities upon it. He has
understood himself as belonging to the world, as one object
among others. Now death has, indeed, made him a part of
the world, and has thus fulfilled the tendency of sin. The
argument stated here is fuller and more explicit than can be
found in Bultmann, but that it is simply a development of his
position may be seen from his treatment of the New Testament teaching that death is already present in sinful existence,
and in his statement that as man's authentic striving is
towards life, 'so it follows that a false mistaken striving
pursues the way to death'.[32]

It is, of course, a fact that the Christian is subject to natural
death equally with the man who lives after the flesh. But the
Christian presumably has been turned from a wrongly to a
rightly directed striving, he has, in Johannine phrase, 'passed
from death unto life'.[33] Does this not seem to argue against
the New Testament contention for a connection between sin
and death? If it were true, would not the Christian be exempt
from death? The question seems to depend on a confusion of
the natural and existential concepts of death. No doubt there
were some Christians in New Testament times who believed
that they would not 'taste of death', in the sense of being
exempt from natural death, and at one time possibly Saint
Paul himself was of their number.[34] But did the disappoint-
ment of their expectation refute their belief in the connection
between sin and death? To this question two answers can be
given. The first is that the Christian is never free from his
share of guilt so long as he exists in the κόσμος. For the κόσμος,
as we saw, enters into the facticity of existence to narrow

---

[31] *S. u. Z.*, p. 238.
[33] John 5.24. I John 3.14.

[32] *Th. des NT*, p. 242.
[34] Mark 9.1; I Thess. 4.15.

down man's possibilities, and even if the Christian is no longer of it, he cannot escape from the sin and death which characterize it. He cannot contract out of war, for instance. The second answer is that, although the Christian is not exempt from death, he is assured of its conquest, and precisely because through his faith in Christ he has gained the being which he had lost under sin. Just as death is already present in the life of sin, so eternal life is already present in the experience of faith. But this second answer can only be properly expounded at a later stage when we have outlined the characteristics of an authentic existence and understood what is meant by faith.

Sometimes Saint Paul has a way of speaking very para-doxically of the Christian life itself as a death in one of its aspects—the Christian is dead to sin.[35] The meaning is plain enough. The Christian has withdrawn from the life after the flesh, he has lost his sinful being, therefore he is dead to sin. The paradox arises from the fact that what the Christian has lost was itself a loss, that to which he has died was itself death. The usage here might seem to be very confusing, but on the other hand, as we shall see, it links up with Saint Paul's thought on the significance of the death of Jesus. In any case it makes no difference to the broad interpretation of the New Testament understanding of death.

17. *The Quest for Meaning*

With this discussion of death we have come to the end of the analysis of inauthentic existence, the life of the natural man. It is a way of being directed towards the world, mis-understanding and deceiving itself, dehumanized and fallen. Or more summarily, its significance may be described as a life of care terminated by death. Both Christianity and existen-tialism are agreed that such a life is meaningless and worth-less—it is inauthentic existence, and worse still, it is sin and enmity against God. Whatever value it may claim is based upon illusion, and from that springs its contentment and

[35] Rom. 6.2.

pride of achievement. The illusion is that man is master of his own destiny and of his world. Sometimes the mood of anxiety breaks in to disclose to man that he is not at home in the world, and that he is not master of his existence. But man flees from this disclosure into the further illusions of collective self-deception—organized illusion, it might be called. Yet all illusions are finally shattered by death. The life that was founded on the earthly and the transient ends in nothingness.

Christianity and existentialism are further agreed that in such an existence as has been described man has lost himself, he has somehow missed his true being. There must, therefore, be an alternative to that fallen existence—the spiritual man is set over against the carnal man, authenticity over against inauthenticity. And this implies that man stands in need of conversion. His whole being must be turned round in a new direction. But when we inquire about that new direction, we find that Heidegger and the New Testament give quite different answers.

Let us first see how Heidegger would direct us to an authentic existence. For his thought, death itself supplies the clue. Instead of fleeing from death, man is to look death in the face, and more than that, he is to accept and choose it as his own pre-eminent possibility. He is to live in the anticipation (*Vorlaufen*) of his own death.[36] To anticipate death, we are told, means neither to commit suicide nor to brood over death, but to make death the unifying factor in my existence, to relate all my possibilities to this one capital possibility. In other words, it is to see and to accept the nothingness of my existence. Admittedly such an acceptance will deliver me from concern with the world and from the tyranny of the public. It will detach me from the pursuit of the earthly and the transient. It will free me from the illusions of the rich man who dreamed of future ease, and also from those of the man who built his house on the sand. But it will only devalue the worldly existence because at the same time it devalues all existence. It will only deliver from illusion by substituting for it an open-eyed despair. To be myself, free

[36] *S. u. Z.*, p. 266.

from the lures of the world, free from the illusions of the crowd, may sound very fine—but to be myself, even my authentic self, is to be nothing, and Brunner is surely right in saying of Heidegger's attempt to find a meaning for life, and of variations upon Heidegger's theme, such as that of Sartre, that they present us with 'a philosophy of despair, hidden in a number of more or less subtle evasions of the problem (of meaning)'.[37]

Indeed, with such a radical devaluation of values, it is hard to see why the term authentic should be reserved for Heidegger's alternative rather than given to the everyday existence of the natural fallen man (for the notion of authenticity seems to imply some kind of value-judgment). True, Heidegger claims to be free from illusion. But the natural man might reply that illusion is a useful defence-mechanism to render existence tolerable. That is what we meant when we said that inauthentic existence could have value even as an illusion.[38] If every existence amounts to nothing at the end, then what is there to choose between one way of being and another? Let those who wish choose heroic despair and resignation—that may please the eccentric minority of existentialist philosophers. But those who have no taste for that sort of thing will prefer to eat, drink and be merry, shutting out the disclosures of anxiety till the last possible moment, refusing to acknowledge their nothingness till death knocks on the door, making life supportable by the carefully nurtured illusion that they are at home in the world.

The Christian alternative to the inauthentic existence of the natural man is, of course, entirely different from Heidegger's. The parting of the ways first appeared in the discussion of the concept of anxiety. For Heidegger, anxiety disclosed man as thrown into a world in which he is not at home; on the Christian interpretation, anxiety does more than that—it also sets man in quest of the ground of his being, it directs him to God. And further, the Christian believes that God meets man in his quest, that he has revealed himself in Jesus

[37] *Christianity & Civilization*, Nisbet, I, p. 73.
[38] *Supra*, p. 111.

Christ, and that through Christ there is opened to man the possibility of an existence in which not only is he delivered from the illusions of a worldly existence, but death itself 'is swallowed up in victory'.[39] The Christian alternative, therefore, is characterized by hope, while that offered by atheistic existentialism sticks in despair.

Does that mean, then, that from this point onwards the philosophy of existence has nothing further to offer to theology in the elucidation of its problems? Do we find that the influence of Heidegger's philosophy upon Bultmann's thought comes to an end when we complete the analysis of the false existence that leads to death, and enter upon the theology of the life of faith? Even Bultmann's most severe critics might be willing to admit that there has been some value in his use of the philosophy of existence to interpret the New Testament understanding of man without faith. And the unprejudiced reader might be prepared to go even further, and say that, thanks to his employment of concepts derived from this philosophy, Bultmann has presented an extraordinarily clear view of the New Testament conception of fallen man, at once intelligible· to modern minds and apparently faithful to the authentic intention of the New Testament writers themselves. To dismiss Bultmann's work as destructive, as some seem inclined to do, is simply to fail to appreciate the very considerable positive contribution that he has made to the elucidation of the Christian theology of man. But how can existentialism and its concepts be used for the interpretation of New Testament teaching on the Christian life itself? Surely to permit its influence to extend into that side of New Testament theology, bearing in mind how Heidegger conceives an authentic existence, would be to introduce something utterly incommensurable with Christian teaching, and therefore misleading.

The question, however, is not to be settled so simply as that. We are still approaching the New Testament with the question of human existence in our minds. While the preceding analysis has been in the main directed to the inauthen-

39 I Cor. 15.54.

tic way of being, it has also had to examine the fundamental ontological structure of man, which lies before authenticity or inauthenticity, and makes it possible for man to be either the one or the other. To that basic ontology belongs, for example, the concept of existence itself, also concepts like understanding, disclosure, affective state and so on. In the New Testament terminology, σῶμα, νοῦς, καρδία are such ontological concepts. In his formal ontological structure, man is the same whether he is Christian or pagan, whether his existence is authentic or inauthentic. It is that in virtue of which it can be said that he is a man.

This may appear to be a dangerous statement, and it may be questioned in some quarters. Does not Saint Paul say that 'if any man be in Christ, he is a new creature'?[40] But what exactly does that mean? Does it mean that the whole constitution of the man's former being is abolished, and that he has been constituted afresh and differently? In that case we cannot speak of conversion. Here we would have no genuine conversion, but the substitution—by inscrutable and indeed inconceivable means—for the former man of an entirely new and different man. Saul of Tarsus and Saint Paul the Apostle would be different persons altogether. No doubt in a sense they were different persons. But it seems equally indubitable that in another and very important sense they were one and the same person—Paul's existence was always somehow his own. The change was an ontical one— the radical reorientation of a personality which yet retained the same basic ontological structure. But what does a radical reorientation of the personality mean? Bultmann called it a new understanding of the self, and from what we have learned of the existential concept of understanding, we take that to mean: the projecting of the self on new possibilities. But where do the new possibilities come from? Were they there already?

This is the really crucial question, and we must be careful about the answer which we give. Ontically speaking, the answer is 'no'. Fallen man has lost the *existentiell* possibility

40 II Cor. 5.17.

of gaining or regaining his true existence. That possibility
(as will be argued in detail later) is given to him by the grace
of God in Jesus Christ. But ontologically speaking, the
answer must be 'yes'. God's gift is only possible in so far as
man can appropriate it—that is to say, make it somehow
his own, so that it must fall within the horizon of his existential
possibility. Otherwise we are not talking about an entity that
exists, but about a mere thing, to which properties may be
added or taken away, as a car may be painted blue or red.
But if man's ontological structure persists through conversion, then the ontological concepts already sketched will
have their place in interpreting the New Testament theology
of the Christian life.

Further, although the content of Heidegger's concept of
authentic existence is so utterly different from that contained
in our understanding of the Christian life, there may prove
to be certain formal structural affinities. Conscience, decision,
the unity of the self—these are instances of subjects on which
both the existentialist philosopher and the Christian theologian have something to say in describing what they conceive to be the true life for man. Here again, therefore, the
theologian may find that the philosopher's analysis of these
phenomena helps to elucidate his own problems.

Finally, let it be said that we were not altogether fair to
Heidegger in the brief summary which we gave of his concept
of an authentic existence, since we said nothing there about
his very important analysis of the temporality and historicity
of man. That subject also will call for attention, and it is one
of vital importance for the theologian, and one that has been
particularly influential with Bultmann. For the Christian
religion rests upon historical events, 'the mighty acts' by
which, the Christian believes, God changed man's situation
and made possible for him the new life. For the theological
understanding of these events there is necessary an understanding of man's existence in its temporal and historical
character.

Thus, although after their common rejection of a life
founded upon the world, Christianity and existentialism take

THE SIGNIFICANCE OF EXISTENCE

different paths in their quest for meaning, there is still a wide area for interaction between the two, and in particular there are still points at which Christian theology may find it necessary to clarify some of its presuppositions by existential analysis. To these problems we must now address ourselves.

PART TWO

THE
CHRISTIAN LIFE AS
AUTHENTIC EXISTENCE

VI

THE TRANSITION TO AN
AUTHENTIC EXISTENCE

18. *The Idea of an Authentic Existence*

THE problem is now to describe an authentic existence, or to answer the question, What is man's true life? This question, remarks Zehrer:

'is the most natural, but also the most radical question man can ask. For which reason he seldom asks it, preferring to assume that the answer is known. When as an individual he asks this question, one can infer that something which gave him security has come to an end. When the question emerges in the historic course of a given culture, it is a sign that the foundations of the culture have become faulty, and that people are no longer unselfconsciously at home in it.'[1]

So long as man is lulled into that contentment—however illusory—which belongs to an existence founded on the world, he is untroubled by ultimate questions about his whence and whither, his why and wherefore—indeed, as we have seen, he avoids such questions. But when the mood of anxiety breaks in to reveal that he is not at home in the supposedly secure world which he has constructed, when everyday existence is disclosed as a life of care terminated by death, the question of existence forces itself upon him. And, of course, that is precisely what is happening on the continent of Europe in the twentieth century. Traditions and institutions which long gave security to life have been

[1] *Man in this World*, Hodder, p. 28.

largely swept away. Man is stripped and isolated, confronted with the question which he formerly concealed from himself: what is my true life? The life of material security is one built upon the sand. Is there an authentic existence, founded, so to speak, upon a rock—or is there just nothingness?

To this most radical of questions Heidegger and Bult-mann—and, of course, many other contemporary thinkers besides—have sought to give an answer. Heidegger's answer, so far as it goes, is ambiguous. He does hold out the possibility of an authentic existence, and thus far his philosophy opens a way of salvation to man in his fallen condition. And yet, since that authentic existence appears to be acceptance of nothingness, it is no true salvation that is offered. God is 'not yet' in Heidegger's thought, and therefore he has not passed beyond the first shock of despair which comes when the illusory and inauthentic character of an existence founded on the world is disclosed. Bultmann, on the other hand, goes to the Christian revelation for his answer to the question. He believes that God has spoken and acted decisively in Jesus Christ, and that therein lies the clue to the problem of human existence. Like Barth, therefore, he looks to the revealed Word of God as the source of truth. But in a way which goes beyond Barth, he approaches that source of truth out of the human situation, from the question of the meaning and end of existence that is agitating a dread-filled mankind.

Let us examine more closely this idea of an authentic existence. That which is authentic is genuine or original (ursprünglich—a term sometimes used by Heidegger). An inanimate object can, strictly speaking, be neither authentic nor inauthentic. Its nature is purely given, and it simply is what it is. True, we can speak of a signature as being authentic, but that implies a reference to human existence. Considered simply as ink on paper, one signature is as real, genuine and original as another. Authenticity is properly a character of something which is not given in its nature, but stands before different possibilities of being. It is, therefore, a character of man (and perhaps also of living things besides man, but that does not concern us here). Man exists authentically when his original possibilities, belonging to his being as man, are fulfilled. His existence is inauthentic when his possibilities are projected on something alien to himself. In that case the self is lost and scattered. Even his original possibilities may be lost or rendered inaccessible. That is fallenness. To restore authenticity would mean: to unify the scattered self so that it is withdrawn from false concerns and stands in its original possibilities.

This idea of authenticity is readily applicable to the biblical understanding of man. We are told that man was formed in the image of God.[2] His original possibility is to be the child of God. But by worshipping and serving the creation rather than the Creator, man has lost that possibility and fallen away from his original being—though we understand, of course, that the term 'original' here may not necessarily have temporal significance. The Christian religion claims to restore to man his original being, and his lost possibility of being the child of God and enjoying communion with God. Understood in this way as deliverance from fallenness, sin and death, together with the restoration of the original possibilities which God gave to man at his creation, the Christian life may fairly be called the authentic existence of man. In it man gains his true being, and the intention of the Creator is realized.

In the New Testament various terms are used for such an authentic existence. Sometimes it is called simply life ($\zeta\omega\eta$). This term is not used for the natural living principle in man —denoted rather by $\psi\upsilon\chi\eta$—but, in Bultmann's own words, stands for 'the authentic being of man'.[3] The commandment of the Creator is life.[4] Whereas man in his fallen existence loses his being and runs into death, when he exists according to the command and intention of the Creator, he gains his being and attains to life in the fullest sense.

Just as we noted that the idea of the connection of sin and death is common to both the Pauline and the Johannine writings, so we find that this opposite idea of life as man's

[2] Gen. 1.26.　　　[3] *Th. des NT*, p. 228.　　　[4] Rom. 7.10.

authentic possibility is also common to these two major streams of New Testament thought. In the Fourth Gospel Christ summarizes the aim of his mission as the bringing of life to men: 'I am come that they might have life, and that they might have it more abundantly.'[5] The concept of life is, of course, central to the whole Johannine teaching. Christ gives life to the world; he is the bread of life; his words are life; he is the resurrection and the life.[6] The purpose of the writer of the Fourth Gospel is 'that ye might believe that Jesus is the Christ, the Son of God; and that believing ye might have life through his name.'[7] Here, too, is the thought that the command of God, the authentic intention of the Creator, for man is life: 'His commandment is life everlasting'.[8] Such life, understood not as a natural phenomenon but as man's authentic God-given existence, is eternal or everlasting, because, being the opposite of death, the concomitant of sin, it is therefore immune from death. Thus the believer has even now eternal life.[9]

Another concept which is used in the New Testament to express the thought of man's authentic existence is πνεῦμα. Man's fallen existence is an existence 'after the flesh'. In Saint Paul's thought, spirit is contrasted with flesh. Thus man's authentic existence is 'after the spirit' (κατὰ πνεῦμα). The Christian walks 'not after the flesh, but after the spirit'.[10] And just as σάρξ meant not a substance but a way of man's being, in which he is oriented to the world, to the visible, the tangible, and the temporal, so πνεῦμα is not a substance either, but that way of being in which man is oriented to God, to the invisible and eternal.[11] For Saint Paul, an authentic existence after the spirit means as radical a devaluation of the things that are cherished in man's fallen existence as we find in Heidegger's authentic existence in the face of death— a Christian nihilism concerning the things of the world, if you like: 'Let they that have wives be as though they had

[5] John 10.10.
[7] John 20.31.
[9] John 3.16; 5.24; 6.47; 17.3.
[11] Cf. *Th. des NT*, p. 331.

[6] John 6.33; 6.35; 6.63; 11.25.
[8] John 12.50.
[10] Rom. 8.4.

none; and they that weep as though they wept not; and they that rejoice as though they rejoiced not; and they that buy as though they possessed not; and they that mix in the world as though they were not absorbed in it: for the fashion of this world passeth away.'[12] The difference is that Heidegger's devaluation is made before nothingness, Saint Paul's before God. It is not everything which is devalued here, for if 'the things which are seen are temporal, the things which are not seen are eternal'.[13] The authentic existence offered by the Christian gospel is not only deliverance from the tyranny of the world and the flesh, but positively a new way of being oriented to God—in other words, life in the sense of that term already explained. And indeed the two concepts of ζωή and πνεῦμα are explicitly connected by Saint Paul, with the implication that this connection is parallel to that between sin and death: 'to be carnally minded is death; but to be spiritually minded is life and peace.'[14]

The detailed structure of the spiritual existence, the eternal life, which the New Testament promises, will only emerge as the argument proceeds. For the present we simply note that it is the opposite of that fallen carnal existence already analysed, and that it claims to be for man his authentic existence, for which he was destined by his Creator.

19. *Conscience*

The immediate problem is the manner in which the transition is made from the one way of being to the other—from the false to the true, the fallen to the original, the inauthentic to the authentic. It is common ground to Christianity and existentialism that such a transition or conversion is possible. The gospel promises that through faith man may be brought from death to life. Heidegger, too, believes that man may be recalled from his fallen existence. 'Inauthenticity denotes a way of being in which man may go astray, and generally does go astray, but in which he need not necessarily and always go astray.'[15]

[12] I Cor. 7.29-31.
[14] Rom. 8.6.
[13] II Cor. 4.18.
[15] *S. u. Z.*, p. 259.

But if man's fallen existence is death, and his true existence is life, and these two are opposites, how can the gulf between them be bridged? Bultmann acutely observes that it was when Saint Paul saw most clearly the gap between the true self and the self that is lost that he came nearest to Gnostic dualism.[16] Yet dualism is no final solution, and it is certainly not the Pauline or the Christian solution. We are not dealing with two completely different and mutually exclusive worlds, but with one world which is still the creation of God, even where it is fallen into sin. We saw already that while the Christian may be spoken of as a new creature, nevertheless there must be some continuity with his former being, in so far as he is the same man whose individual existence is always his own. Something which belongs to him and constitutes him passes from death unto life, and is still his on both sides of the transition.

To use a somewhat gross analogy, let us imagine a local authority engaged in slum clearance. There is a derelict property on a certain site. The authority has several possibilities open to it. The slum may be pulled down, the debris carted away, and an entirely new building erected on the site. Or again, the old building might be repaired and modernized, so that it would remain substantially as it had been, but brought up to present-day requirements and rendered habitable for a few more years. Or finally, the building might be pulled down to its foundations, and the old material—perhaps stonework fashioned by masons of several generations ago, who were masters of their craft— used to put up a new house on a different and altogether better plan.

Applying this analogy to the problem of conversion, it may be said that in the first case, in which the old is replaced by something entirely new and different, there is no true conversion. That is so because there is no continuity, and the process would have to be described as substitution or replacement. In the second case there is no true conversion either. The old remains essentially as it was, and all that has taken

16 *Th. des NT*, pp. 195-196.

place is a measure of rehabilitation, a temporary readjust-ment. In the third case we do seem to have something which could properly be called conversion. There is continuity in so far as the same material has been used, yet there is also discontinuity in so far as the old house has been demolished and a new house conceived entirely afresh has been put in its place. What persists through conversion is, so to speak, the material of man's being, his basic ontological structure as being-in-the-world, but ontically his being is entirely reoriented, so that there is a genuine break with the past, and he is at once the same person and a different person.

Our problem is now more sharply defined. It is to explore the character of this ontical or *existentiell* reorientation, which, we may find, is effected from outside man altogether; and at the same time, to show how this reorientation lies within the horizon of man's existential possibilities, so that what is described is a genuine conversion and not a substitution.

We begin the discussion with an examination of Heidegger's view of the way in which the transition from an inauthentic to an authentic existence is to be effected. Man is lost—he is scattered in the public and in the world of concern. His possibilities—his rules, tasks, standards and so on—are already decided for him. His is a life without genuine choice, decided by no one in particular—and yet in a sense he has himself chosen that irresponsible existence. To exist authen-tically he must return from this lost condition to his original possibilities—which means that he must recover choice. But in order to find himself, Heidegger thinks, he must be shown to himself in his authentic possibility. Is there any testimony in man's own being which directs him to his authentic possibilities? Heidegger thinks that there is. Such a testimony, he claims, is given by what we call the voice of con-science.[17]

So what we have here is a continuation of the existential analytic. Another phenomenon, conscience, is to be analysed. It will—so it is contended—show man his authentic possi-bilities, and through heeding its voice, he will enter into

[17] Cf. *S. u. Z.*, p. 268 ff.

these possibilities. We refrain from criticism for the present until we see how Heidegger's approach to the problem develops.

Conscience is a notoriously difficult phenomenon to understand. Butler made it central in his ethical theory, but he seems simply to have assumed it, and gave no clear statement of what conscience is, or how it is related to man's nature as a whole. Kant identified conscience with practical reason, and so gave it a definite place in his scheme of human nature. Yet conscience is surely not reason alone. We associate it with feeling also—with remorse and uneasiness, for instance. On the other hand, we find Mill concentrating on this element of feeling in conscience to the neglect of the cognitive aspect of the phenomenon. Conscience is 'a feeling in our own mind', according to his view, and particularly the feeling of pain which accompanies any violation of duty. Whatever criticisms we may make of Heidegger's view of the function of conscience, we shall see that at least he introduces some clarity into the very confused notions that have been held as to what conscience is. His ingenious theory of conscience succeeds in relating it to the whole structure of the being of man, and does justice to both the cognitive and affective aspects of the phenomenon.

Heidegger's analysis of conscience begins from the fact that it gives us to understand something.[18] It discloses, and therefore it belongs to that group of phenomena already discussed which together constitute the disclosure of man to himself—understanding, mood or affective state, anxiety or dread. Conscience gives man to understand something, and that something is himself—it is an important way in which man is disclosed to himself.

Conscience has the character of a call or summons. Who is it that is called? Quite clearly, the call is addressed to man —to fallen man lost in the crowd and in the world. He is summoned out of his worldly concern, his self-deception, his irresponsibility, his false security, to his original possibilities that have been lost to him. Who is it that calls in

18 S. u. Z., p. 270.

conscience? Not someone else who is with me in the world, not some external power breaking in upon me. Man is the caller as well as the called. It is the authentic self that calls. But if man has lost himself, how can there be an authentic self to summon him? That question rests on the misunderstanding that the self is an object, a thing of some sort. But if the self is possibility, then the authentic self is still there as possibility even when man has lost himself. So long as he exists and is man, he has the basic possibilities of being himself or losing himself. That still belongs to his ontological structure even when the ontical possibility of being his true self has been lost. If the voice of conscience seems strange and external to man, that is because he has fallen so far into the world that he has forgotten and ceased to understand his authentic possibilities. He is estranged from himself, and can no longer recognize his true self. But when, in the mood of anxiety, he is isolated from the crowd, when he is confronted with the fact of his own individual existence, when his sense of security and being at home in his world is shattered, this call is heard in the distance—the summons to his original possibilities.

Conscience therefore, on Heidegger's view, is the call of the self to the self—the authentic self to the fallen self. It belongs to the very structure of man's being as having a relation to himself. When he falls away from himself, the being of man becomes more or less split—an idea familiar to Saint Paul also, who conceived the life after the flesh as the strife of self against self. It seems to be an intelligible idea only if the self is conceived as possibility. How otherwise could we conceive the self as splitting into an authentic self and an inauthentic self, which are two in so far as they are at war with each other, and yet one in so far as they are both always mine? But if the self is possibility, we can understand how the authentic self is still there as possibility even when I have decided for the world and my actual self is fallen and inauthentic.

Corresponding to the call of conscience, there must be a hearing, an understanding of the summons. It is recognized that conscience may be—and perhaps often is—mistaken. It is open to perversion. The deception of conscience, Heidegger thinks, lies not in the call, but in how this is heard and understood. It may, for instance, be distorted by the influence of the public. What the crowd does is assumed to be right. But if conscience is ever to be genuinely understood at all, it follows that even in his fallenness man must have the possibility of an authentic hearing. Without that possibility of understanding and appropriating the call, man can never be summoned out of his fallen way of being back to his original possibilities. This is an important point, and we shall meet it again when we come to consider Bultmann's view of the transition to an authentic existence.

This authentic hearing understands the call of conscience as a summons to guiltiness (*Schuldigsein*). Here we meet what appears to me to be possibly the most obscure and paradoxical of all Heidegger's concepts. It is paradoxical because we do not think of conscience as summoning to guilt, but rather to its opposite. It is obscure because Heidegger understands guilt in a sense so entirely removed from the common understanding of the term that it may well be asked whether he would not have been wiser to employ some different term. To be guilty, in the common-sense understanding of the expression, implies that something is owing for which I am answerable. But this, Heidegger thinks, is an interpretation based on the claims and counter-claims of practical concern—that is to say, it is a fallen understanding of guilt, related to the world out of which fallen man understands himself. Guilt may be the failure or lack of something that can and ought to be, but this idea must be detached from the realm of practical or worldly concern and understood in relation to the individual's own being. What is it, then, that is lacking? It is not authentic being either. Guiltiness, we are told, does not belong to fallen existence, any more than it is understood in fallen existence. The summons of conscience to guiltiness is precisely a summons out of the fallen existence that is based on worldly concern. What is lacking appears to be the power to master the possibilities for which conscience demands that we accept responsibility. For '*Dasein* projects himself upon possibilities, but they are the possibilities into which he is thrown. The self has never power to be the ground of its possibilities, it takes over the ground. This negation of power belongs to man's facticity.'[19] Guiltiness thus comes before every guilty act. As soon as I accept responsibility, I am guilty, because I already understand that I lack the power to discharge my responsibility. Therefore I usually flee from my responsibility.

What of conscience as we commonly understand it? We speak of experiencing a good conscience or a bad conscience. We think of conscience as warning us against some wrong action that is contemplated, or as causing remorse for wrongdoing committed in the past. Conscience is understood as a kind of internal censor, the function of which is to conform us to moral courses of action. But Heidegger thinks that the usual pronouncements of conscience are nothing but the voice of *das Man*, the standards and customs of the crowd into which the individual has merged himself to be rid of his own responsibility. The genuine utterance of conscience is heard when, in the mood of anxiety, the individual is isolated from the crowd and confronted with his own being as possibility thrown into the world.

The idea that the day-to-day pronouncements of conscience are nothing but the voice of the crowd, and therefore worthless as reflecting the rules of a fallen humanity is, it need hardly be said, an extremely dangerous one. There could be an echo of Nietzsche here, and something not unlike the Nazi idea, derived rightly or wrongly from Nietzsche's teaching, that the masters, those who have resolved to fulfil the possibilities of their being, are emancipated from the shackles of a slave-morality. What the doctrine actually means for Heidegger remains obscure, and it would, of course, be most unfair to interpret his teaching in the manner just suggested, but at the same time it must be pointed out that it opens the way to such dangers—a kind of moral nihilism. There is, however, another interpretation of

19 Cf. *S. u. Z.*, p. 284.

Heidegger's teaching which is more likely to commend itself to Christian thought. Is it not the case that conscience has been heard at its purest when it speaks as the conscience of an individual protesting against that which is accepted by the conscience of the mass? That has been true even within the Christian Church. The great Reformers of the sixteenth century—Luther's 'Here I stand. I can do no other. So help me God', comes to mind—or more recently the pioneers of social amelioration in the nineteenth century were men and women whose consciences rebelled against the code of conduct which the Church at large accepted. The voice of conscience stands in real danger of being perverted so as to become simply the reflection of the conventions and usages of the social environment. It could express the rules of fallen humanity, based on the claims and counter-claims of an existence based on worldly concern. Our Lord, in speaking of the Mosaic laws of divorce, remarked that they had been given 'for the hardness of your heart'[20]—they were laws adapted to man's fallen condition. His own moral teaching is based on the law of love which called men to go beyond the accepted code, and their own consciences so far as they were moulded by that code. Heidegger's views here may, therefore, be interpreted not so much as an attack on moral codes as an appeal to let conscience be heard as it arises out of the being of the individual, uninfluenced by the conventions of the crowd. Conscience speaks authentically in the isolation of the individual from fallen society—and, for the Christian, this isolation comes about when he stands in his individual responsibility before God. We notice here, of course, the absence in Heidegger's theory of an authentic community, a group which is not fallen. The excessive individualism of his view of conscience would seem to need correction from the Christian point of view, which sets forth the Church as such an authentic society, reinforcing and, if need be, correcting the consciences of its individual members. But how far the empirical Church measures up to this standard is another question altogether, as the illustra-

[20] Mark 10.5.

tions given above of men whose individual consciences rebelled against the practice of the Church showed.

In the critical examination of this original theory of Heidegger on conscience, let us first set down what appears to be of value in it. (*a*) Conscience is here clearly related to the whole structure of man's being. As existing, man has a relation to himself, and conscience arises from the tension between the basic possibilities of his being—to exist authentically or to exist inauthentically, to be himself or to lose himself. (*b*) Conscience is a mode of disclosure, involving both cognitive and affective elements. It is related to that basic anxiety in which man is confronted with his own being. In conscience, what is disclosed is the possibility of the authentic self, and man is summoned from fallenness into that original possibility. (*c*) Man's impotence is recognized. For man, to be responsible is equivalent to being guilty. He is free and yet not master of his freedom, and before any act of guilt he is already guilty because he has accepted a responsibility which he cannot fulfil.

Our criticism of Heidegger concerns not so much his actual concept of conscience as the function which he assigns to it in making it the bridge from fallen to authentic existence. Is conscience able to play the part which, on Heidegger's theory, is demanded of it? If we can show that it is not, serious damage will have been done to Heidegger's argument at this vital point where it makes the transition from the analysis of fallen existence to that of authentic existence.

Everything turns on the question of how far the fallenness of man's being is conceived by Heidegger to have proceeded. In some passages he seems to make it quite clear that fallenness, first introduced into the existential analytic as a bare possibility of existence, is in actual fact radical and universal. Fallenness is one of the three constituent structures of care, which is the everyday being of man. 'Fallenness belongs to care itself, and is never merely accidental in all understanding of the self.'[21] The understanding is fallen, conscience itself is

[21] *S. u. Z.*, p. 295.

fallen. But in that case, could there be any way out from fallenness at all?

There may be a way out because, on Heidegger's view, there remains to fallen man the possibility of an authentic hearing of the call of conscience. That possibility arises when the individual is isolated in the mood of anxiety from the crowd and from preoccupation with the world, and brought to face the question of his own existence. The Christian theologian also must allow some kind of authentic hearing even to fallen man if the message of the gospel is to reach him.

But here again the difference between ontological and ontical possibilities is relevant. Even in his fallen condition, man can still hear the call of the authentic self, because, so long as he is man, authenticity and inauthenticity are possible ways of being for him. But while authenticity remains an ontological possibility in fallenness, it has ceased to be an ontical possibility. That is to say, it is a bare formal possibility for man, in the sense that he is so constituted in his being that he might exist authentically. It is not, however, a concrete *existentiell* possibility for which he can decide now, because as fallen he has come into a situation in which that possibility is no longer open to him. As Heidegger himself says, fallen man is deprived of the power of choosing his original possibilities.[22] To recover the choice of these possibilities would mean in the first place to choose choice (again this is Heidegger's own phrase), but that is precisely what is impossible when the power of choice is lost.

Conscience, as Heidegger has described the phenomenon, can at best awaken in fallen man the awareness of a lost possibility of being. It can disclose to him his ontological possibility of authenticity. But it cannot by any means empower him to choose that possibility. It cannot bring before him the *existentiell* possibility of authenticity for which he can decide. And it now appears that only some Power outside man, some Power not fallen as man is fallen, can bring to man this concrete possibility of regaining his authentic being. And yet even such a Power could only hold

22 *S. u. Z.*, p. 268.

out that *existentiell* possibility because it falls within the horizon of man's existential possibility of authenticity, and can therefore be appropriated by man and made his own.

Here for the second time we observe Heidegger's existential analytic approaching to the very frontiers of religion. His deep understanding of the fallenness of man, and of man's impotence so that responsibility already implies guilt, are factors in his thought which seem to demand for their completion a doctrine of God. On Heidegger's own view of man, it seems to me that man cannot lift himself, and that his authentic being can only be restored, if at all, from outside himself. Yet once again Heidegger does not cross the frontier when he reaches it, but turns aside to this unconvincing theory of the function of conscience as bridging the gulf from fallenness to authenticity. And again Heidegger's thought takes the direction that it does because of precisely the same emphasis which we noted on the previous occasion when the existential analytic came very close to a religious interpretation of existence—namely, in connection with the phenomenon of anxiety. There Heidegger saw man disclosed in his facticity, adrift on the sea of what is, whereas the Christian sees man disclosed in his creaturely relation to God, the ground of his being. Here also it is facticity which dominates Heidegger's thinking—man accepting possibilities into which he is already thrown, powerless to order an existence for which he is none the less answerable. The Christian, on the other hand, turns again to the ground of being, and finds that God supplies the power which he lacks in himself.

Conscience cannot support the weight which Heidegger seeks to rest upon it. Even if it discloses to man his authentic being and summons him to his original possibilities, it does not empower him to attain to them. Fallen man needs not the disclosure of a bare existential possibility, but the placing of an *existentiell* possibility within his grasp. And if he is told that the former is sufficient, then one who has known the frustration of the struggle between self and self might reply with Augustine, 'Where was my free will all these years?' Conscience gives only the former, it cannot give the other.

Yet setting aside the exaggerated claims which Heidegger makes for it, conscience obviously has its own function in the transition from inauthentic to authentic existence. That function is preparatory in its nature. The call of the authentic self (if this be accepted as a suitable description of the basic phenomenon of conscience) creates dissatisfaction with a fallen existence. It arouses uneasiness, it dispels the contentment of a life preoccupied with the world, it awakens responsibility, and directs man to the quest of his authentic being and original possibilities. The function of conscience, therefore, resembles that of the closely related phenomenon of anxiety, in the isolation of which the voice of conscience is heard. But whereas anxiety discloses to man his finitude— or in theological language, his creatureliness—conscience discloses to man his fallenness—or in theological language again, his sinfulness. Both initiate the quest for a new orientation of the being of man. But conscience of itself cannot, any more than anxiety, effect such a reorientation. It discloses the possibility, but that possibility is not one which is as yet within the reach of fallen man. At the most, man is disturbed by the call of conscience and directed away from the world in which he has lost himself, but he is impotent to withdraw himself from concern with the world. He has lost the *existentiell* possibility of authenticity, and while the testimony of conscience prepares him for the understanding and accepting of such a possibility were it somehow to be presented to him from outside himself, that testimony cannot itself make the possibility an actual one for man in his fallen situation. If we were to use the metaphor which Saint Paul employed to describe the function of the law, we might say that conscience is 'our schoolmaster to bring us unto Christ'.[23] The analogy must not be pressed too far, but it serves to indicate that the work of conscience must be completed by religion. Just as we suggested that anxiety is met by God's act of revelation, so conscience is met by his act of grace.

[23] Gal. 3.24.

This would certainly seem to be in line with the New Testament understanding of conscience. There conscience appears as a universal phenomenon of human existence, rooted in the structure of man's being as such. It is found in Jews and Gentiles alike, and its function is to bear witness, as if it were a kind of law written in the heart.[24] There are two points of contact between this New Testament view of conscience and that of Heidegger. In both cases its utterance is described as a testimony arising out of man's own being, and in both cases also it is specifically connected with the affective state in which man's being is disclosed to himself——Angst in Heidegger, καρδία in the New Testament.[25] But the function of conscience is differently understood in each case. For the New Testament, it brings before man the demand for righteousness, but there is no suggestion that conscience can make man righteous. Indeed it is recognized that conscience can be weak and its pronouncements variable.[26]

Bultmann believes that the concept of conscience (συνείδησις) is one which Saint Paul may have introduced into Christian thought, although, of course, the phenomenon of conscience had always been known. Bultmann's treatment of conscience is interesting, because here we see very clearly the influence of Heidegger upon his thought. As the concept of σῶμα was interpreted to mean that man has a relation to himself, so the concept of συνείδησις is also interpreted as a relation of man to himself; specifically, it is a reflective, critical relation, in which man is conscious of his own conduct and judges it in the light of a demand.[27] Bultmann endeavours to illustrate this Heideggerian conception of conscience from those Pauline passages in which συνείδησις is mentioned, but this seems to be a case where his philosophical presuppositions have been allowed to fill the gaps in exegetical evidence. Of course, Saint Paul does not put forward any theory of conscience (which it was not his concern to do), but simply uses the concept without troubling

[24] Rom. 2.15.   [25] For the connection of these concepts, *supra*, p. 67 ff.
[26] I Cor. 8.7.   [27] *Th. des NT*, p. 213.

151

to define it. And in that case Bultmann's interpretation is justifiable—it is not repugnant to anything that Saint Paul says about conscience, and at the same time it clearly relates this concept to the other anthropological concepts of the New Testament. But perhaps Bultmann should have been more careful here to point out the assumptions by which he reaches his interpretation, instead of presenting it as if it were the obvious interpretation of conscience which anyone might be expected to find on reading the New Testament with no special philosophical assumptions such as Bultmann himself undoubtedly has.

While Bultmann accepts Heidegger's theory of the nature of conscience, he is as clear as anyone about the inadequacy of conscience to fulfil the function which Heidegger assigns to it, and is fully aware that at this point existentialism and Christianity go different ways. Indeed there could be no more searching criticism of this side of existentialist teaching than that which Bultmann himself has given us.[28] Briefly his argument runs as follows. Christianity and existentialism are agreed that man is fallen, and that his salvation must lie in a radical surrender (*Hingabe*) of his self-made world and its fancied security. But existentialism seeks salvation in a self-made righteousness to which man is directed by conscience—for example, the disillusioned acceptance of death in Heidegger's thought. But this self-made authenticity is no true surrender. It is still this-worldly in its orientation, it rests on human power as much as does the self-made instrumental world. It is on a level with the righteousness of the Jews or the wisdom of the Greeks, both of which Saint Paul regarded as being at bottom subtle manifestations of that confidence in the flesh which is at the root of fallenness. Man's salvation must come from beyond man himself. But here, as Bultmann points out, we touch on a difference not only between Christianity and existentialism, but between religion and all philosophy. Philosophy believes that if man is shown the good and if he understands it and recognizes it to be good, he will follow it, and there is nothing to prevent

[28] *K. u. M.*, vol. 1, pp. 37-38.

his attaining it if only he sets his will upon it. Religion, with its deeper insight, understands that man may know the good and even will the good, and yet depart from it and be powerless to attain it.

We conclude, therefore, that conscience has its part to play in effecting the transition from fallen to authentic existence, as indeed the New Testament recognizes, but that part is subordinate and preparatory, and cannot have the place which existentialist philosophy assigns to it. Salvation comes from beyond man himself, not from anything in his own being. Here, therefore, the existential analytic can no longer help us. It shows us, indeed, man's impotence, but the answer to his situation lies outside its reach. And with this we pass from conscience to the religious concept of grace.

20. *Grace*

If conscience is one of the most obscure and confused concepts in the realm of ethics, the same might be said of grace in the realm of theology. On some theories it appears as a mysterious power—which comes near to being hypostatized—that enters men in some undefined way and takes control of them. As such it can be 'conveyed' in the sacraments, it can be 'latent' or 'active', it can be 'stirred up', it can 'infuse' righteousness. These all look like animistic ways of speaking, and while no doubt they point to realities of Christian experience, they can hardly be said to bring conceptual clarity to the understanding of what the experience of grace is. Or again, grace may be said to be a quality of God, and may be contrasted with his wrath. But to speak of grace as a bare quality does not explain the experience of it in Christian living. A quality is perceived, but experience of divine grace is more than the perception of a certain quality in God.

Bultmann says that grace is not a special quality of God, and the New Testament does not suggest that we are to think of him as gracious rather than wrathful.[29] But wrath is not a quality of God either—it is an event, namely, his

29 *Th. des NT*, p. 283.

judgment. God has created man responsible, with the possibility of gaining his true being or losing it. Man's responsibility is not only to himself but to his Creator. He is placed before God, and, as we already noted, to fall away from himself is to fall away from God, and to defy the command of God which is life. In Saint Paul's words, 'Every one of us shall give account of himself to God.'[30] My existence is not purely my own affair. When I lose myself, at the same time I lose God and am cast off from him, I undergo his judgment and experience his wrath.

To believe in the grace of God, in Bultmann's view, is to believe in the possibility of being saved from his wrath. Grace also, then, is an event, which corresponds to that other event which we call the wrath of God. Grace is the event in which God restores to me and places within my grasp my lost possibility of authentic being, that is to say, the being which God intended in creation and from which man has fallen away into sin. Such grace is an act of forgiveness which delivers from past guilt and breaks the power of sin over human life. For it was because of past sins that man was fallen into a situation in which to choose his authentic being was no longer an *existentiell* possibility for him. But into that situation came the event of God's grace, restoring the possibility and therefore blotting out the past, in the sense that man was delivered from that alienation from himself and from God into which his past had brought him. The event of grace, therefore, means both a deliverance from the past —forgiveness—and a new possibility for the future, from which, because of his past, man was hitherto cut off, so that it could only be restored to him from outside himself.

With the concept of grace ($\chi\acute{a}\rho\iota s$) we see how the New Testament—and with it, of course, Christian thought in general—understands the possibility of a transition from fallen to authentic existence, and the irreducible difference which here separates Christian theology from atheistic existentialism. For the Christian it is God who gives to man the *existentiell* possibility of authentic being, though admit-

30 Rom. 14.12.

154

tedly the gift can only be given because man in his fallen
existence retains the existential possibility—if not, he would
have ceased to be man. And with that existential possibility
goes the possibility of having conscience, and the possibility
of understanding and appropriating the gift of grace. But
the fuller discussion of that belongs to the analysis of faith.
For the present we simply note that in all genuinely Christian
theology the transition from fallen to authentic existence is
the work of God, not man. Hence Saint Paul could say, 'By
the grace of God I am what I am'.[31]

Closely connected with the concept of grace is the other
New Testament concept of justification, the making just
(δίκαιος) or righteous of someone who was in the opposite
condition, which also implies a notion of transition. It is in
connection with this concept that the contrast of the Christian
view of man's attaining his true being through grace with all
other possible views comes out most clearly. The Jews sought
a legal righteousness, based on fulfilling the demands of the
law. The non-theistic existentialist seeks a righteousness or
authenticity based on effort of will and stern resolve. Both
depend upon human striving, yet both are impossible of
attainment because of human fallenness. Saint Paul on the
other hand says, 'We conclude that a man is justified by faith
without the deeds of the law.'[32] The kind of righteousness
visualized here is neither legal nor ethical, but, in Bultmann's
phrase, forensic. It implies a new relation of man to God,
who is his Judge. And the new relation consists precisely in
this, that man counts for nothing all his own striving and
achievement, and recognizes that his true life is God's gift
to him. He ceases to live by his own power, and surrenders
himself to God. And this understanding of the Christian life
is one on which Bultmann lays great emphasis.

Grace, on Bultmann's interpretation, is to be understood
as an event. But what event? It is the event constituted by
the mighty acts, the saving events (*Heilgeschehen*) which God
wrought in Jesus Christ. These mighty acts, coming into the
human situation from outside, that is to say, from God

[31] I Cor. 15.10.　　　　　　　　　　[32] Rom. 3.28.

himself, made possible forgiveness in so far as man was delivered from enslavement to his own past, from which he could never have freed himself, and at the same time made possible a new life in so far as Christ brought back to man his lost possibility of authentic existence as the child of God. For Bultmann, therefore, the work of God in Jesus Christ, or in other words, the grace of God given in Christ, is unique and decisive for human existence, and constitutes the only way to man's salvation. This is worth pointing out, because Bultmann's radical criticism of some traditional elements in the Christian faith may cause the careless student of his thought to lose sight of the fact that on this central issue Bultmann stands firmly on the ground of historic conviction. Bultmann—and here again we point out that he has much in common with Barth—is actually far more orthodox, in the best sense of the term, than much of the liberal theology of last century which tended to think of the coming of Christ as simply the highest manifestation of God, continuous with and not differing in kind from the manifestations of God in conscience, in nature, and in non-Christian religions. But for Bultmann it is an event on a different plane altogether. It may be called supernatural in the sense that it is a true intervention from outside into man's situation—and in no other way can man be saved, if the preceding analysis of his being is anywhere near the truth at all. Bultmann is influenced by existentialism and he makes no secret of it, as we know, but that does not prevent him from seeing perfectly plainly the place where Christianity and existentialism part company, and the distinctive indispensable element in Christianity as a supernatural religion which no philosophy can supply.

To return to the argument, grace is an event, namely, the act of God in Christ. But is not that a past event, whereas grace is surely present? Can we accept this simple identification of grace with the saving event which occurred once for all nearly two thousand years ago? Bultmann's reply to that would be that grace—and, of course, that means the saving event itself—is present whenever the Word is proclaimed and authentically heard, so that to the hearer of the Word is restored his lost possibility of gaining his true being. That possibility is placed before him as something for which he can decide—and for which he may, in fact, decide in the act of faith. It is in this way that the mighty acts touch his existence now, and so grace is present.

Here we have evidence of the strong evangelical and Protestant influence in Bultmann's thought. His concern is with the proclamation of the gospel to the world. It follows that he attaches great importance to preaching, and the sacraments also he regards as ways of proclaiming the Word. No doubt the Word can be proclaimed and heard in other ways also—for instance, simply in the reading of the New Testament. But in whatever way the Word may be proclaimed and heard, the point is that, in such proclaiming and hearing, grace is present to me, the saving events are significant to my existence now. To say that anything is significant for my existence means that it presents me with a possibility—and that is precisely what the divine grace does, as we have seen. It presents to man the possibility of attaining his true being. We noted at the very outset that Bultmann goes to the New Testament with the question of human existence in mind. The question is, What does this mean for my existence? or alternatively, What possibility is presented to me here? If the saving events are considered merely as objective historical happenings which occurred some nineteen centuries ago, I might be filled with admiration on hearing the record of them, just as I might be by reading of the trial and death of Socrates in Athens at an earlier time. But that is very different from my being given a present possibility—indeed I might rather despair because, let us say, the possibility of Socrates' courage and nobility is one which would be beyond me. In the case of the mighty acts, in order that a possibility may be presented to me now, or—which is the same thing—in order that the event may be significant for my existence, it is necessary, as Bultmann contends, that grace, which is itself the saving event, should be present to me in the proclaiming and hearing of the Word. But if that is so, then the saving events are not merely past

157

historical happenings—not just facts of history, as we commonly understand that expression. Thus, of the resurrection of our Lord, Bultmann claims that belief in the resurrection is identical with the belief that the Risen One is present in the Word now proclaimed.[33] The past event is at the same time present event, and it is the present event that is significant for my existence—it is the grace by which I can experience forgiveness and have the possibility of new life.

But is this not the abandonment of the position stated earlier, when it was said that Bultmann identified grace with the saving events wrought by God in Jesus Christ? These events had a once-for-all character (*Einmaligkeit*) and can be assigned to a definite period of history. But now it appears that grace is a whole series of events, and repeats itself every time the Word is proclaimed and heard. But Bultmann would deny that there is any contradiction here. We have not a series of different events, but one event—albeit an event of a peculiar kind. Bultmann calls it an eschatological event. It is past, in the sense that some nineteen centuries ago God acted in a decisive way and intervened in man's situation. It is present, not merely in the sense that there remain with us the abiding consequences of what happened in the past, but more importantly in the sense that God acts now in a decisive way and intervenes in my situation, and only for that reason can the event be called a saving event, significant for my existence and relevant to men today.

But what meaning can we attach to this concept of an eschatological event? How is it possible for such an event to be both past and present—and, presumably, future also? Before we can answer these questions or go more fully into Bultmann's treatment of the mighty acts, it will be necessary to revert to the existential analytic, and consider Heidegger's views on the nature of history, which, I believe, have had considerable influence on Bultmann at this point. For already a wide vista of new problems has opened out before us—the problems of the understanding of human existence in its temporality and historicity.

[33] *Th. des NT*, p. 301.

VII

EXISTENCE AS TEMPORAL
AND HISTORICAL

21. *Temporality and Historicity*

THE being of man was defined by Heidegger as care. But it was pointed out that this could not be regarded as the final analysis, because the argument had been confined to man's everyday inauthentic existence. We must now see how Heidegger goes on to the question of a more original interpretation of the being of man. Or to put the question in another way: what makes care possible?[1]

It will be remembered that care, whilst it is a unity, has a threefold structure, and is constituted by possibility, facticity and fallenness. To show what makes care possible would be the same as showing what articulates these three structures in the unity of care. Then we would have penetrated to the original being of man in virtue of which his existence can be either inauthentic—characterized by care—or authentic. Possibility implies something which is ahead, and before which man stands. In his everyday fallen existence man has lost his authentic possibilities and has fled from his responsibility. But so far as his possibilities are restored to him, he stands before a future. Thus possibility is grounded in the future. Facticity, on the other hand, implies something which is already there. Man always finds himself already in a situation. Again in his everyday existence he flees from the disclosure of his true situation. But so far as he is brought to face the disclosure of his situation, he understands that what he is relates to what he has been. His facticity is grounded

[1] Cf. *S. u. Z.*, p. 324 ff.

159

in the past. Fallenness is primarily related to the present. Avoiding acceptance of either his authentic past or future, man loses himself in the concerns of the present, scatters and dissipates his being in the possibilities that are to hand.

This past, present and future which emerges from the threefold structure of care Heidegger calls temporality (*Zeitlichkeit*). This is the original being of man. It makes care possible as his inauthentic way of being, and it must make possible also his authentic way of being, though we have still to see how exactly the latter is constituted. Yet to say that man is temporality does not mean that he exists as an object in time. Man's past and future belong to him in a way in which the past and future cannot belong to a rock, let us say, or to any object within time. And in man lies the possibility, as we shall see, of bringing his past, present and future into a unity.

Because man is temporal in this special way, he is also historical (*geschichtlich*). History is possible for him because his temporality is not just a being within time (*Innerzeitigkeit*) but rather a being constituted by past, present and future in such a way that at any given moment not only the present but the past and future as well are disclosed to him and are real to him.

But what is history?[2] Here we have a term frequently used by theologians but rarely examined and subjected to that ontological analysis which we saw to be the prerequisite to clear theological thinking. The term has an obvious ambiguity (which can be avoided in German, where there are two possible terms) in that it may mean either the historical reality (*Geschichte*) or the scientific study of it (*Historie*). Heidegger is concerned with history in the former sense, that is to say, with the stream of historical happening. How is it to be understood?

He distinguishes four meanings that are commonly attached to history. (*a*) The term is used for the past, as when we speak of something, rather contemptuously perhaps, as 'belonging to history'. We mean that it is no longer relevant,

[2] Cf. *S. u. Z.*, p. 378 ff.

and no longer affects the present. (*b*) But the term can have the opposite meaning as well, in common speech. When it is said, for instance, that we cannot escape from history, here history still means the past, but the past as somehow still alive and present with us. The past has, therefore, a double sense—it belonged to a time beyond recall, yet something of the past may still be with us, such as an ancient poem. Thus in the second sense history is regarded not so much as the past simply as past, but rather as that which has its origin in the past and is still present. History is understood as becoming, a connection of events extending through past, present and future. (*c*) History may again be understood as the development of human relations, man's culture in its many forms as distinct from nature, though in a way the latter can also belong to history as battlefield, site of a cult, and so on. (*d*) The historical is identified with the traditional, whether the origin of the tradition is understood or not.

Conflicting though these different common understandings of the meaning of the term 'history' are in some respects, Heidegger notes that they all have something in common— they relate to man as the subject of historical happening. But if that is the case, then history is to be understood existentially. That means that it is not to be understood under the categories applicable to things—causality and so on—but under the existentials which describe the possible ways of being of man. History is nothing but man's way of being as historical. But why then is practical historical research generally directed to things—tools, works of art, places of worship and other material objects that have survived from some ancient culture? That is because man is not a bare subject, but always being-in-the-world. These tools and other objects which are of historical interest Heidegger calls the secondary historical. The primary historical is man himself.[3] This is an important distinction for our purpose.

Let us now try to see the significance of this distinction. Suppose we are in a museum of antiquities, say, household utensils.[4] They belong to a past time, yet they are still extant

[3] *S. u. Z.*, p. 381.   [4] *S. u. Z.*, p. 430.

in the present. What makes them historical? Certainly they have changed with age—they are worn or broken or worm-eaten—but that does not in itself make anything historical. They are no longer in use, yet that of itself does not make anything historical either. 'What, then, is past in them?' asks Heidegger. 'Nothing other than the world, within which they belonged to an instrumental system, and were to hand and were used by *Dasein* in his concern with the world.' The world is no longer, but the object that was within that world is still extant. And the object is now accounted historical solely because it belonged to a past instrumental world of men. Its historicity is derivative or secondary, and stems from man, who is the primary historical.

But if this be so, then history cannot be an objective connection of events. Objects only enter into history so far as they have been of concern to man, and man himself, the primary historical, is never an object. Man exists, he stands before possibilities. The stuff of history—if we may so speak—is therefore existence, and that means possibility. But is this not absurd? Surely history is constituted by fact, not possibility. But in what sense is man a fact? Not as an object with fixed properties, but as an existent projecting himself on a chosen possibility.

With this existential understanding of the historical in view, Heidegger contends that the science of history (*Historie*) is concerned with the study of the possible.[5] It is the disclosure of man in his historic possibilities, and the more history understands possibilities, the more penetrating it is. But history is not concerned with all and every possibility. It is—as is universally recognized—selective. According to Heidegger, it is concerned with man in his authentic possibilities, when he has risen above the level of everyday existence to something great and heroic. And further, it is argued, history is concerned with such authentic possibility as repeatable (*wiederholbar*), as possibility for man existing today. Thus history is oriented to the future. The possibility which is studied by history 'is not taken as a shadowy example, but

[5] *S. u. Z.*, p. 394.

disclosed as resolved destiny which can be repeated so that the power of the possible is felt in present existence, that is to say, belongs to it in its futurity.'[6] Though past worlds have lost their significance for our present existence and the objects that have survived from them are consigned to the museum, man's authentic possibilities do not perish with his instrumental world, but can be present to us in our world.

Heidegger's own attitude to the history of ontology might be taken as an example and application of his understanding of the character of history in general. He tells us that he is attracted to the philosophizing of the Greeks, which he understands as the restless quest for being.[7] But the original sources of philosophy have been covered up and concealed by the deadening influence of tradition, which is accepted without being understood and appropriated.[8] His own philosophy he understands as an attempt to recover the original possibility of an inquiry into being as such.

Strange and paradoxical as it may seem at first sight, Heidegger's philosophy of history will bear closer examination, and is not to be lightly dismissed. If the subject of history is man, and man as existing differs in his being from nature, then it follows that the methods and concepts employed by the historian must be suitable to his subject, and must differ from those employed in the scientific investigation of nature. In other words, the historian must use the concepts (*Begrifflichkeit*) of existentiality. Actually, Heidegger was not the first to realize that. He openly acknowledges his debt to Dilthey and Yorck,[9] who were already aware that history does not lend itself to the scientific methods which are applicable in the study of nature.

And it could be argued that much actual historical study has followed the lines indicated by Heidegger, even if unconsciously and with no explicit theory in mind. The historian must select his material. But what is the criterion of his selection? He would say that he selects what he con-

[6] *S. u. Z.*, p. 395. [7] *S. u. Z.*, p. 2.
[8] *S. u. Z.*, p. 21. [9] *S. u. Z.*, p. 398 ff.

siders to be significant. The question is, then, Significant for what? It is surely reasonable to say that it is what is significant for human existence. But we saw already that to be significant for existence means simply to present a possibility to the existence of someone.[10] Thus such history as we have described does have as its theme the possible. The lessons of history, as we call them, may be understood as simply the understanding of authentic possibilities (whether realized or not) which were once actually open in an *existentiell* situation, and which are still repeatable and so present.

Let us now return to Bultmann. While he does not explicitly mention Heidegger's philosophy of history, it is not difficult to show that some such understanding of history underlies his interpretation of New Testament theology. And indeed that is to be expected in the existential approach to theology, in which the theologian goes to the pages of the New Testament, including its historical passages, with the question of human existence in mind. In the first of his two essays on demythologizing, Bultmann describes the world which we meet in the writings of the New Testament.[11] It is essentially the world of Babylonian cosmology—the flat earth surmounted by the inverted bowl of the firmament, and sandwiched between heaven above and the underworld below. Strange invisible powers are at work both in human affairs and natural events, angels from above and demons from below. Miraculous and occult happenings are attributed to their agency—yes, and everyday happenings too, such as illness. As he moves through this world, the modern man, it would not be unfair to say, finds himself back in Heidegger's museum of antiquities, for it is a world which is no longer. Its concepts are as remote from his understanding as the flint tools in Heidegger's museum are from his daily occupation. They represent the projects of a former understanding of the world, but they are unintelligible to the man of today. When he is ill, he sends, not for an exorcist (if any can be found) but for a medical practitioner. The world of the New Testament has passed away and ceased to be meaning-

[10] *Supra*, p. 157. [11] *K. u. M.*, vol. I, pp. 15-16.

ful. The Copernican revolution and all the discoveries that have been made since then have changed the world-view of the ordinary man completely.

Bultmann says that the world-view of the New Testament is mythical. No doubt it is, but it would be misleading not to realize that the modern world-view has its myths as well, and may be perfectly unintelligible to men who live two thousand years after our time. A strange object in the sky is not interpreted now as a sign from the gods, but as a flying saucer. But this is incidental, and not the point at issue here. Whether more or less mythical than the world-view of modern men, the world of the New Testament is not our world but a museum of antiquities.

But, of course, it does not therefore follow that the New Testament has nothing to say that is significant today. What we have considered is, in Heidegger's terminology, the secondary historical. It is in the New Testament only the background for what it has to say about the saving events. Yet even these events are interwoven into the background. The story of the ascension, for instance, as narrated in Saint Luke's Gospel and the Acts of the Apostles, implies the New Testament world-picture. As far as the type of mythical element that we have so far considered is concerned—for we shall see that there is another—the problem of demythologizing might be expressed as the problem of disentangling the primary historical from the secondary historical in the New Testament. The primary historical consists of possibilities of existence which are repeatable, present to me today as they were present to others in the past. The central theme of the New Testament is such a possibility—the possibility of forgiveness and the new life which God offers to men in Christ. It is that in the New Testament history which is significant for the existence of modern man, that is to say, a present possibility of decision for him. What Bultmann is striving to do is to spotlight this essential primary historical in the New Testament, to separate it from the now meaningless secondary historical, and so make it a real possibility of decision for man today. And if that be so, his work is not destructive of the historical element in the New Testament, but the reverse.

We are now also in a position to understand better what Bultmann means by an eschatological event. It appears to be very close to Heidegger's concept of repeatable authentic possibility, which for him is the most important element in history. Such a possibility, as we saw, is understood by Heidegger as one 'which can be repeated so that the power of the possible is felt in present existence'. Even so the power of divine grace and the possibility which it restored to man, first actualized in the coming of Christ, is felt again whenever the Word is proclaimed and heard. In this way the event of grace can be understood as both past and present. But at the same time we must remember that for Bultmann the eschatological event has a unique character in so far as it proceeds from God, whereas for Heidegger there have been no doubt many authentic repeatable possibilities in history. Thus the two concepts—eschatological event and authentic repeatable possibility, though structurally similar, are not quite identical.

Having thus clarified the existentialist understanding of history, we turn now to the task of examining more closely the concepts of the mythical and the historical, before we go on to see how the view of history outlined in the preceding pages may be used for the interpretation of the mighty acts.

22. *The Mythical and the Historical*

God has acted in a decisive and unique manner in Jesus Christ. That is the foundation of the Christian religion, and because of that it stands on a different level from all human philosophies, actual or possible. But how are the mighty acts to be understood theologically? Bultmann's interpretation seems to depend on the possibility of distinguishing three elements in the New Testament account of these acts of God.

Firstly, there is the mythical element. But what is a myth? The term seems to be a very confused one. The mythical is defined by Bultmann as a way of thinking in which the other-worldly and divine are represented as this-worldly and human.[12] But this is scarcely a wide enough definition, for as Professor Henderson points out, there are secular myths, such as the Nazi myth of the master-race and the Marxist myth of the classless paradise into which the divine does not enter at all.[13] This objection would also apply to the definition of myth as stories of the gods. Bultmann himself says that the world-picture of the New Testament is a mythical one.[14] But what does he mean by myth in this sentence? He goes on, as we have seen already, to speak of the flat earth under the vault of the firmament—in other words, the Babylonian cosmology. But this is not myth within the sense of his own formal definition. It is primitive science or primitive world-view, not a description of the divine in terms of this world, but a description of this world itself as these early thinkers imagined it to be.

Having regard to this confusion in Bultmann's usage, we shall have to look for the meaning which he attaches to the term myth not only in his formal definitions but also in the broad way in which he speaks of the mythical. We are not attempting a definition of myth in general, but simply describing what Bultmann—consciously or unconsciously—comprehends under the term, as that is sufficient for our purpose here. We take it to include: (a) what might be called myth proper, the representation of the divine and other-worldly in human and this-worldly terms; (b) everything in the New Testament which implies those first-century concepts which now belong to a world that is no longer, and are not acceptable or intelligible to the modern mind.

To the first type of myth we shall return later. As to the second, a difficulty immediately arises, for who is going to say just what is and what is not acceptable and intelligible to the modern mind? On some matters there might be fairly

[12] *K. u. M.*, vol. I, p. 22 note.
[13] *Myth in the New Testament*, S.C.M. Press, pp. 52-53.
[14] *K. u. M.*, vol. I, p. 15.

general agreement. The story of the ascension which we already instanced is literally intelligible only if we accept the Babylonian cosmology, and since we live in the post-Copernican era, it is literally unintelligible to us—though, of course, that is not to deny that it may be intelligible in some other way. There are other matters on which there would be very little agreement. Consider, for instance, the miracles of Jesus. Bultmann apparently rejects them as not acceptable to the modern mind. 'We cannot use electric light and wireless, or claim modern medical and clinical treatment in cases of illness, and at the same time believe in the New Testament world of spirit and miracle.'[15] But that is to ignore the fact that in this scientific age thousands go to Lourdes every year, and that in Protestant Churches also there is a very real interest in what is called spiritual healing. There seems to be nothing unacceptable about it to many modern minds. And apart from that, many of us have no difficulty both in appreciating the developments of modern thought and the advance of medical science, and in believing that our Lord had a power of spiritual healing—without, of course, necessarily believing in demons!

The truth is that at this point we perceive in Bultmann's thought not the influence of existentialism but the hangover of a somewhat old-fashioned liberal modernism. He is still obsessed with the pseudo-scientific view of a closed universe that was popular half a century ago, and anything which does not fit into that tacitly assumed world-picture is, in his view, not acceptable to the modern mind and assigned to the realm of myth. Let us frankly acknowledge that there is myth in the New Testament, in both senses of the term which we described, but Bultmann himself is perhaps too ready to assign to the mythical element in the New Testament narrative events which may really belong to the second element, to which we now turn.

This second element we shall call the objective-historical (*historisch*). The narrative element in the New Testament, as Bultmann acknowledges,[16] is entirely different from the

15 *K. u. M.*, vol. I, p. 18.   16 *K. u. M.*, vol. I, p. 41.

mythical narratives of Greek or Hellenistic deities, since it centres in a definite historic person, Jesus of Nazareth. The mighty acts may therefore be studied as objective happenings by the scientific historian, as indeed the Apostles' Creed implies when it states that our Lord 'suffered under Pontius Pilate'. The event is given a definite place in world history.

Among the mighty acts, the cross is the one which can most readily be understood as an objective-historical event. That Jesus aroused opposition by his teaching, that he was betrayed, arrested, tried and put to death—there is nothing mythical about that, considered as a fact and apart from interpretations of it. It is perfectly intelligible and acceptable as it stands, whether one's world-view is that of the first or the twentieth or any other century. But is theology particularly interested in the objective-historical? Faith in the cross is something entirely different from a belief that the cross is a fact of history, and it is with the exposition of the content of faith that theology is concerned.

Attempts have, of course, been made to isolate the objective-historical element in the New Testament, and the results of this research are very interesting. As a good illustration, we might take the work of the French scholar Guignebert.[17] Applying the most rigorous methods of scientific history and textual criticism, Guignebert has pretty well dealt the death-blow to all theories which regard the figure of Jesus as a purely mythical construction, and has proved beyond all reasonable doubt his objective-historical reality. Beyond that, however, the positive results of his investigation are meagre in the extreme. With a ruthlessness which goes far beyond anything in Bultmann, he destroys the New Testament record, and presents us with the allegedly historic Jesus—an attenuated figure very far removed from the Jesus of Christian faith.

But let us suppose for a moment that the results of his investigation had been different—and, of course, different conclusions have been reached by scholars of a more conservative mind than Guignebert. Suppose he had proved not

17 See his book, *Jesus*, Kegan Paul.

only the objective-historical reality of Jesus, but had also substantially verified the New Testament record as a whole and shown that it gives an account of events which actually took place at a given time in world history. Would that really make much difference for religious faith or for theology? It would not, and frankly, it would be intolerable if it did. For then not only the theologian but the ordinary Christian believer would be at the mercy of the historian. Faith would be founded on historical research, on the probability of certain events having taken place at a certain period in world history. That certainly seems to be the unenviable position in which those theologians find themselves who stake their case on the objective-historical. But we say that the results of historical research would not make much difference, one way or the other, and for this reason. Guignebert approaches his subject-matter with the most admirable detachment—and, of course, that is the only proper attitude for the scientific historian. His investigation is purely objective. But, as we saw already, the theologian is never detached from his subject-matter.[18] As the interpreter of faith, he speaks from within faith. His relation to his subject-matter is not objective but existential. And should he come to understand it objectively, he has ceased to be a theologian and has become a philosopher or an anthropologist. Now in particular, the mighty acts, when regarded as objective events or objective-historical happenings, cease to be saving events—but it is precisely in their character as saving events that theology is interested.

That is not to say, of course, that there is no value at all in the objective-historical understanding of the New Testament record. There could only be saving events if there had been certain objective events—a point which Bultmann is perhaps inclined to overlook. The objective-historical does have a certain relevance to theology, as we shall see. The full understanding of the mighty acts as saving events is bound up with the understanding of them as objective events in the world, related to certain prior, contemporary and subsequent

[18] *Supra*, p. 58.

events. Yet we begin with saving events which imply objective events—not with objective events which are transformed into saving events. It is not the objective-historical element in the mighty acts that is of primary importance for theology.

This primacy belongs to the third element, which we shall call the existential-historical (*geschichtlich*). By this we mean that element in them which makes them significant for my existence, that is to say, which sets before me a present possibility. In Heidegger's language, it is 'the authentic repeatable possibility' which lies in the mighty acts, in Bultmann's language it is their eschatological character in virtue of which they are not merely past happening but God's present act of grace in my situation.

Heidegger, as we saw, makes the existential-historical the primary subject-matter for all historical study. History (*Historie*), he maintains, when it is authentic history, is concerned not with facts but with the possible. Its primary task is not to investigate past events as such, or to show their origins, relations, interactions and consequences, but rather to disclose man in his historic possibilities, and above all in his authentic repeatable possibilities. Presumably he would approve of the historical work of Spengler, for instance, who analysed the destiny of ancient cultures to elucidate the future possibilities of western culture. Such history ceases to be a purely academic or objective study, and acquires a certain pragmatic character. It is, Heidegger claims, concerned with the future more than with the past. No doubt there are historians who will disagree with Heidegger's view of their subject, just as there are some who accept it, but they can be left to argue the matter out among themselves, since the wider question of history in general does not concern us here.

Our business is with the more limited application of the existentialist philosophy of history to the historical events which enter into the field of Christian theology, and here it does seem true that it is the existential-historical understanding of these events which is of importance. In so far as the

171

cross and resurrection are saving events and proclaimed as such, they are not past occurrences of world history but open to man as present possibilities—namely, of forgiveness and a new life. They are thus understood as existential-historical happenings.

This follows also from one of the first principles of the existential approach to theology which we noted at the very outset. There it was said that in this type of theology the orientation of the question (*Fragestellung*) is to human existence, and we noted Bultmann's statement that when he goes to the Bible the question to which he seeks an answer is the question of human existence. Or in the New Testament language, the question may be expressed, 'What must I do to be saved?'[19] The answer to that question is not simply that great events—the cross and resurrection—once took place, but that great events—forgiveness and the new life—can take place now. That alone gives the questioner a possibility of salvation for which he can decide. But the events are here understood in their existential-historical character. The historical statements of the New Testament are understood not as the record of past objective occurrences, but as significant for my existence.

But does the primacy of the existential-historical for theology mean that we can do without the objective-historical and the mythical altogether? In the New Testament the three elements are all interwoven. Can theology either dispense with any one of them or isolate any one of them?

We begin again with the mythical element, bearing in mind the confusion in Bultmann's use of this term, and that it covers for him both concepts which belong to the first-century world-view, and ways of speaking in which the divine is represented as this-worldly. We note to begin with a fundamental difference between the positions of Bultmann and Guignebert as regards their attitude to the mythical element in the New Testament. Guignebert is interested only in the objective-historical, and the mythical element in the record is dismissed by him as without significance, a mere

19 Acts 16.30.

legendary accretion which has to be removed in order to reveal the objective-historical content of the New Testament. On the other hand, while Bultmann also counts much of the record as mythical, he does not deny that it has value, and his aim is to restate its content in a form free from mythical expression, if that is possible. The value of myth lies for him in this, that it seeks to express the existential-historical content of the event of which it speaks, to point to the significance of the event for human existence. But he thinks that myth is a very imperfect instrument for the purpose which he assigns to it. The myth is therefore to be translated into a statement which concerns my existence. And further, Bultmann thinks that the New Testament itself leads the way in demythologizing, in that it sometimes expresses the significance of the myth for human existence in a form which does not appear to be mythical.

We have had an example of such demythologizing already in connection with Saint Paul's concept of the creation. He speaks in some places in Gnostic terms of the world having fallen under the dominion of demonic powers. We understand these demonic powers not as external to man but as proceeding from him in his fallen condition. And since Saint Paul himself was no dualist, we may accept Bultmann's contention that the Gnostic terminology was already demythologized for him. He gives me to understand what happens when I worship and serve the creature more than the Creator—and here it is Saint Paul himself who supplies the demythologized or existential interpretation of the demonic. Again, preachers for generations before Bultmann have no doubt demythologized the story of the ascension, so far as it implies the Babylonian cosmology. It has been interpreted in its significance for the existence of the believer, as symbolizing the lordship of the risen Christ over the world. But this interpretation also is already found in Saint Paul[20]—though admittedly in a passage which contains obvious reference to the first-century world-view.

It will be noted, however, that both of these examples

[20] Phil. 2.9-11.

concern only one of the two types of myth which we saw to be comprehended under Bultmann's loose employment of the term—namely, concepts belonging to the first-century world-view. It would therefore seem possible to eliminate that mythical element in the New Testament which arises from the use of such concepts by the New Testament writers. Such concepts belong to a world that no longer is, they are not meaningful for us, and, as in the examples given, they can be removed and the meaning of the New Testament teaching is thereby made intelligible to modern minds.

But what about myths of the other type, in which the divine is represented as this-worldly? This is myth according to Bultmann's own formal definition, and perhaps it is the only myth in the New Testament in the strict sense of the term, for Bultmann's extension of the term to cover first-century world-concepts may be unfortunate. Can this other type—the more important type of myth—be eliminated?

Bultmann himself seems to concede that we can speak of God's actions only in mythical terms.[21] And the reason for that has already been stated.[22] The everyday categories of human understanding are applicable to objects in nature (*Vorhandenheit*). The existentialists have tried to analyse the categories—or existentials—applicable to the being of man himself (*Existenz*). But that still leaves us without categories applicable to the ground of being, being itself beyond both *Vorhandenheit* and *Existenz*, that is to say, God. We can only speak of him by analogy or symbolically in categories drawn from *Vorhandenheit* or *Existenz*, as when we say that he is the First Cause or that he is our Father in heaven. But already in the use of such symbols we are into the realm of the mythical. Even to make such a simple statement of the Christian message as that 'God has sent his Son' involves (*a*) a symbol drawn from *Vorhandenheit*, the idea of sending or transferring from one place to another; and (*b*) a symbol drawn from *Existenz*, the idea of sonship, a relation between two human beings. But clearly it is impossible to get away

[21] Cf. *K. u. M.*, vol. I, p. 40.   [22] *Supra*, p. 77.

from such metaphors, so long as we seek to speak directly of God and his acts. Human thinking is such that here myth and symbol are inevitable.

But it may be replied that we need not and ought not to speak directly of the acts of God. We can express it all in terms of the significance for our existence of his acts. That God has sent his Son can be translated into statements about the possibility for me of forgiveness and a new life.

Leaving aside for the moment the question whether we can so easily surrender the possibility of speaking directly about the activity of God, what happens when we confine ourselves to making statements of an existential order? Do we really get away from myth even then? We saw earlier the difficulties which beset the communication of existential knowledge, and that it is frequently expressed in poetry, stories, myth and so on rather than in the exact propositions suitable to the communicating of scientific knowledge. It seems that as soon as we cease to speak of stocks and stones we must begin to use symbols and metaphors. Heidegger himself has confessed the difficulty of communicating the findings of his existential analytic, and has excused the strangeness of his terminology.[23] Even in his exact analysis of existence, there is an abundance of symbolic language, borrowed from the world of nature. Man is 'being-in-the-world' but in a non-spatial sense, his existence is characterized by 'thrownness', he 'projects' his possibilities, he is 'fallen'. These are only a selection from his metaphors, some of which are crude enough. And at the most crucial part of his argument, it will be remembered, he fell back on an ancient classical myth for the clarification of his meaning.[24] Hence we conclude that even if it were possible to translate all statements about the activity of God into statements about the existence of man in relation to God, it would still not be possible to get away from symbols, or from the myths which are constructed out of symbols.

We therefore reject the project of a demythologized Bible. Such a Bible would presumably be an analytic of Christian

[23] *S. u. Z.*, pp. 38-39.   [24] *Supra*, pp. 113-114.

existence—almost a baptized version of *Sein und Zeit*, as Bultmann seems to imply when he says that 'Martin Heidegger's existential analysis of man seems to be only a secular philosophical exposition of the New Testament view of man.'[25] But this would defeat Bultmann's own purpose of rendering the teaching of the Bible intelligible to the ordinary man of the twentieth century, because if the symbolic language of the Bible is difficult for the modern mind to grasp, the symbolic language in which any existential exposition must be couched is even more difficult. If the Bible is remote from the thinking of men today, an existential analytic is even more remote. Heidegger's work is difficult enough for anyone with a training in philosophy, and to the man in the street it must seem like a book sealed with seven seals. Yet a demythologized Bible, in which everything was translated into existential statements, could scarcely be less difficult. It would require to use the same obscure symbolic language as Heidegger employs, or language very like it. And because that language would be symbolic, it would be more accurate to speak of transmythologization than of demythologization.

Compare the two statements, that man in his being is compounded of possibility and facticity, and that man was formed of the dust of the ground and into his nostrils was breathed the breath of life. We would certainly agree that to the trained mind the first of these statements is more exact than the second. But to the ordinary man of the twentieth century the first statement would be unintelligible. He might misunderstand the second statement by taking it literally, but there is a reasonable chance that its relatively simple symbolism would still convey to his mind the meaning which is intended, without his having to master existentialist terminology. It would certainly seem far easier to convey the meaning to him by explaining the symbolic language of the biblical writer than by replacing that language by a new and more difficult way of speaking.

But we have still to discuss the important question whether,

25 *K. u. M.*, vol. I, p. 33.

in fact, we can give up speaking directly about God's activity, and confine ourselves merely to making statements about human existence. And it must be denied that we can. Bultmann believes—as every Christian theologian must—that God has acted in Jesus Christ. All existential analysis of Christian faith and experience assumes this proposition. If it is taken away, Christianity ceases to be a religion and becomes another philosophy of existence—which Bultmann expressly denies that it is. Yet the presupposition itself can only be expressed in mythical form—as that Jesus Christ is the Son of God, or that God has sent him. We can never, therefore, eliminate the mythical, and indeed we reach the conclusion that all existential exposition of the Christian faith rests upon an assumption which is only capable of mythical or symbolic expression.

We have here criticized some of the excesses to which Bultmann's theories are inclined to lead him. This is simply part of the wider criticism that Bultmann tends to over-emphasize whatever in Christian teaching is congenial to existentialist treatment, and to pass over whatever resists such treatment. We maintain that the mythical element cannot be eliminated—apart possibly from some first-century concepts which we have agreed to include under the heading of myth in the widest sense. Yet when that criticism has been made, and the limits of demythologizing laid bare, we can now acknowledge the value of Bultmann's teaching on its positive side. The myth must be related to my existence —and indeed to treat it as literal statement of fact might amount to a kind of idolatry. The business of the preacher is to present the myth in its existential significance, the business of the theologian is to analyse the experience of faith. Yet on the other hand we deny that the myth is exhausted in its existential significance. It conceals and at the same time expresses the real activity of God beyond my existence or any existence.

We turn next to the objective-historical. Can it be eliminated? The argument here follows a similar line to the one employed to show the indispensability of myth. There it was maintained that every existential proposition about the Christian faith implies a mythical proposition about the real activity of God. Here it is argued that every existential-historical event implies an objective-historical event. That is made quite clear in Heidegger's philosophy of history. He tells us that history is concerned with the possible. But that does not mean that history can roam where it will, or that it is indistinguishable from legend and fiction. History is concerned with repeatable possibility, and for a possibility to be repeated, it is necessary that it must once have been actual. To say that history is concerned with the possible does not release it from the course of real happenings, that is to say, from the facts.

Bultmann frankly acknowledges that the existential-historical significance of the cross has its origin in the objective-historical event of the crucifixion of Jesus.[26] But he makes it clear that he attaches little importance to the objective-historical happening as such. That may have meant much to the first preachers of the gospel who had themselves witnessed it, but now, he considers, our concern is with the existential-historical aspect of the cross, and the objective-historical happening has only theoretical interest for historical research.

We would be perfectly willing to agree with Bultmann that Christian theology and Christian preaching must be primarily concerned with the cross as an existential-historical event, for only so can it be a saving event and significant for my existence today. Yet we must protest at the tendency here to exclude the objective-historical element altogether. True, Bultmann is right in refusing to make theology—and Christian faith—dependent on historical research. But there is a sense in which the existential-historical implies the objective-historical. To preach the cross as saving event is to propagate an illusion unless the origin of that saving event was an actual happening—namely, God's once-for-all act at Calvary. Bultmann, I believe, recognizes this, but tends to obscure it by excessively subordinating the objective-historical

[26] *K. u. M.*, vol. I, p. 43.

to the existential-historical.[27] The question arises even more acutely in connection with the resurrection, but that will be dealt with later.

The argument here links up with and reinforces an earlier criticism of Bultmann.[28] It was said that he stripped our Lord of the numinous character which the records assign to him, and represented him as little more than a teacher of practical philosophy, and we contended that this picture of the historic Jesus is inadequate. We now see more clearly why that is so. The existential-historical (the Jesus of faith) presupposes an objective-historical origin (the Jesus of history). Admittedly we are primarily concerned with the Jesus of faith. The Fourth Evangelist represents our Lord himself as having said, 'It is expedient for you that I go away',[29] and this seems plainly to indicate the transition from the objective-historical life of Christ, limited as to time and space, to the existential-historical life, which is not so limited. Yet the latter implies the reality of the former, which cannot be dispensed with.

We cited the work of Guignebert as typical of the most radical scientific historical criticism to which the New Testament records can be subjected, and we noted his

[27] The discussion here may seem to require further clarification. We are trying to contrast two possible positions. The first is that of the man who begins from his experience of a saving event as present in the hearing and receiving of the Word in the act of faith, and who infers from that an origin for that event in objective world-history. But he may not be particularly interested to know the precise 'how' of that objective event though he believes 'that' it took place, for, as Tillich says, 'propositions about a past revelation give theoretical information; they have no revelatory power.' (*Systematic Theology*, vol. I, p. 141.) The second position is that of the man who begins with the assertion that an objective event once occurred, and bases his faith—or his theology—on that. The latter seems to be dependent on the results of historical research in a way in which the former is not, yet the former has not abandoned the objective-historical altogether because, as Bultmann says, Christianity differs from Greek myths in having its origin in an objective event of world-history. But here the guarantee of the once-for-all event in world history is provided by the reality of the present saving event, which posits the once-for-all event as its origin. Both faith and theology are thus liberated from dependence on historical research.

[28] *Supra*, pp. 22-23.
[29] John 16.7.

acceptance of the objective-historical reality of the life of Jesus, though he reduces that historic life to even more shadowy dimensions than does Bultmann. But it appears to me that as soon as the historian admits the objective-historical reality of the figure of Jesus, he must also admit that he was a big enough figure to found the Christian religion—or to put the same thing in another way, he must recognize an objective-historical which can support the weight of the existential-historical. This would certainly seem to be applicable to Bultmann's thought, for his recognition of the existential-historical significance of the life of Jesus implies a sufficient objective-historical origin. That is not to say, of course, that every incident recorded about Jesus must be objective fact, but it does argue that there must be a greater degree of continuity between the Jesus of history and the Jesus of faith than Bultmann seems willing to allow.

In answering in the negative the questions whether we can dispense in theology with the mythical and the objective-historical, we have also answered our third question, which was whether the theologian can isolate the existential-historical. We have seen reason to believe that this is the primary concern of theology in its treatment of the mighty acts, but that it cannot be the exclusive concern follows from the indispensability to theology of both the mythical and the objective-historical. For it has been shown firstly that every existential statement of the content of Christian faith assumes a proposition about the real activity of God, a statement about God which is not reducible to a statement about human existence, and which, from the very nature of our thought and language, is necessarily symbolic or mythical in its formulation; and it has been shown secondly that every existential-historical event has its origin in an objective-historical event which took place once for all in world history, and if that connection were absent there would be no genuine existential-historical happening but only a philosophical speculation, perhaps an illusion, a floating possibility unrelated to reality.

23. *The Mighty Acts*

Having now clarified the three possible ways in which the theologian may speak of the mighty acts, and having shown that all three ways are, in varying degrees, relevant to theology, we return to the mighty acts themselves. But immediately one further preliminary problem confronts us. We generally speak of the mighty acts in the plural. Bultmann prefers to think of one unitary act centred in the cross, to which both the resurrection and the incarnation must be related for them to have significance. This concept of a unitary act in which the cross is pre-eminent seems at first sight acceptable enough. Clearly the mighty acts are a unity in that they all belong to Christ. And further, as Bultmann shows, their unity is explicitly stated in the New Testament. Saint Paul frequently brings cross and resurrection together in a unity, and nowhere more significantly than in his remarks on baptism.[30] Cross and incarnation are likewise brought together.[31] Thus it would seem legitimate to consider the mighty acts as a unity centred in the cross.

But we have mentioned this apparently minor point because, as it appears to me, Bultmann goes on to make a somewhat doubtful use of his unitary conception of the saving events. Why is he so insistent on this concept of a unity in which the incarnation and resurrection are subordinated to the cross? Partly no doubt the reason is simply that Bultmann recognizes in the cross the essence of the Christian gospel—the radical surrender of self-sufficiency on the part of the Christian, which is at the same time a surrender to God. The resurrection as the new life follows from acceptance of the cross, and the incarnation means that God himself has spoken and acted in the cross. Yet the reason seems also to be partly that, as noted already, the cross is the mighty act which is most easily intelligible as objective-historical happening. And while Bultmann tends to give a very subordinate place to the objective-historical or even to

[30] Rom. 6.2-5; cf. also Rom. 4.25; I Cor. 15.3-4.
[31] Cf. II Cor. 8.9; Phil. 2.6 ff.

pass over it, we saw that he does recognize that the existential-historical has its origin in an objective-historical
happening. Now he appears to be unable to believe that we
can attach any objective-historical meaning to the birth and
resurrection stories of the New Testament. Yet since he
certainly does attach existential-historical significance to
these stories, he must find some objective-historical event as
their origin. Hence the importance which he attaches to the
unity of the saving acts and the primacy of the cross, which
provides—in his view—the objective-historical origin for
incarnation, atonement and resurrection alike. But this is a
very doubtful proceeding, and it is questionable whether the
objective-historical event of Calvary by itself can bear the
weight of the whole eschatological event of incarnation-
atonement-resurrection. We shall return to Bultmann's
use of the unitary concept of the mighty acts and our criticism of it when we discuss the resurrection.

But first we consider the cross. It may readily be understood
as objective-historical event, but clearly such understanding does not take us very far by itself. The non-Christian
as well as the Christian may believe that Christ 'suffered
under Pontius Pilate', but so long as attention is confined
to the objective-historical, the cross has not the character
of a saving event.

The New Testament speaks also of the cross in symbolical
or mythical terms, drawn from the Jewish cult. Christ is the
sacrifice whose blood atones for sin. He bears the punishment
of sin in the sinner's stead, and so releases the sinner from
the punishment that is his due. The complicated history of
the doctrine of the atonement in Christian theology shows
the extraordinary difficulties which beset the theologian when
he tries to interpret such statements as statements of fact.
When it is realized that we are dealing with what is called
myth, two courses are open. One is the way of liberal
modernism, which either strains to breaking point or simply
disregards the New Testament teaching, and finds the
meaning of the cross in its moral influence or in the principle
of self-sacrifice, or in some such 'modernist myth', as Taylor

has called such a theory.[32] The other way is the way of
Bultmann, who does not discard the mythical but seeks to
translate it into the existential-historical.

And it is the New Testament itself, he claims, which gives
the lead here in translating the myth into existential terms.
Saint Paul bursts open the categories of Jewish thought.
'Christ hath redeemed us from the curse of the law . . . that
we might receive the promise of the Spirit through faith.'[33]
The thought of the death of Jesus as a sacrifice which frees
from the punishment of sin is here translated into the understanding of his death as 'the means of liberation from the
powers of this world, the law, sin and death'.[34] In this way
the cosmic dimensions of the cross are made to appear. To
believe in the cross of Christ is not to believe that an objective
event once happened (which even the non-Christian
believes), nor yet is it to believe in a mythical representation
of that event, but, in Bultmann's words, it is 'to accept
Christ's cross as one's own, to be crucified with Christ'[35]—
and here again, of course, the existential interpretation of
the myth is found in the New Testament itself.[36] In this
way the cross is present to me, it is no mere past event but
an eschatological event, the authentic repeatable possibility
which was first given to man at Calvary and is still offered to
him in the proclaiming of the Word. It offers to me now the
possibility of forgiveness and liberation from the powers of
this world—and that for my existence, Bultmann would say,
is the significance of the myth of the atoning sacrifice.

But does this existential interpretation exhaust the myth?
Certainly it makes clear its significance for me, it makes it
meaningful, and Bultmann is to be congratulated in drawing
attention to the primary importance of this aspect of the
saving events for Christian theology and preaching. Yet it
seems to me that there is a residual truth in the myth which
cannot be translated into any existential form because it
refers to something beyond existence. The truth is that this

---

[32] *The Atonement in New Testament Teaching*, Epworth, p. 62.
[33] Gal. 3.13-14.   [34] *Th. des NT*, p. 292.
[35] *K. u. M.*, vol. I, p. 42.   [36] Gal. 2.20.

act of forgiveness cost something to God, that there is a mystery of divine activity here which cannot be expressed in any other way than by myth and symbol. It was the Son of God who died, and with this we come to the incarnation.

Clearly we have here no objective-historical event comparable to the cross. The evidence of the birth-stories is scanty and conflicting. Their meaning would appear to be that the person and work of Jesus Christ do not originate from within the world but from God. Precisely in that lies the hindrance to any objective-historical understanding of the event of the incarnation. Because it is an intervention in world history, it is different from any event within world history, and therefore is to be differently understood. It is an activity of God and therefore cannot be expressed except mythically. 'The Word was made flesh', 'God sent forth his Son', 'God was in Christ'[37]—these are different symbolic ways of expressing the truth of the incarnation, the last of which is perhaps the most literal expression that could be found, though the symbolic element is there also in the preposition. Here is a mystery of the divine activity which the categories of human thought cannot grasp, so that we must be content with the mythical expression. Nor can we here translate into existential terms the entire truth of the myth. If we say that Christ is for us God, that still implies that God was in Christ, and we cannot get away from it. Even if he does not say so explicitly, it seems clear that Bultmann recognizes that at this point demythologizing is impossible. We noted his criticism of the existentialist attempt to reach authentic existence out of the resources of fallen human existence, and the place which he gives to God's act of grace intervening in the human situation. It is the act of grace—the sending of Christ and giving him up to death on the cross—that must be expressed in mythical form since it enshrines the deepest mystery of the Christian religion, that God was in Christ.

Must we have an understanding of Christ as the Son of God, that is to say, must we believe in the incarnation, before

37 John 1.14; Gal. 4.4.; II Cor. 5.19.

we can perceive the cross as saving event? If that were true, it would considerably upset Bultmann's arguments, and particularly his view of the unity of the mighty acts as centred in the cross. Bultmann himself is very much aware of this problem.[38] His argument is that it is because God speaks to us in the cross, and offers us there a new understanding of ourselves and a possibility of new life, in place of the old life of self-sufficiency, that we recognize the Crucified One as the Son of God. This argument appears to me to be sound, except that I think it should be expanded to include not only the cross, admittedly the climax, but the total person and work of our Lord. It must have been the numinous character of his life and ministry as well as of his death which created belief in his divine provenance. That numinous character is plainly discernible in the Gospel records, and it must have been discernible in the historic Jesus also. So again we find ourselves returning to the attack on Bultmann's picture of the historic Jesus, and being compelled to maintain that there must be sufficient continuity between the Jesus of history and the Christ of faith to account for the origin of that faith. The cross must have been the culmination of a process of revelation already going on. Yet as the culmination, the final unfolding of the mystery, the cross holds the key position, since it is in the light of the cross that the whole mission and destiny of Christ become intelligible to us, and we can recognize that 'God was in Christ', restoring to man his lost possibility of being the child of God.

We turn finally to the resurrection. Can we have any objective-historical understanding of it? Bultmann thinks not. 'Is it not a completely mythical event?' he asks.[39] And here we must take Bultmann to task for what appears to be an entirely arbitrary dismissal of the possibility of understanding the resurrection as an objective-historical event. He dismisses it because of some prior assumption in his mind. What is that assumption? It is not the influence of existentialism here, because existentialism has nothing to say about the possibility of such an event at all. It is the other influence which

[38] Cf. *Th. des NT*, p. 298 ff.   [39] *K. u. M.*, vol. I, p. 44.

we noted before, the hang-over of liberal modernism, as we called it. The resurrection, however we might understand it, would be miraculous in character, and Bultmann has decided in advance that in this scientific age we cannot believe in miracles, and therefore we cannot believe in the resurrection as an objective event that once happened, even if we can believe in it in some other way.

The fallacy of such reasoning is obvious. The one valid way in which we can ascertain whether a certain event took place or not is not by bringing in some sweeping assumption to show that it could not have taken place, but to consider the historical evidence available, and decide on that. But Bultmann does not take the trouble to examine what evidence could be adduced to show that the resurrection was an objective-historical event. He assumes that it is myth. On his own theory, therefore, it is to be translated into the existential-historical. But we saw that every existential-historical event implies an objective-historical event as its origin, and Bultmann seems to have cut away any objective-historical ground for the resurrection. He tries to get round this difficulty, however, by referring it back to the cross as its objective-historical origin. 'Can mention of the resurrection of Christ be anything other than the expression of the significance of the cross?'[40] It was for this reason that we questioned his insistence on the unity of the mighty acts. Can we, in fact, rest everything on the objective-historical event of the cross alone? Would not the cross by itself have meant the defeat of good by evil, so that it could not serve as the origin for saving events? We are reminded of Saint Paul's argument: 'If Christ be not raised, your faith is vain.'[41] And that he believed in an objective-historical resurrection in some sense or other seems clear from his appeal to witnesses[42]—though Bultmann dismisses the significance of this appeal in a remarkably arbitrary fashion.[43]

Our argument that the resurrection must be understood in some sense to have been an objective-historical event is

[40] *K. u. M.*, vol. I, p. 44. [41] I Cor. 15.17.
[42] I Cor. 15.5-8. [43] *Th. des NT*, p. 300.

therefore twofold. Firstly, the question is to be decided not on general grounds of probability—for, after all, we remember that these were unique events in which God was at work —but on the historical evidence available. Slight though it is, it seems to me that the Easter stories together with Saint Paul's appeal to witnesses make it undeniable that Christ appeared to his disciples after his death—in what way we do not presume to say, nor do we think it needful to inquire. And, secondly, to accept the resurrection as an existential-historical event seems to me to make it necessary to postulate an objective-historical event additional to the cross as its sufficient origin. No doubt there is a mythical element in the New Testament ways of speaking of the resurrection, but to suggest that here we have something entirely mythical with no objective-historical basis additional to the cross seems quite unwarranted.

However, having once criticized Bultmann for what we consider to be his reckless and arbitrary denial of an objective-historical element in the resurrection, we now turn to the appreciation of his positive teaching on the subject. Briefly that teaching is that for Christian faith and for theology as the exposition of Christian faith the primary understanding of the resurrection is the understanding of an existential-historical or eschatological event. Just as faith in the cross was said to be not simply the belief that Jesus was once crucified but rather that in the cross God offers me a possibility of existence now, so belief in the resurrection is not simply belief that a miracle once happened but belief that a miracle of new life can happen now for me—though in both cases, as we have specifically argued, the latter belief implies the first.

But the objective-historical understanding of either the cross or the resurrection has no more than theoretical or speculative interest. When we spoke before of the difference between objective and existential knowledge,[44] we said that the knowledge of God is existential, the understanding which belongs to a divine-human encounter, and that when God is

[44] *Supra*, p. 56 ff.

objectified as, for instance, in the philosophy of Descartes, he ceases to be God in the religious sense and becomes yet another object in the world of objects. Presumably something of that kind was meant when someone said that the next greatest folly to denying God's existence is the attempt to prove it. Much the same might be said of the resurrection. Attempts to reach an objective understanding of it, to prove that the tomb was empty, and so on—of which there are not a few examples in the commentaries—are simply beside the point, for in its character as saving event the resurrection is to be understood existentially. Bultmann says of such attempts to reach an objective understanding of what happened on Easter morning that they 'can neither be proved nor made illuminating'.[45] They cannot be proved because they all involve very doubtful speculation on matters about which the New Testament writers deemed it wise to say little or nothing. They cannot be made enlightening, because even if a complete proof and a convincing account of the resurrection as objective event were to be reached, it would neither increase nor diminish the faith of the believer, who is concerned primarily not with past happening but with that which is significant for his existence now.

For faith, the resurrection is present. It is understood not as past objective happening, but as the present possibility of new life which God offers in Christ, and for which man may decide. This is the existential-historical understanding of the resurrection which is an eschatological event, an event containing authentic repeatable possibility. 'The belief in the resurrection of Christ,' says Bultmann, 'and the belief that in the proclamation of the Word Christ himself—yes, God himself—speaks, are identical.'[46] Bearing in mind the reservations that we have made earlier, we may say that this statement sets out the essential significance of the resurrection for Christian faith. We do not prove—or accept without proof—that something once happened, and go on to deduce what that happening now means for us. We begin with the present possibility which Christ offers in the proclaiming

[45] *Th. des NT*, p. 300.   [46] *Th. des NT*, p. 301.

and hearing of the Word, and from that we infer that something did once happen, but precisely what that something was is a matter for academic speculation only and of no particular relevance to faith.

We have endeavoured to analyse the mythical, the objective-historical, and the existential-historical elements in the mighty acts. We have seen that none of these three elements can be dispensed with, but that for the understanding which belongs to faith the existential-historical has the primary relevance. In such understanding God's act of grace in Christ is present to me. In the proclaiming of the Word God speaks to me through Christ, and summons me to accept the possibilities of forgiveness and renewal made available in the cross and resurrection.

Does Bultmann destroy the historical element in Christianity—as, for instance, Thielicke has argued?[47] Christianity is distinctively a historical religion, and we have on several occasions protested against Bultmann's excessive devaluation of the objective-historical origins of Christian faith, which he tends to reduce to a very insignificant place. He does not, however, eliminate this element, nor can he eliminate it, since his existential-historical interpretation implies an objective-historical happening which took place once for all. He asserts, as we have seen, that the mythical element in Christianity differs altogether from the myths of Greek religion in that it refers to a definite historical person. And his whole argument as to the distinction between Christianity as a religion and existentialism as a philosophy rests on the belief that in Jesus Christ God entered world history in a special and decisive way.

The question, however, must be carried further than that. When it is asked if Bultmann destroys the historical element in the New Testament, it is implied that we know what is meant by the historical element, that is to say, the question already assumes an understanding of what the historical is. And further, the question seems to understand it as what we have called the objective-historical, the facts of world

47 *K. u. M.*, vol. I, p. 159 ff.

history. But we have already outlined Heidegger's philosophy of history, and seen that on his view the concern of historical study is not with fact but with possibility. Clearly some such understanding of the historical is operative in Bultmann's thought. It was not our business to pronounce upon the validity of Heidegger's view as a theory of history in general, but we did say that it was the kind of history that is relevant to theology. The question of existence is not answered by a fact but by an *existentiell* possibility. Now if we accept such a view of the historical and identify this much-abused term with what we have called the existential-historical, then Bultmann is so far from destroying the historical element in the New Testament that it might rather be claimed that he is making clear for us what the genuine historical element in the New Testament really is.

Lest there be any misunderstanding on this point, let us be quite clear how widely Bultmann's attitude to the historical differs from another attitude with which the careless reader might confound it, because of certain very superficial resemblances. I refer to the attitude to the historical of nineteenth-century absolute idealism, and of the theology which fell under its influence.

That attitude is stated by one of our most noted English idealist philosophers, F. H. Bradley, with his usual admirable clarity.[48] Christianity, he supposes, is a universal and eternal truth, 'conscious of itself above time, and yet revealing itself in the historical growth of spiritual experience'. Suppose one were asked to compare such a conception of truth with the truth about some happening in time.

> I will not instance such events as the virgin birth and bodily ascension of Jesus of Nazareth, but I will take the historical assertion that Jesus actually at a certain time lived and taught in Galilee and actually died at Jerusalem on the cross. And by 'actually' I mean that if we had been there, we should have seen those things happen. All such

[48] In Terminal Essay VIII, appended to Second Edition of *The Principles of Logic*, O.U.P., pp. 688-690.

events are, if you view them as occurrences, of little importance. Inquire by all means whether and how far there is good evidence for their happening. But do not imagine that Christianity is vitally concerned with the result of your inquiry. Christianity, as I conceive it, covers so much ground, fills such a space in the universe, and makes such a difference in the world that, without it, the world would be not so much changed as destroyed. And it counts for much that this eternal truth should have appeared on our planet (as presumably elsewhere) and should here (we hope) be developing itself more and more fully. But the rest, if you will take it as mere event and occurrence, is an affair so small—a matter grounded by the very nature of its world on so little—that between the two things there can hardly be a comparison.

This might fairly be called a destruction of the historical element in Christianity. It is based on the assumption that truth is not to be found in the realm of the temporal. There we can only have symbols pointing to some eternal truth. Christianity is identified with a philosophical truth which, apprehended in its purest form, would no longer have need of Christian symbolism and would make no reference to Christ, or his life or death. Whether Christ actually lived or not is—on this view—of no moment, since religious events have no value in themselves, but are symbols only which stand for timeless truth, 'incarnations of eternal reality'.

But this view of the idealists is poles apart from Bultmann's position. The idealist identifies the essence of Christianity with a high philosophy of the universe, but for Bultmann Christianity is a religion with saving power. For the idealist the mighty acts become mere optional symbols of supra-rational truth, but for Bultmann they constitute God's unique act of grace. For the idealist the significance of these acts for the individual is a purely intellectual one, but for Bultmann they summon to a decision, in so far as they present a possibility of existence. Thus when his view is compared with that of idealist theologizing, it will be seen that it is not

Bultmann who destroys the historical. His aim is not to destroy the historical foundation of our religion, but to exhibit it in its cosmic dimensions as authentic repeatable possibility, significant for the existence of men today. In his own words, it is the case 'of a historical Person and his Destiny being raised to eschatological rank'.[49]

[49] *Th. des NT*, p. 301.

VIII

CHRISTIAN EXISTENCE

24. Faith

WE have seen how, according to the New Testament teaching, God has in Jesus Christ intervened in the human situation and restored to mankind the *existentiell* possibility, which had been lost through sin, of gaining his authentic being, that is to say, of becoming the child of God. For the individual this is a possibility that is offered now when he hears God speaking to him in the proclamation of the Word. With respect to the past, it is the possibility of forgiveness. The sin which cut him off from his true life is blotted out by God's act of grace in restoring that true life as a possibility within his reach. With respect to the future, it is the possibility of entering on a new life. To accept the cross and resurrection of Christ is to surrender self-sufficiency and to live in dependence on and in communion with God. We must now attempt the existential description of this new life, the authentic existence of man as the New Testament understands it to be, and we begin with faith, which is the attitude in which man enters upon it.

Bultmann gives a preliminary definition of faith in the following terms: 'Faith is the decision in face of the grace which confronts us in the proclamation of the Word.'[1] On this view, therefore, faith is closely connected with decision —and in our quotation, almost identified with it.

It may at once be asked, however, whether the important place here given to decision in the Christian life is legitimate. Is it true to the New Testament teaching, or is it even consistent with Bultmann's own interpretation of that teaching?

[1] *Th. des NT*, p. 265.

A genuine decision is something that a man must make for himself—it is his own, if anything is. If, therefore, decision is the essential step towards entering the true or authentic existence for man, does that not imply that entry into such an existence is something which man must do for himself? And is it not the teaching of the New Testament, as Bultmann himself understands and expounds it, that that is exactly what man cannot do, and that God alone can do for him? If decision plays the part here assigned to it, what becomes of the concept of grace?

And further, does this not look like an improper influence of existentialism upon Bultmann's interpretation of New Testament thought? For decision or resolve (*Entschlossenheit*) has a very important place in Heidegger's concept of an authentic existence.[2] The fallen self, it will be remembered, dwells in the present.[3] But this was described as an inauthentic present, in so far as absorption in immediate possibilities implies a flight both from the past and from the future. It is a flight from the past because it is a forgetting of facticity. It is a flight from the future because it is an avoiding of possibilities, and especially the capital possibility of death. But when man authentically hears the call of conscience (for there is a possibility of authentic hearing even in fallen man[4]) he is brought into the authentic present which is the moment (*Augenblick*) of decision. The moment differs from the inauthentic present in this, that it is not a bare present but carries with it a disclosure of the past (what has been, the limitation of facticity) and of the future (what can still be, the possibility that remains open). Fallen man who is in the inauthentic present is characterized by irresolution—he jumps from one immediate possibility to another. His existence is not his own, but is at the mercy of chance circumstances in the world on which it is founded, and so it lacks coherence. But when conscience summons man into the moment of decision, and his total situation is disclosed to him, genuine resolve becomes possible. Such resolve unifies the self which is scattered in the irresolution of fallenness.

[2] Cf. *S. u. Z.*, pp. 295-313.   [3] *Supra*, p. 159.   [4] *Supra*, p. 143.

The unification is brought about because in resolve past, present and future, the threefold structure of existence as temporality, are brought together. Resolve looks to the past in accepting facticity. That means that a genuine resolve is never for an impracticable ideal, but for a possibility which is still open in the situation. Resolve looks to the future because it is the projecting of the self forward on such an authentic possibility. And the resolve is accomplished in the authentic present, the moment of decision in which both past and future are disclosed.

We have attempted here to give a purely formal account of the concept of resolve. In Heidegger, of course, resolve is related to the concrete situation of the anticipation of death. It is anticipatory resolve—the projecting of the self upon the capital possibility into which it is thrown, namely, death. But not all existentialists would accept this connection of resolve with death, and therefore we may find it convenient to have before us the bare formal existential structure of resolve, as outlined above, without reference to Heidegger's view that it is the resolute acceptance of death and the nothingness of human existence that constitutes authentic existence. That will be especially the case if we use the existential concept of resolve to elucidate the place of decision in Christian existence, which is directed not to death but to life.

Clearly resolve is, in Heidegger's philosophy, a purely human phenomenon. It represents indeed man's extreme effort in the direction of self-sufficiency, his ultimate striving to rise above the void into which he is thrown. He is 'condemned to be free', in Sartre's well-known phrase which neatly combines the facets of facticity and possibility, and he decides to accept his fate. For even the resolve which accepts death as the capital possibility, in the light of which all possibilities are to be evaluated, is not a passive acceptance of nothingness. It is despairing man's last endeavour to be superior to his destiny. It makes him, says Heidegger, 'powerful to exist, it scatters every concealment of himself, and along with dread there is joy in this possibility.'[5] Now, quite

[5] *S. u. Z.*, p. 313.

obviously, decision can have no such place in the Christian life which denies man's self-sufficiency and asserts that he cannot of himself attain to an authentic existence. Has Bultmann, therefore, been led away by the influence of Heidegger at this point to an exaggerated emphasis on decision?

That does not necessarily follow. Let us not overlook the great difference between Heidegger and Bultmann on this matter of decision. The possibility upon which man projects himself in authentic resolve is, according to Heidegger, a possibility derived entirely from his own resources. But the authentic possibility, for which, on Bultmann's view, man is summoned to decide, is one entirely derived from God, presented to man by God's act of grace in Christ. In a sense, therefore, the decision itself is God's gift, in so far as God's grace alone makes possible the decision. This is explicitly recognized by Bultmann himself: 'Faith is the work of God, in so far as the grace which comes from him first makes possible the human decision, so that this decision itself can be understood only as God's gift, without on that account losing its character as decision.'[6] This last clause has its importance also, for some element of genuine decision there must be. Man is not an object, he exists. If God, therefore, will give to man salvation, he cannot impose it upon him as he might impose a property upon an object—at least, not without taking away man's distinctively human character, his existence, and so reducing him to the level of an object or an automaton. God's gift of salvation can only be given as a possibility for which man can decide. The decision itself may be considered to be God's gift, since God alone made it possible, yet on the other hand it is also man's own, since he had the alternative of rejecting the possibility which God offers.

No doubt in actual Christian experience the element of decision is sometimes more, sometimes less pronounced and present to consciousness. Yet some genuine decision there must always be, an accepting and appropriating of the gift

[6] *Th. des NT*, pp. 325-326.

of grace which comes to man as possibility. That would be true even of those brought up in a Christian environment who might find it difficult to recall any definite act of decision. In their case the moment of decision, as Heidegger calls it, has been of extended duration. Yet genuine decision there must have been if they have appropriated the gift of grace and are not passive inheritors of a dead tradition. Goethe's well-known lines are relevant here:

Was du ererbt von deinen Vätern hast,
Erwirb es, um es zu besitzen. [7]
[Earn the heritage of your fathers in order to possess it.]

But if decision has its own place in the Christian life, and if to accord it that place is not inconsistent with recognizing the place of the divine grace—as we have tried to show—then it would be unfair to say that by emphasizing decision Bultmann has fallen back into the belief in man's self-sufficiency, which he himself has been at such pains to oppose. It might, however, be fair to say that Bultmann tends to over-emphasize the importance of decision, as in the sentence we quoted in which he states bluntly that faith is the decision which man makes in the face of grace. The exaggeration of the place of decision is probably due to his preoccupation with existentialism. Yet too much importance should not be attached to what is intended as merely a preliminary definition of faith. Bultmann modifies his position later, as when he speaks of the decision itself being in a sense the gift of God, and more especially in his phenomenological analysis of faith, at which we must look shortly, and in which he draws attention to other constituent structures of faith besides decision. Bearing this in mind, we may agree with Professor Henderson that 'to emphasize decision is not to do something alien to the Christian tradition—provided one does not neglect other elements equally vital in that tradition.' [8]

Does Heidegger's existential analysis of the structure of resolve, considered formally and apart from its connection

[7] *Faust*, Part I.
[8] *Myth in the New Testament*, S.C.M. Press, p. 24.

with death, shed any light on the character of Christian decision? It may be said that it does in two ways. Firstly, it was said that in the moment of resolve man's total situation is disclosed to him—the past (facticity), which in his fallen existence he forgets, and the future (possibility), which he avoids. Saint Paul's entire Epistle to the Romans may serve as an illustration. In it the situation of mankind—which is also the situation of the individual[9]—is brought before us. Man is disclosed in his facticity, which the Christian interprets as creatureliness, and in his sin, which consists in worshipping and serving the creature more than the Creator. And it is in the disclosure of this situation, with man stripped of his illusions and made aware of his own helplessness, that the message of the Christian gospel is exhibited as the only genuine future for mankind, involving an acceptance of creatureliness, a surrender of self-sufficiency, and a dependence on God. It is surely not unreasonable to say that Saint Paul's exposition brings the reader into the moment of decision, and that this moment displays the characteristics revealed in Heidegger's analysis—a disillusioned awareness of my total situation, past, present and future.

Secondly, there is the point which Heidegger makes about the relation of resolve to the unity of the self. In resolve, the self which was scattered in fallenness is integrated. So in the act of faith or committal there is a unifying of the self which was dissipated in the world. The self is now projected on its authentic possibility of life in dependence upon God. Yet this unity also may be thought of as the gift of God, since his act of grace alone makes it possible for man to commit himself to him. Thus Saint Paul says: 'I am crucified with Christ: nevertheless I live; yet not I, but Christ liveth in me.'[10] The self, when it seeks to be sufficient unto itself, disintegrates, but the cross and resurrection afford the possibility of a reintegration which so transforms the self that here Saint Paul can say that it is not he who lives but Christ who lives in him. We shall return to the question of the unity of the self in connection with the subject of hope.

[9] *Th. des NT*, p. 266.　　　　　[10] Gal. 2.20.

We must now turn to the other elements in faith besides decision. Christian faith, as Bultmann points out, is always related to a quite definite ground—it is faith in the saving work of Christ. 'It is therefore not piety or a general trust in God, but the receiving of the Word.'[11] To receive the Word means that it is authentically heard or understood, so that another constituent element in the structure of faith must be understanding. 'Faith cometh by hearing',[12] and to hear means to understand and make my own the knowledge which God has gifted to man through Christ.

What is this knowledge? Bultmann describes it as a new understanding of the self. The old understanding of the self as sufficient to itself is given up. That old understanding may have taken several different forms—concern with the world and striving for the mastery of things, or the Jewish quest for righteousness through observance of the law, or the confidence of the Greeks in human wisdom, or even, we might add, the *existentiell* resolve of man to be himself from his own resources. All are in different ways a trusting in the flesh, in Pauline language. To accept the cross and resurrection of Christ is to abandon all such understandings of the self, and to enter into a new understanding in which the self is seen in relation to Christ, surrendered to him and living not in its own power but in the power of God. The clearest New Testament statement of the change from the old to the new understanding of the self is perhaps that in which Saint Paul, speaking of 'the excellency of the knowledge of Christ Jesus my Lord', expresses for himself the wish that he may 'be found in him, not having mine own righteousness, which is of the law, but that which is through the faith of Christ, the righteousness which is of God by faith: that I may know him, and the power of his resurrection, and the fellowship of his sufferings, being made conformable unto his death.'[13]

Is this interpretation of faith as a new understanding of the self too intellectual? We must recall the earlier discussion of understanding.[14] There we distinguished between

11 *Th. des NT*, p. 313.   12 Rom. 10.17.
13 Phil. 3.8-10.   14 *Supra*, p. 54 ff.

199

objective understanding and existential understanding—the understanding of things and the understanding of existence. And just as religious faith is not belief in a set of propositions but faith in a Person and his work, so the understanding which is a constituent of faith is not objective or academic understanding of a fact, but an existential understanding, a disclosure of the self to itself in every aspect of its existence and in its relations to God and the world. It is, in fact, that understanding of myself which belongs to the disclosure of my total situation given in the moment of decision, as already described. The understanding of the self of which Bultmann speaks is a practical understanding, closely related to decision. To have a new understanding of the self, in the sense in which Bultmann and Heidegger use the expression, does not mean to adopt a new philosophy of life, but to undergo a complete re-orientation of the self. By speaking of a new understanding of the self, Bultmann makes it clear that he means a change in which 'the new "I" is constituted in place of the old', or again, 'the direction of the will is reversed'.[15] The charge of intellectualism in stressing the element of understanding in faith can only be made if understanding is taken in the narrow sense of objective understanding—which it often is in common speech. But it is precisely against this narrow intellectualism that Heidegger and the existentialists in general have protested, and their broader use of the term is clearly the one which Bultmann has in mind when he speaks of that new understanding of the self which belongs to faith as one of its basic structures.

The practical character of such understanding is made evident when we consider its close relation to obedience, which Bultmann considers to be another important element in the New Testament concept of faith.[16] The promotion of obedience 'to the faith' was understood by Saint Paul to be a main purpose of his apostolate.[17] In surrendering his self-sufficiency, man commits himself to God for the direction of his life. The new understanding involves a new way of life. And it is in this act of obedience that Bultmann considers that

[15] *Th. des NT*, p. 311.   [16] *Th. des NT*, p. 310.   [17] Rom. 1.5.

man enters on an authentic existence, in the existentialist sense of that expression—that is to say, man becomes himself. The free act of obedience is 'a deed in the authentic sense, in which man is himself in what he does'.[18]

We have insisted on the existential character of the new understanding which comes with faith, and have shown that its practical expression is obedience. Since, however, it is understanding, it ought to be possible to say what is understood. There is genuine knowledge contained in faith. This knowledge is recognized in the New Testament as a gift of the Spirit.[19] It is a gift because man has not discovered it for himself, it has been revealed to him by God in his act of grace. Yet it is recognized also that the Christian can and should increase in such knowledge.[20] Thus Bultmann says that, as well as being a gift, it is a task.[21] It is a task confronted by all the difficulties which beset the expression and communication of an existential knowledge, and we have only to read Saint Paul's own Epistles to understand how difficult the task is.

For here we have come to the relation of theology to faith. Christian theology proper—as distinct from the pretheological inquiry which clarifies and secures the ground for it—is the systematic elucidation and exposition of the knowledge that is given with faith. It is not speculation separated from faith, but rather faith explaining itself. 'The Christian knowledge is the understanding of the self under divine grace . . . an *existentiell* self-understanding in faith.'[22]

Bultmann sums up his existential interpretation of faith by saying that faith is not only a relation of man to God, but a relation of man to himself.[23] That man always has a relation to himself was, of course, an idea contained in the basic concept of existence which was examined at the beginning of our inquiry and which was verified, so far as New Testament thought is concerned, by the analysis of the Pauline concept of σῶμα. In the treatment of faith we began from the thought of man's new relation to God made possible by

18 *Th. des NT*, p. 312. 19 I Cor. 12.8. 20 Rom. 12.2; Phil. 1.9
21 *Th. des NT*, p. 322. 22 *Th. des NT*, p. 323. 23 *Th. des NT*, p. 319.

God's act of grace. That new relation is the condition of man's justification, and of the life of obedience in which he attains his authentic being. But in attaining his authentic being, he has entered into a new relation with himself. The basic possibilities for man are that he can be estranged from himself (inauthentic existence) or at one with himself (authentic existence), and it is only his relation to God in faith that can give him a right relation to himself, or make him at one with himself.

Here the argument has followed a direction opposite to that which was used in the consideration of sin. We began then from the thought of man fallen away from himself, at war with himself (the relation which characterizes an inauthentic existence), and proceeded to the conclusion that he was also fallen away from God, at war with God, since he had defied God's command to life. In the consideration of faith we have begun with man's reconciliation to God, and have worked back from the new relation to God to his new relation to himself in an authentic existence in which he is at one with himself.

Faith, as it has been described, is not an act that takes place once for all, but issues in the life of faith—the steady orientation of the self to the authentic repeatable possibilities made available to man in the cross and resurrection of Christ. So long as he is in the flesh, man is never delivered from the temptations of the world, and since he has no power in himself to overcome them, he is always in danger of slipping back into an inauthentic existence.[24] But so long as he looks to God he has a power not his own and exists authentically as the child of God. This authentic existence is actualized in the concrete relations of the individual life, and at some of these we must look in the following pages. But this authentic existence may be fairly described as man's recovery of his true being, made possible by God's act of grace in Jesus Christ. Thus Bultmann can say that 'salvation is nothing else than the fulfilment of man's authentic intention to life, to his true self, which had been perverted by sin.'[25]

[24] Cf. I Cor. 9.27. [25] *Th. des NT*, p. 266.

God has given to man the power to fulfil his own command unto life—the indicative is joined with the imperative. God has granted what he himself commanded when he created man in his own image and set him before his possibilities.[26]

It will have been observed that in the preceding argument the quotations have been taken exclusively from the writings of Saint Paul, so far as the New Testament is concerned. The reason is simply that Saint Paul has worked out the concept of faith more fully than have the other New Testament writers, but, of course, it would be quite wrong to suppose that it is peculiarly his. Some such concept of faith must be found in all genuinely Christian theology.

With differences of emphasis and terminology we find a very similar understanding of faith and its importance for Christian existence in the Johannine writings. There the verbal form—'to believe'—is preferred to the noun. 'That ye might believe' is a continually recurring phrase to express the purpose of Christ's works and mission, and to express the purpose of the writer himself in composing the Fourth Gospel.[27] This faith, just as much as the faith of Saint Paul, is existential in character, and so is the knowledge which it apprehends.[28] The truth which enlightens the believer is not a bare intellectual truth but the truth of existence, not a philosophy but a saving knowledge. This truth is identified with Christ himself—he is the truth. To believe on him is nothing other than to accept and make one's own the possibility of life which he came to make available to men. Here in somewhat different language we have essentially the same understanding of faith as we find in the Pauline writings.

Even Bultmann, who—in spite of the title of his book—believes that the New Testament contains several theologies rather than a single theology capable of being expounded as a whole, recognizes the essential agreement between the Pauline and Johannine concepts of faith, though terms used by the former (grace, justification) are lacking in the latter.[29]

[26] Cf. Augustine, *Confessions*, X, 40.   [27] John 1.7; 11.42; 17.21; 20.31, etc.
[28] Cf. *supra*, p. 66.   [29] *Th. des NT*, pp. 416-423.

But though they do not use these terms, the Johannine writings make their own valuable contribution to the understanding of the life of faith. The allegory of the vine and its branches, for instance, brings out in its own way the relation of indicative and imperative as clearly as does Saint Paul in his more technical theological language.[30] But it is sufficient for our purpose here to note that the Johannine understanding of faith or believing does not contradict in any material particular the concept of faith already set out from the Pauline writings.

25. *Characteristics of the Life of Faith*

We must now try to set out some of the characteristics of the life of faith as we find them described in the New Testament, comparing them where necessary with the corresponding characteristics of authentic existence as conceived by existentialist philosophy. And first among these characteristics we shall examine the thought of freedom.

The being of man is such that we cannot conceive an authentic existence for him unless in that existence he is free. He can only be truly himself when he stands before genuine possibilities of decision. Thus Heidegger claims that the act of anticipatory resolve in the face of death brings freedom —freedom from illusion and from the tyranny of the public, freedom for the world and for death itself.[31] Similarly in the New Testament, we find in both the Pauline and Johannine writings the claim put forward that the act of Christian faith brings freedom to the believer: 'Where the Spirit of the Lord is, there is liberty'; 'Ye shall know the truth, and the truth shall make you free.'[32]

It is notable that both in existentialism and in the New Testament teaching the freedom of an authentic existence is contrasted with the lack of freedom in an inauthentic existence. We seem here to find illustration of a recurring dictum of philosophy, namely, that virtue alone is free and vice is servitude. Heidegger, as we saw before, thinks that

[30] John 15.1-8.   [31] *S. u. Z.*, p. 298, etc.   [32] II Cor. 3.17; John 8.32.

when the individual is merged in the public he loses the power of choice, his possibilities are taken away from him, and his decisions are made for him. Saint Paul explicitly contrasts 'the bondage of corruption' with 'the glorious liberty of the children of God',[33] and we noted already that he considers slavery to be one of the characteristics of the life without Christ. The Fourth Gospel has a corresponding contrast between the servitude of sin and the freedom which is given by the Son.[34]

But if this is so, how do we meet the standard criticism of the view that virtue is free and vice is servitude—namely, that if man is to be held responsible for bad actions as well as good ones, he must be free in both? The objection can be answered if we recall what was said about inauthentic existence. The individual is enslaved to the depersonalized mass, but in that mass, as Heidegger has expressed it, man unfolds his own dictatorship. He has lost his freedom because he fled from it. He wanted to lose it and chose to lose it. But once lost, he cannot regain it, because that would mean to choose choice—and it was at that point we suggested that, although Heidegger does not acknowledge it, his understanding of man brings us to the place where either the divine grace must intervene or all thought of an authentic existence be given up entirely. In the New Testament man is represented as enslaved to the personified powers of sin and death, and to the rulers of the κόσμος. Yet again, as we saw, though there may be some Gnostic terminology here, there is no Gnostic dualism. The powers to which man is enslaved are powers of his own making, and he has chosen to serve them. Yet once that fatal choice has been made, the power of choice is itself lost, and man cannot of himself reverse his decision. We reach the paradoxical position that man is responsible for his own irresponsibility. He has chosen to surrender freedom, but once freedom is surrendered, it cannot be recovered and man is enslaved—unless indeed some Power outside himself restores freedom to him. But the point is that if man has surrendered his freedom, he is

[33] Rom. 8.21.   [34] John 8.33-36.

responsible for his enslavement. This arises not from facticity, for which man could disclaim responsibility, but from fallenness, or in other words, not from his being bound up with the world in his existence, but from his having chosen the world, and having lost his being with its freedom to the world in that act of choice.

The Christian concept of freedom involves us immediately in another paradox, for this freedom is at the same time the service of God. The act of faith which appropriates the gift of freedom is the act of surrender and obedience to God. A man who is a slave in earthly society becomes free in the Lord, and a man who is free in earthly society becomes a slave of Christ.[35] When we contrast this with Heidegger's somewhat arrogant conception of freedom, we see that the difference arises simply from the absence of God in Heidegger's philosophy. For Heidegger, man's freedom in a hostile world must have something of a defiant character. But for the believer, freedom is found when he turns from the worship of the creature, which meant slavery, to the worship of the Creator, 'whose service is perfect freedom'. Man is free when he finds his true being as a child of God, to whom his relation finds expression in obedience. To be free is to obey God's command to life.

Bultmann defines Christian freedom in typically existentialist language: 'Freedom is nothing else than being open for the genuine future.'[36] As a formal definition of freedom, this would presumably be acceptable to Heidegger, but because of the absence of God from his philosophy, the content of Christian freedom is quite different from that of the freedom envisaged by the existential analysis, although, as regards its formal structure, it is almost exactly parallel. This last point is important if we accept the view that theology has its ontological presuppositions,[37] and that its statements about man and his possibilities should be capable of being brought into relation with man's own understanding of himself as clarified in the existential analytic. Christian freedom is as an *existentiell* possibility the gift of divine grace,

[35] Cf. I Cor. 7.22.   [36] *Th. des NT*, p. 331.   [37] *Supra*, p. 6 ff.

yet that the gift can be given, it must lie within the horizon of man's existential possibility. That it does indeed lie within this horizon will become clear from a comparison of the New Testament concept of freedom with Heidegger's. The formal structure is threefold in both cases.

The first element is freedom from the depersonalized collective body, liberation from the tyranny of the fallen mass of mankind. As we saw in the discussion of conscience, this may mean for the existentialist a revolt against the generally accepted moral code. This can be a most dangerous doctrine, though in the case of Heidegger there are reasons which would make it unfair to press this point too far. But if we recall again the pernicious influence which the philosophy of Nietzsche had in Germany in inculcating the belief that there is a morality for the masters and a morality for the slaves, we shall understand that whatever the philosopher's intentions may be, whenever he teaches a doctrine of freedom from public conventions, he is at once opening the door to the most undesirable consequences, and these seem to be inevitable if God is absent from his message. In the New Testament it is taught that the Christian believer is made free from the law.[38] No doubt there were some who misunderstood this teaching as opening the door to licence.[39] But the danger of such misunderstanding is negligible compared with the danger inherent in the teaching of the existentialist philosophers, for whereas with them God is absent, in the New Testament it is God himself who has given this freedom through Christ. The Christian believer is freed from the law, considered as external restraint, precisely because his inward delight lies in obeying freely the will of God. We come back here to our Lord's own teaching, which contrasted the law as the traditional collective usage of the Jews with the authentic will of God, which the law had obscured rather than expressed. And his demand was for radical obedience to God, which would issue in going beyond the demands of the law rather than in ignoring them.[40] Thus in one of its aspects Christian freedom is a concrete actualizing of the

[38] Gal. 5.18.   [39] Gal. 5.13.   [40] *Supra*, p. 21 ff.

existential possibility of liberation from the depersonalizing power of convention, yet since it is a freedom founded on God, such liberation can never be disruptive of morality, as it may easily prove to be in the absence of God.

The second element is freedom from the world of things, into which inauthentic man is fallen. To resolve to obey conscience (in his own special sense of the term) and to live in the anticipation of one's own death is, in Heidegger's view, the way to deliverance from concern with the material world. But as we have already seen, he does not show how fallen man can make the resolve, and in any case there is no valid reason for rejecting the comforting illusions of the worldly life if in the end all existence amounts to nothing- ·ness. Heidegger's analytic has disclosed here an existential possibility of freedom, but only an act of grace can make it an *existentiell* possibility. This we do find in the New Testament teaching, that the Christian believer has, in fact, freedom from sin.[41] He is 'open for the genuine future' in the sense that God's act of grace in the cross and resurrection of Christ breaks into man's fallen situation to restore choice and set man before his lost authentic possibility of life. 'The power of the flesh binds man to the past, the power of the spirit gives the freedom which discloses the future.'[42] Freedom from sin does not mean that temptation is removed—it remains so long as the believer is in the world, and he may succumb to it. But he is free from it in the sense that another possibility is now open to him, and he overcomes it so far as he is per- petually appropriating the gift of grace and living in the possibilities of the cross and resurrection. 'Looking unto Jesus,' that is to say, oriented to these possibilities given in him who is the Mediator of grace and the Author of faith, the believer 'runs his appointed course with steadiness'.[43]

The third element in freedom relates it to death. The difference between the existentialist and Christian view- points comes out here in the different prepositions which are employed. Heidegger speaks of freedom 'for' death. By this he appears to mean that death can be removed from the

[41] Rom. 6.18.   [42] *Th. des NT*, p. 331.   [43] Heb. 12.1-2 (Moffatt).

208

realm of contingency and made a true possibility in the existentialist sense of the term—something upon which I can choose to project myself. This is done in anticipatory resolve. I accept my facticity, the fact that I am thrown into death, and I take it up into my resolve and project myself upon this capital possibility, which is the possibility of the impossibility of my existence. All other possibilities are evaluated in the light of it. This is, of course, a hard doctrine, but presumably those who accept it do find themselves free in the face of death. In having the courage to accept death and the nothingness of their own being, there is no doubt that in a sense they rise above death and are freed from the fear of it. The New Testament, however, speaks of freedom 'from' death.[44] But it is 'the spirit of life in Christ Jesus' that brings this freedom. Again the formal correspondence between the New Testament and existentialist concepts of freedom is accompanied by a difference of content which arises from the absence of God in the latter and the supreme importance of God's act of grace for the former. The Christian believer is freed from death because, in the possibility opened to him in the resurrection of Christ, he has been brought into life, and since that life is founded upon God, it is eternal. Death cannot separate man from the love of God made known in his act of grace, the purpose of which was to give life to men.[45]

With the mention of freedom from death, we have come to another characteristic of the life of faith, namely, hope. There could scarcely be genuine hope apart from a belief in God, and therefore we find that Heidegger has little place for hope in the scheme of authentic existence, and suggests that its function is simply to lighten the burden of being.[46] But the Christian, believing both that he is the creature of God and that God acted in Jesus Christ for his salvation, has the gift of hope.[47] The Christian hope is especially the hope of the life to come, or rather, the continuation beyond this present world of the life in Christ already begun. Sin, we saw, is the falling away from the self, which is also a falling away from God, and so sin leads to death. But if in the Christian

[44] Rom. 8.2.   [45] Rom. 8.38-39.   [46] S. u. Z., p. 345.   [47] Rom. 15.13.

life there is freedom from sin, the self is unified and brought into communion with God. Heidegger, too, believes that in a resolved authentic existence the self attains its unity. But the Christian goes on to interpret the consequence of this unity and the communion with God which goes with it as the opposite of the disunity which arises with sin—that is to say, if the way of sin leads to disintegration and death, the way of faith leads to life. Life is the command of God as Creator, and at the same time his gift in the risen Christ. Death and suffering prevail in this world, but the Christian is directed beyond to the invisible world of God, and has hope.[48]

Joy and peace are further characteristics of the life of faith as it is described in the New Testament writings.[49] And here again we note that Heidegger mentions these in his account of the formal structure of an authentic existence, though of course with the usual difference of content. There is joy, he claims, in the dread-filled resolve to live in the anticipation of death[50]—and no doubt there is, though it would seem to be the somewhat grim joy of knowing that every comforting illusion has been shattered and the worst freely accepted. He also claims equanimity as a character of authentic existence, and carefully distinguishes it from indifference, on the ground that the latter is grounded in a failure to observe and appreciate, while the former rests on resolve.[51] In spite of the difference of content, it is not difficult to see the formal existential structure which is common to both the existentialist and Christian concepts of peace (or equanimity) and joy. They arise from that unity of the self which in the one case is attained in resolve (Heidegger), or that unity of the self which is at the same time a communion with God and follows from the committal of the self to God in faith—the other case, the Christian 'joy and peace in believing'.

The life of faith is above all characterized by love. Love is said to be greater than hope or even faith itself; that we should love one another is Christ's commandment; and the presence in a man of love for his brethren is the token that

---

[48] II Cor. 4.18.
[50] S. u. Z., p. 313.

[49] Rom. 15.13; John 14.27; John 15.11, etc.
[51] S. u. Z., p. 345.

he has entered into the new life.[52] Considering the central importance of love in the New Testament teaching, it is surely rather remarkable that Bultmann seems to have relatively little to say about it in his exposition of that teaching. Is there a reason for this reticence? Is it not rather strange that freedom figures much more prominently in his account of the life of faith than does love?

Let us begin by noting what he says about the love of God.[53] He practically identifies this with grace, which he understands as an act. The love of God then is, in his view, not so much a feeling or a disposition or even an attitude of God towards men as simply an act or event, namely, the sending of Christ. Is this, however, an adequate account? We usually think of God's love as the motive of his act, and the act as the manifestation of his love, rather than that the two are one and the same.

Bultmann rightly says that it is God's act of love towards us that gives to us the *existentiell* possibility of loving. The love of the brethren, as the New Testament teaches, follows from the appropriation of God's gift of love in faith. Is this love of the brethren, then, an act also, like the love of God? Or if, as we suggested, Bultmann's concept of the love of God is inadequate, is his concept of Christian love among the brethren also inadequate?

For a fuller account of his views on Christian love, we have to go elsewhere than to his systematic exposition of the New Testament teaching on the life of faith.[54] He rightly contends that love is not an emotion, as it is often understood to be. If love is Christ's commandment, it cannot be an emotion, for I cannot experience any particular emotion at will, and so I could not obey the command. Neither is love an ideal, nor yet is it a universal love of mankind. Love is always the demand made now in a particular situation, and that demand is understood in the context of a relation between I and Thou.

[52] I Cor. 13.13; John 15.12, etc.; I John 3.14.
[53] *Th. des NT*, p. 286.
[54] Essay, 'To Love Your Neighbour', *Scottish Periodical*, 1947 (tr., R. Gregor Smith).

Here Bultmann touches on the important Christian concept of the neighbour. The neighbour is one who is always there already. Man is not an isolated subject who must form relations with others—he is always already 'being-with-others'—and here we have no difficulty in recognizing in Bultmann's exposition the concepts of *Mitdasein* (equated with the neighbour) and *Mitsein* or being-with-others which we have already met in Heidegger.[55]

Love is absent when I approach the Thou (*Mitdasein*) as if he belonged to the world (*vorhanden*), or in the 'enforcement of the I in face of the Thou'. This is a false relation between persons, and presumably leads to Heidegger's inauthentic being-with-others, *das Man*. Love is present when I understand my connection with my neighbour as a Thou in each situation as it arises. Love is 'an understanding of the self in relation to the Thou', and since this understanding is in a definite concrete situation, it involves decision. We now see the relation of love to faith. This loving understanding is also the new understanding of the self in faith, and the decision of love is made possible by the decision of faith. Love of my neighbour is made possible by the love of God—and again Bultmann reminds us that by the love of God he does not mean some eternal quality of God, but his act of love in a definite situation. And the New Testament itself provides a neat summing up of the argument here: 'Herein is love, not that we loved God, but that he loved us, and sent his Son to be the propitiation for our sins.'[56]

Can we say more explicitly what this attitude of love to one's neighbour, this being open for one's neighbour means? There is clearly a strong admixture of Heidegger's existentialism in Bultmann's exposition of the concept of love, and perhaps it will clarify matters if we look more closely at Heidegger's position. For him, as for Bultmann, man is always already being-with-others (*Mitsein*), and my neighbour is never an object within the world but always a co-existent (*Mitdasein*). My relation to him (*Fürsorge*) is of a different order from my relation to things (*Besorgen*).

[55] *Supra*, p. 89 ff.   [56] I John 4.10. Cf. Bultmann's Essay, pp. 48-55.

Heidegger does not speak of love, but he does speak of authentic being-with-others, which we take to be the nearest approach to a concept of love in his philosophy. The duty of a person who exists authentically with others is 'to liberate them, to become their conscience as it were and recall them to themselves.'[57] Now we saw that Bultmann identified the love of God with his act of grace in which he restored to man the possibility of attaining his true being. Is the Christian love which God's act of love originates in those who accept the gift of grace to be understood in a similar way—in which case it would be very close to Heidegger's idea of authentic being-with-others, which recalls the other to his true being? In other words, does love consist in helping the individual to be himself? Or is this altogether too individualistic an account?

We note that Tillich, in his ontological analysis of love, which has certain affinities with Bultmann's approach, says that 'the highest form of love and that form of it which distinguishes eastern and western cultures is the love which preserves the individual who is both the subject and the object of love'.[58] Presumably there is no greater benefit that one man can convey to another than to help to bring the other into his true being. In that case Christian love would seem to be indistinguishable from Christian witness. And since Christian witness has very wide limits, it may well be that every act of love done in the name of Christ would fall within it—it would be a proclaiming of the Word, recalling the other to himself through love, the Christian counterpart of Heidegger's idea of becoming the other's conscience, as it were.

Yet while acknowledging the force of these considerations, we would still contend that Bultmann's view both of the love of God and of Christian love among the brethren is inadequate, and betrays the infection of existentialist individualism. It is inadequate because it has no place for fellowship or communion. It is true that Christian love can never be selective—our Lord himself answered the question,

[57] Cf. *S. u. Z.*, p. 298, also p. 122.   [58] *Love, Power and Justice*, O.U.P., p. 27.

Who is my neighbour? Is there not a quality of love, a sharing of being or a participation in being, which belongs only to those within the community of Christian believers, founded on their communion with God in Christ, and about which Bultmann has said nothing? The New Testament would certainly appear to indicate that this is so when it speaks of a fellowship of the Spirit which is also a fellowship with one another, and of believers being 'all one in Christ'— a unity which is made possible by their faith in Christ.[59] The Christian is open to his neighbour whoever the neighbour may be in any particular situation, he may hope by his act of love to bring the neighbour into the fellowship, but we still have to realize that the neighbour may not yet be within it, and the love which binds the fellowship itself together Bultmann has left out of account. In speaking of fellowship, however, we have really passed to another subject, the question of the Church or the Christian community, and it is in that connection that the question whether Bultmann shows an excessively individualist bias will have to be pursued.

Meantime, we sum up the discussion of the life of faith in the Christian individual. As well as faith, including its constituent structures of decision, understanding and obedience (following Bultmann's analysis), we find that freedom, hope, joy, peace and love are important characteristics of Christian existence as described in the New Testament. Formally these may be considered to be existential possibilities of man, as may be shown by a comparison with Heidegger's analysis of an authentic existence, but concretely they have a uniquely Christian content in that they arise as the gifts of God's act of grace in Jesus Christ. They are possibilities of man which are only actualized as 'the fruit of the Spirit'.[60]

[59] II Cor. 13.14; I John 1.3; Gal. 3.28.   [60] Gal. 5.22.

IX

EXISTENCE IN THE
COMMUNITY

26. *The Church*

IT is surely rather remarkable that in a major work devoted
to the exposition of New Testament thought and to the
analysis of its concepts, the index of nearly one hundred and
fifty Greek terms should omit the word κοινωνία, which
might have been supposed to have some importance. Yet
that is true of Bultmann's *Theologie des Neuen Testaments*. This
curious circumstance alone might tend to confirm what was
said in the discussion of love about there being an excessive
bias towards individualism in Bultmann's thought, stemming
from the influence of Heidegger's existentialism. It might
even indicate a weakness in the existential approach to
theology in general. It is true that Bultmann has quite a
few things to say about the Church, and much of what he
does say is extremely relevant and valuable. Yet it seems
equally true that there is a certain inadequacy in his whole
treatment of this theme.

To clarify the subsequent discussion of the Church proper,
we begin by summarizing a short essay in which Bultmann
has expressed his views on the nature of human community in
general.[1] In this essay, he tells us, his approach to the problem
of community is not sociological but ontological. He distinguishes four types of community: (*a*) the natural community,
rooted in blood and soil, of which the family and the nation
are examples; (*b*) the historical community, which arises out

[1] 'Formen menschlicher Gemeinschaft' (Tübingen, 1952), (E.T. 'Forms of
Human Community', *Essays*, R. Bultmann, S.C.M. Press, 1955).

of common experiences and common tasks. The state is the obvious example here. (c) The cultural community, founded upon a common body of ideas, whether they be scientific, philosophical or artistic; (d) the religious community, which is based upon faith.

The presupposition of a genuine community, he believes, is selfhood. The community must ensure the freedom and responsibility of personality, it must be the setting for individuality, unlike the false community of *das Man* which destroys these things. In his survey of the first three types of community he shows how they can be—and often are—perverted through a process of depersonalization in which the specifically human and personal element is destroyed. The obvious illustration for the first type is what the Nazis made of the doctrine of 'blood and soil' which reduced even love and marriage to the level of cattle-rearing or horse-breeding.[2] The apparatus of the totalitarian state is the threat to personality contained in the second type of community. For the third type, the peculiar danger lies in dogmatism, the fixation of ideas.

Genuine community, it is contended, is rooted in religious faith. If the presupposition of community is selfhood, then community must have a foundation of faith because, as we saw, it is through faith that man attains his true self, or alternatively expressed, it is God who makes the gift of the self.[3] And here, of course, we come to the paradox of individualism and community. Man can only receive this gift from God when he is taken out of every (more or less perverted) human community and placed before God in radical isolation (*Einsamkeit*). 'If any man come to me and hate not his father, and mother, and wife, and children, and brethren, and sisters, yea, and his own life also, he cannot be my disciple.'[4] The way to God involves the decision of faith which is taken in isolation, and is a surrender of the world and of the old understanding of the self which was based on the world and on relationships within the world. Yet this nihilism, if we may so call it—for Bultmann draws

[2] *Op. cit.*, p. 263 ff. [3] *Ibid.*, p. 270 ff. [4] Luke 14.26.

216

attention to the obvious relation between the radical surrender of Christian faith and the despair of the self and the
world in such thinkers as Nietzsche, Heidegger and Sartre—
is the founding of a new community, which is a community
in the transcendent, or a community in God. When man is
freed from concern with the world (for it is this concern
which divides men) he is free for a new relation with his
neighbour. I find myself on the other side of despair (Sartre),
in my end is my beginning (Eliot). These sayings are taken
by Bultmann to be echoes of our Lord's own teaching that it
is through losing his life that a man finds it.[5] And for the
Christian this finding is made possible through God's act of
grace.

The Christian believer, delivered from the world and
entered on the new life, is free for a new relation with his
brethren, and belongs to the community of those who are
called, the ἐκκλησία. Yet this community, the Church, is in
continual danger of degeneration. For the Church, in one
sense invisible, is in another sense a visible community in
space and time which cannot avoid being institutionally
organized. And as soon as that happens, there arises the
threat of convention and officialdom, and above all, Bultmann thinks, the threat of orthodoxy which transforms the
knowledge of God in faith to a dogma.

Bultmann, however, visualizes the community of the
Church as passing over into a wider community which
reaches out beyond the boundaries of the Church, the community of love. This, as we saw, is not an ideal Utopia
grounded on universal human love, but rather the love of
one's neighbour which consists in being open for those whom
we meet in actual situations. But if this being open for one's
neighbour rests on a detachment from worldly concern,
then, Bultmann contends, there is community even between
the nihilist and the believer, because for both worldly
differences have ceased to matter, they are delivered from
the old self and set free for genuine relations with each other.

Like the salvation of the individual, which was described

[5] Matt. 16.25; John 12.25.

on the basis of the existential analysis as simply man's fulfilment of his authentic intention to life,[6] so the Christian community is held to be simply the fulfilment of what is already adumbrated and intended in all human community. 'Faith brings to light the hidden community of all men.'[7] Man is created to be himself, and that means to be himself in the community.

We do not at this stage comment on Bultmann's views on community, but bearing them in mind, we turn to the more detailed examination of his concept of the Church. There are two broad types of understanding of the nature of the Church, which Quick has termed the utilitarian and the organic views.[8] On the utilitarian view, the Church exists primarily for the sake of its mission of proclaiming the Word, and its organization is secondary to that purpose, and adaptable to changing circumstances. On the organic view, the Church is primarily a community or fellowship of believers, a Christian society with a more or less fixed pattern of organization.

It will not surprise us to find that Bultmann leans towards the first of these two possible understandings of the Church. That accords both with the Protestant and the existentialist influences in his thought. Yet at the same time Bultmann strives to maintain a high conception of the Church, and does not allow himself to be carried to extremes, even when these might seem to be the logical consequences of some of his own positions.

The origin of the Church he finds in the mighty acts themselves. Those who had entered upon the new life in Christ were conscious of being separated from the world, and so of belonging together to an eschatological community. It was not the need for organization that produced the Church, but rather the consciousness of belonging to the Church led to the growth of an ecclesiastical organization.[9] And Bultmann makes it clear that he considers that some kind of organization is a necessity.

---

[6] *Supra*, p. 137, see *Th. des NT*, p. 266.   [7] *Op. cit.*, p. 273.
[8] *Doctrines of the Creed*, Nisbet, p. 330.
[9] Cf. *Th. des NT*, pp. 91-106, 304-306, 440-446.

The double significance of the Church, Bultmann suggests, is already to be seen in Saint Paul's writings. Sometimes he speaks of the whole Church, sometimes of individual congregations. In the first sense, Bultmann thinks, the Church is conceived as something which does not belong to this world, it is the instrument for proclaiming God's grace, while in the second case it is conceived as embodied in actual communities within the world. This is not quite the same as Quick's distinction of utilitarian and organic views of the Church, though it is related to it, but like that distinction, it must not be pressed too far. Bultmann here seems to make the distinction too radical. On the one hand, the individual congregations were conscious of belonging to the wider Church. And on the other hand, the universal Church itself might be thought of as an organization which is in some sense at least within the world. For the first Jewish converts the Church was the new Israel, the continuation of the authentic tradition of God's chosen people on earth. For the Hellenistic converts, to whom the notion of a new Israel would be unfamiliar and meaningless, the Church was the body of Christ, σῶμα Χριστοῦ. And though both terms imply a separation from the world, they also imply some kind of organized community within the world. We notice, however, that Bultmann traces the concept of the body of Christ to Gnostic origins, and holds that it expresses primarily the unworldly nature of the Church. But that seems to be a strange explanation when we remember that the term σῶμα itself was interpreted by Bultmann to mean man's way of being in virtue of which he is in the world.[10] Are the terms σῶμα and σῶμα Χριστοῦ completely unrelated? The idea of the body of Christ is said to be not so much that of differences being combined in a unity (which as Bultmann points out would be true of any human society) but rather that the members so far as they belong to Christ are not differentiated from each other by those things which make a difference in the world—nationality, wealth, social position and so on.[11]

Wherever the Word is proclaimed, there is the Church.

[10] *Supra*, p. 40 ff.   [11] *Th. des NT*, pp. 304-305.

Its primary function is thus to witness, to recall men to themselves. This is in line with the concept of love already analysed. God's love towards men was identified by Bultmann with the sending of his Son, that is to say, with his act of grace, so presumably Christian love is the communicating of this grace (remembering that the Word is proclaimed in many other ways besides preaching) so that men are brought to themselves and assisted to find their authentic being.

But here we come back to the question of the love which subsists within the Church, binding its members in one. It could be wished that Bultmann had given us a more positive account of the fellowship of the Spirit—or for that matter a more positive doctrine of the Holy Spirit. But these are matters on which he remains silent. Is it really adequate to say that the unity of the body of Christ arises simply from the fact that worldly differences have ceased to mean anything for the believers? True, it is the concern for the things of the world together with the belief in self-sufficiency that makes for divisions between men, and when individuals surrender their self-sufficiency and concern with things to live in obedience to God, the differences disappear and they are free to come together in unity. But here is the difficulty. If the body of Christ is defined in the negative sense that worldly differences have ceased to count, how does it differ from that wider community of which Bultmann spoke in which nihilists and existentialists and Buddhists and all who have turned away from worldly concern, as well as Christian believers, are free for genuine relations with one another? Actually I can find no difference at all. As Bultmann defines it, the body of Christ has nothing specifically Christian about it.

This is a very serious criticism to make, but it seems to be just. Surely we are entitled to ask for a more positive conception of the unity of fellowship and love in the Christian community than we find in Bultmann's theology? He is perfectly right, of course, in saying that the fellowship of the Church is not to be found in any social programme belonging to this world.[12] But on the other hand, as the late President Roosevelt pointed out, man's chief problem is how to live with his neighbour. An important part of the witness of the Church, or in other words an important way of proclaiming the Word, must be simply the manifestation within the Christian community of a spirit of fellowship and love which cannot be found outside of it. And about this distinctively Christian fellowship, it seems fair to complain, Bultmann has nothing adequate to say.

Here, however, we have struck upon a fundamental problem in the theology of the Church. What is the relation of individualism and community in the Christian life? The existentialists have a strong tendency towards individualism. We know what Kierkegaard thought of an organized state church. We find Zehrer in our own day somewhat rhetorically suggesting that Christians will have to go out to the deserts or the catacombs to carry on their witness.[13] And while Bultmann certainly would not go to the lengths of either of these two, the individualist influence is strong in him also.

It must be admitted that a certain suspicion of the organized Church is not entirely without justification. As a matter of historical fact, that Christian fellowship and love which ought to bind the believers in one has been perhaps least in evidence when the Church was most fully organized, and perhaps most in evidence when the Christians were driven into deserts or catacombs. And there appear to be two reasons for this state of affairs.

The first is that the Church tends to usurp what rightly belongs to the individual. The task of the Church in the proclamation of the Word is to bring the individual into the moment of decision. But, in fact, the Church has frequently taken away from the individual the real possibility of decision. It can make the gospel a tradition to be unthinkingly accepted. When it has done so, it has fallen into precisely the same condition as the cult of Israel against which the prophets contended, or the Jewish legalism which our Lord criticized.

[12] *Th. des NT*, p. 305.　　　[13] *Man in this World*, p. 312.

221

Or again, the Church may take away from the individual the new understanding of himself in faith, by transforming the existential knowledge which belongs to faith into a set of dogmas to which assent is to be given, whether they are understood or not—and it is this petrified orthodoxy which, as we saw, Bultmann considers to be the chief danger in organized Christianity. Or again, the Church may destroy that freedom which we saw to belong to the life of faith by multiplying the rules which are inevitable in any organized body. It was against such a destruction of the liberty of the Christian man that Luther protested. A direct existential relationship of the believer to God in Christ is an essential and vital element in the Christian religion. There are some things that the believer must understand and do for himself, if his faith is authentic, and the tendency, even in Protestant churches, has been for the Church to encroach on the sphere which rightly belongs to the individual.

The second reason is that the Church, as an organization, tends to approximate to the pattern of *das Man*. As a community within the world, the Church must evolve some kind of machinery for its affairs, a system of government and administration. It must own property, it must enter into relations with other associations of men, especially the state. Bultmann and everyone else, except a few extremists, admit the necessity for these things. But as soon as all that happens, some measure of depersonalization is almost inevitable. All the familiar phenomena which Heidegger described as characteristic of an inauthentic being-with-others reappear within the Church. It may become marvellously efficient as a mechanism and yet be completely deficient in fellowship and in the other marks of the life of faith. That seems to be the price of collective organization. And, of course, in its relation with secular organizations, the Church may easily become entangled in the whole social mechanism, and so incur share in deeds which it should be the Christian's duty to oppose— and indeed it would not be difficult to cite examples from history where individual Christians have protested while the official Church acquiesced, and only long afterwards were these individuals vindicated and the conscience of the Church as a whole caught up with them. At its worst, the Church can become a business, as happened in the later Middle Ages, and then we have the terrible spectacle of what must be paradoxically called a fallen Church. That is an exceptional state, but just as the Christian individual is exposed to temptation as long as he is in the flesh, so is the Church as long as it is in the world, and it appears that the collective body is always more vulnerable than the individual. As a collective organization, the Church shows a steady tendency, against which it must always be striving, to fall back into the world.

But because the empirical Church is exposed to such dangers and has in large measure failed to manifest the fellowship of the Spirit, are we to abandon the organic concept of the Church altogether, and think of it as simply the sum of individual Christians whose unity is somewhat negatively expressed by saying that for them worldly differences no longer matter? Let us remember that, on the other hand, it is this admittedly imperfect organized Church which makes possible the proclamation of the Word in many ways and in many places where it could not have been heard but for the organization or the machinery, if you care to call it such. As against Zehrer's preference for the deserts and the catacombs, we may set Latourette's conviction that the great era of the Church was the nineteenth century, when tremendous expansion was accompanied by and made possible by a high degree of organization. Mission and organization depend on one another. The Church's witness to the world must have behind it the Church's own internal organic structure. The functional and organic views of the Church, and their precursors in the New Testament, are not rival theories but complementary aspects of the life of the Church. Sometimes one may be emphasized at the expense of the other, but both are necessary to the life of the Church.

In the same way, community and individualism are both necessary in the Christian life. It is in his relations with others that the faith of the individual receives its concrete

223

expression. Even Heidegger, individualist though he be, acknowledged, as we saw, that being-with-others is not something external which is added on to the being of the individual, but belongs to man's being as such—though admittedly Heidegger does not develop this point very far. Paradoxical though it may seem, Heidegger is probably right in suggesting that the existential basis of authentic community lies in liberation, in helping the other to become his true self. Further than that, he has put the problem on its proper level—the level of personality. But he has not followed up his own clues. Bultmann seems to be on similar lines when he thinks of the body of Christ as made up of individuals for whom earthly differences have ceased to matter—they are made free for genuine relations with each other. But like Heidegger, he has nothing positive to contribute to the understanding of Christian κοινωνία. Neither of them has gone beyond the fringes of the problem, and one feels that for both of them it is individual existence that is really interesting. This is perhaps one of the weakest points both in existentialist philosophy itself and in any theology which attacks its problems from the existential approach. However admirable its treatment of individual Christian experience, it fails to make the transition to the Christian community. But in criticizing Bultmann for the inadequacy of his thought at this point, let us remember that Christian community is an unsolved problem not for him alone but for the Church at large, and that not only the concept but—let us confess it —the reality of κοινωνία is all too often lacking in the Church.

27. The Word and Sacraments

To the Church are committed the Word and the sacraments—these are indeed the vehicles for its mission and the basis of its organization. We have already seen something of the key position which the Word holds in Bultmann's exposition of Christian theology, and we must now examine what he says about it more closely.[14]

14 Cf. *Th. des NT*, p. 302.

The Word is not a world-view, nor yet is it a record of past events. No doubt it implies a world-view and no doubt it implies that certain events have once taken place, but essentially it is a κήρυγμα. It confronts the individual, it questions his understanding of himself, it demands from him a decision. For in the Word the saving events, and therefore the grace of God, are present. The Word sets before the hearer now the possibilities contained in the cross and resurrection, and brings him into the moment of decision. 'How shall they believe in him of whom they have not heard? And how shall they hear without a preacher? And how shall they preach, except they be sent? ... Faith cometh by hearing, and hearing by the word of God.'[15]

From the point of view of the existential analytic, we may say that the Word holds in Bultmann's thought the place which Heidegger assigns to conscience. We saw that Heidegger placed upon conscience a heavier burden than it is able to bear. Bultmann is right in claiming that only the Word— and that means the Word of God—can fulfil the function which Heidegger referred to conscience. That function is to summon man out of his fallen existence and set him before his authentic possibility. It is therefore quite literally the Word of life.[16] It is in virtue of the Word that the cross and resurrection are eschatological or existential-historical events, for it is through the hearing of the Word that the possibilities contained in these events are real possibilities of decision for me now. Yet, on the other hand, the Word can only be proclaimed now because these events did, in fact, once take place, and the Word can only be the Word of God because, in fact, God acted in these events.

Bultmann therefore adheres to the importance of preaching in the Protestant and Evangelical tradition. In the proclamation of the Word, it is the risen Christ, yes, God himself who speaks.[17] Grace is present in the proclamation, the saving deed itself is present, for as saving deed it is an eschatological or existential-historical event and therefore not tied to a particular point in time. This high concept of

15 Rom. 10.14-15, 17.   16 Cf. John 6.68.   17 *Th. des NT*, p. 301.

preaching is, of course, found in the New Testament. 'We are ambassadors for Christ, as though God did beseech you by us: we pray you in Christ's stead, be ye reconciled to God.'[18] The Word which is proclaimed is God's Word, and in it God speaks to men, as he spoke in the Incarnate Word.

Here also there is a definite view of what preaching ought to do. Its function is to bring men into the moment of decision, to disclose to them their own selves in the light of the cross and resurrection. From what we know of apostolic preaching in the New Testament, Bultmann again would appear to be loyal here to the New Testament understanding of preaching. It is an *existentiell* proclamation which brings the hearer to confront the gift of grace. True, much has passed for preaching in the Church that would not conform to this understanding of it, but that is a judgment of what the Church has made of the gift of the Word entrusted to it. It would not be too much to say that the whole aim of Bultmann's theology, including his views on demythologizing, is to spotlight the essential κήρυγμα of the New Testament for the men and women of our time, and to bring it before them as the one relevant possibility that is still open for a bewildered world. His aim, that is to say, is an evangelical one.

The concept of the Word described here seems to imply also a high view of the Church. The preacher is sent—he is commissioned for his task, and the commission is given to him by the Church, the community of those who have heard and have been called by the Word, and to whom the Word is committed. The Word is proclaimed by the Church, which means that God speaks through the Church. But in that case would not Bultmann have to allow more to the idea of the Church as σῶμα Χριστοῦ than he does? Would he not need to acknowledge more substance to this concept, since it is the body of Christ, the Church, which now proclaims the Word and so becomes mediator of the grace which had its origin in the cross and resurrection? Let us be clear, however, that this does not mean that Bultmann would need

[18] II Cor. 5.20.

to allow more to the visible or institutional Church than he does, because the essence of the Church does not lie for him in its organization or its succession or anything of that sort, but quite simply—in its proclaiming of the Word! Where the Word is proclaimed, Christ is present, the cross and resurrection are present, the Church is present and speaks 'in Christ's stead'.

There is another aspect of the Word which should not be overlooked. In the proclaiming of the Word, judgment has begun. In this sense, too, the saving deed which it proclaims is eschatological. The Word is 'sharper than any two-edged sword . . . and is a discerner of the thoughts and intents of the heart.'[19] The Word proclaims the grace and love of God. But, as Bultmann points out, these do not exclude what the New Testament as well as the Old Testament calls the wrath of God, and which Bultmann, corresponding to his treatment of grace and love, considers to be an act, not a quality, and namely, the act of judgment. This act goes on now in the proclaiming of the Word, for according as men either accept or reject the grace which the Word brings before them, they take the way that leads either to life or to death.

In Bultmann's thought, the Word is very closely connected with the sacraments of baptism and the Lord's Supper. If we think of the sacraments as means of grace, then it is clear that Bultmann's understanding of the sacraments must be oriented to his concept of grace as God's act in which through Christ he restores to man his true being. The sacraments are therefore essentially the same as the proclamation of the Word in which grace is present to the hearer. The sacraments are special modes of this proclamation in which, in addition to the spoken word, certain visible elements are employed and certain visible actions performed. They are nothing but concrete manifestations of the Word, and the grace which they convey consists in bringing the recipient into the authentic possibility of his being—namely, making him at one with God and with himself.

Bultmann's view of the sacraments has the two great

19 Heb. 4.12.

merits of simplicity and intelligibility. Perhaps it will be objected that he has over-simplified the matter and deprived the sacraments of their distinctive character. But in what way has he done so? True, he has not perplexed and mystified us with talk of substance and accident, but since these concepts are in any case of philosophic rather than of biblical provenance, it is no matter for regret that he has dispensed with them. The question is here related to existence rather than to metaphysics. It is, 'What do the sacraments mean for my existence?' Or alternatively, 'What possibilities do they open to me?' It is true also that Bultmann has dispensed with all obscure animistic conceptions of grace, and that he leaves no room for a mechanical or automatic sacramental efficacy. But again, what fault can we find with that? If Bultmann has eliminated magic and metaphysics from the understanding of the sacraments, he has certainly not tried to eliminate the essential mystery and miracle of the sacraments—the mystery, namely, that God himself speaks and acts in the sacraments, and the miracle of present grace that brings the believer into the new life opened to him by the cross and resurrection of Christ, so that he lives in the power of God. These points will now be illustrated from the individual sacraments, and we shall find that nothing in Bultmann's understanding of them deprives them of any character which might be considered essential to their sacramental nature.

Baptism, according to the New Testament, is a burial with Christ, and a rising with him through faith.[20] It is, in other words, an entering into the possibilities of the cross and resurrection, of forgiveness of sins and newness of life. But in giving us part in the death and resurrection of Christ, the sacrament of baptism has the same function as the proclaiming and hearing of the Word. In it the believer receives through faith the gift of grace.[21]

Yet as a special mode of the Word, baptism must have its special character. That character seems to lie in this, that baptism brings out the polarities of Christian existence as at

[20] Rom. 6.4; Col. 2.12.   [21] *Th. des NT*, pp. 306-308.

once individual and communal. Baptism is an individual experience, in which the individual is placed over against God. Yet at the same time baptism is the gateway into the Church. The individual believer is in baptism received into the body of Christ.[22]

One obvious difficulty which seems to arise out of Bultmann's view of baptism concerns the practice of infant baptism. If baptism is a way of proclaiming the Word, it implies a corresponding hearing and act of faith on the part of the baptized person, and presumably the young child is not yet capable of either. One possible way out of this difficulty would be to hold that infant baptism is only made complete in confirmation, just as we suggested that in the case of a child brought up in the Christian faith, the moment of decision may be of extended duration. One can, of course, see many difficulties in such a line of argument, but apart from it, it seems that Bultmann's understanding of baptism would exclude children from this sacrament and reserve it to those who had reached an age at which the making of an *existentiell* decision had become possible.

The sacrament of the Lord's Supper is understood by Bultmann in much the same way as he understands baptism.[23] It is a way of proclaiming the Word in which the elements of bread and wine and the ritual acts have their place along with the spoken word. And again in this sacrament the polarities of the Christian life are exhibited. The consecrated elements are given to the individual, and receiving them in faith, he as an individual is the recipient of Christ with the benefits of his cross and resurrection. Yet, on the other hand, in its character as a common meal the Lord's Supper discloses the individual within the body of Christ, the fellowship of faith. The doctrine of a real presence is also safeguarded on Bultmann's interpretation of this sacrament —not indeed through any theory of transubstantiation or consubstantiation or anything of the sort, but because this is a proclaiming of the Word, and in all proclaiming of the Word the crucified and living Lord is present and himself

22 I Cor. 12.13.   23 *Th. des NT*, pp. 309-310.

speaks. The sacrament is not a mere memorial of a past event—Christ is present, though not, of course, localized in the elements or anywhere else.

This discussion of the sacraments allows us to see the place of worship in the Christian life. Christ is present with the worshipping Church, and there is consciousness both of the individual relation of each to him, and of the unity of the Church as the community of those whom he has called out of the world. In worship is the perpetual appropriation of grace, the steady orientation of the self towards the possibilities of the cross and resurrection in virtue of which the believer lives not of himself but in the power of God, and can fight against the temptations of the world. This is the foundation of an authentic existence, as opposed to that inauthentic existence which is founded on worldly concern. And so far as the believer appropriates the grace thus made available to him, he enters upon and continues in the life of faith, freedom, hope, joy, peace, love and fellowship.

CONCLUSION

X

RESULTS OF THE INQUIRY

28. *The Perspective*

AN attempt to assess the value of the existential approach to theology must begin by indicating the place which such an approach, as exemplified in Bultmann's work, occupies among recent trends in theology. According to Tillich,

> 'A theological system is supposed to satisfy two basic needs: the statement of the truth of the Christian message and the interpretation of this truth for every new generation. Theology moves back and forth between two poles, the eternal truth of its foundation and the temporal situation in which the eternal truth must be received. Not many theological systems have been able to balance these two demands perfectly. Most of them either sacrifice elements of the truth or are not able to speak to the situation. Some of them combine both shortcomings.'[1]

It would hardly be unfair to say that much of the liberal modernism which prevailed at the beginning of the present century had the demerit of combining both the shortcomings to which Tillich refers. On the one hand, it had sacrificed elements of the truth in attempting to combine and harmonize the biblical teaching with the philosophical and scientific thought of the day. On the other hand, it did not speak to man's real situation as a fallen and sinful creature, since it was infected with the optimistic view of man which then prevailed in secular thought. Or alternatively, if it did speak to a situation, it spoke to an inauthentic situation without recognizing it as such.

1 *Systematic Theology*, Nisbet, vol. I, p. 3.

As an illustration, let us take the so-called moral influence theories of the atonement which were being put forward around that time. On the one hand, these theories failed to do justice to the New Testament teaching on the death of Jesus, and simply passed over whatever elements in that teaching seemed to them to be not congenial to the temper of thought in their generation. And, on the other hand, they failed to do justice to the factor of sin in the human situation, and supposed that if man is shown the ideal of goodness he will follow it and eventually perhaps attain to it as his moral evolution proceeds.

It may not be without significance that two of the major theological developments that have taken place since that time have each followed upon one of the two great wars which convulsed the world in the first half of the twentieth century. And further, both of these developments have emerged on the continent of Europe, where the crisis of modern civilization has been far more acutely experienced than either in the British Isles or in America.

The first development was the theology of Karl Barth in the period after the First World War. The great and invaluable contribution which Barth made to Christian theology lay on the side of its *kerygma* or message. He called a halt to the process of amalgamating and diluting that message with the human speculation of the day, and referred theology back to its true source in the revealed Word of God. The practical value of his theological work was soon attested in the stiffening which it afforded to those elements in the German Church which resisted Nazi pressure. Barth was right in rescuing the kerygmatic character of theology which was in danger of being lost, and in causing the Church again to hear the Word of God over against the voice of human speculation. But the danger in such a kerygmatic theology is that it may lose touch with man's actual situation. It is in danger of lapsing into a complacent orthodoxy which is curiously irrelevant to the modern mind. It should be said in fairness that this criticism applies more to the disciples of Barth than to their master himself. To quote Tillich again:

CONCLUSION

'Barth's greatness is that he corrects himself again and again in the light of the situation and that he strenuously tries not to become his own follower. Yet he does not realize that in doing so he ceases to be a merely kerygmatic theologian.'[2]

After the Second World War there took place a further development in theological thought, and of this we have taken Rudolf Bultmann as representative. It would be a complete misunderstanding to think that Bultmann has gone back to the attitude which prevailed before Barth. On the contrary, he accepts with Barth the *kerygma*, the revealed Word of God, as the foundation of Christian theology. His thought is based upon the New Testament. But as he sees it, the *kerygma* is always understood in the answering situation of faith, and it is in that actual situation that it is to be interpreted. Let him speak for himself:

'Faith is nothing other than the answer to the *kerygma*, and this is nothing other than the Word of God addressed to us, questioning and promising, directing and pardoning. As such it does not offer itself to critical thought, but speaks in concrete existence. That it never appears except as a theological exposition depends on this, that it can never be expressed except in a human language formed by human thinking. But that is precisely what confirms its kerygmatic character; for that makes it clear that the propositions of the *kerygma* are not universal truths but are addressed to a concrete situation. They can therefore only appear in a form which is moulded by an understanding of existence (or the interpretation of such an understanding). And correspondingly they can only be intelligible for one who can understand the *kerygma* as a Word addressed to him in his situation—and to begin with, it is understood as question and demand. Expressed differently, the *kerygma* is only intelligible as *kerygma* when the understanding of the self which it has awakened is understood as a possibility of man's understanding of himself in general, and so becomes the call to decision.'[3]

[2] *Op. cit.*, p. 5.   [3] *Th. des NT*, pp. 580-581.

235

In this important if somewhat involved statement in which Bultmann sums up his conception of the theologian's work, he makes clear his intention of holding the balance in his theology between *kerygma* and situation—as Tillich also claims to do by his method of correlation. If our simplified account of the course of theological thinking in the first half of the present century is accepted, it will be seen that in intention at least Bultmann has advanced beyond the positions both of liberal modernism and of Barthianism. He has accepted Barth's correction of the older position in founding his theology on the *kerygma* of the Christian revelation, and at the same time he has corrected the excesses of a kerygmatic theology in attempting to interpret the *kerygma* in relation to man's contemporary situation. Whether, of course, his intentions are always fulfilled is quite another question, and we suggested already that at some points the liberal modernist influence still exerts a very strong influence in his thought.

The situation also has changed during the fifty years under review. The facile optimism and confidence in human power which marked the earlier period has largely disappeared, and has been replaced by a mood of anxiety which sometimes comes near to despair. The question of man's own being, which, as Zehrer says, was not being asked fifty years ago because the answer was assumed to be known, is now being asked anew. This mood finds its philosophical expression in existentialism, which is not just another speculation but rather contemporary man's self-analysis, and which, therefore, no theologian who speaks to the situation can afford to ignore.

We now have before us both the place of Bultmann's work in the perspective of recent theological thought, and also a fairly comprehensive view of his work and its relation to existentialist philosophy. We have seen some of the strong points and some of the weaknesses and inadequacies in his exposition. We are therefore in a position to attempt some evaluation, and we shall take as the basis of the discussion Bultmann's own statement of his position, which has already

been quoted in full.[4] Leaving aside certain aspects of the
existential approach to theology which have already been
sufficiently discussed and criticized—for instance, the relation
of theology to the historical, and the relation of individualism
and community in the Christian life—we concentrate now
upon two main topics—the understanding of man and the
question of demythologizing.

29. *Existentialism and the Christian Understanding of Man*

We begin with Bultmann's statement that the propositions
(*Sätze*) of the *kerygma* 'can only appear in a form which is
moulded by an understanding of existence (or the interpretation of such an understanding)'. This last phrase, we
take it, means the philosophical interpretation of an understanding of existence. However much theology differs in some
respects from the natural sciences, it resembles them in this,
that it sets out with its presuppositions and basic concepts,
and that progress in it consists in the continual clarifying and
fuller understanding of these concepts. It must continually
examine that 'understanding of existence' which moulds the
form in which the *kerygma* is expressed. It must understand
the situation if the *kerygma* is to be shown as relevant to it,
yet such understanding is not, strictly speaking, theology, as
we pointed out before, but a pre-theological or ontological
understanding which can alone secure the ground on which
the theological structure proper is to be raised. To quote
another sentence from Bultmann's statement: 'The *kerygma*
is only intelligible as *kerygma* when the understanding of the
self which it has awakened is understood as a possibility of
man's understanding of himself in general, and so becomes a
possibility of decision.' Or, in other words, the Christian life
into which the *kerygma* summons us must be shown as an
existentiell possibility lying within the horizons of man's
existential possibilities.

But it is not theology but the philosophy of existence which
says what these existential horizons are. And the philosophy

[4] *Supra*, p. 235.

of existence is not a speculative metaphysic but phenomenological self-analysis. 'It is not a speculation detached from
man, but man himself, as he understands himself.'[5] The
theological exposition of the *kerygma* must take note of man's
understanding of himself in general if the new understanding
given in faith is to be shown as a real possibility for man.
This is what Schrey means when he speaks of the philosophy
of existence as a corrective to theology. His language is
perhaps ill-chosen, but he makes his meaning plain: 'Since
there is a personal identity before and after the act of faith,
and the new reborn man is nevertheless still a man, the
expressing of the new understanding of the self in faith has
its ontological foundation in the understanding of man as he
was before the act of faith.'[6]

But this is precisely what Bultmann has attempted to do,
with a large measure of success, as it appears to me. Within
the context of ideas (*Begrifflichkeit*) afforded by the existentialist
analysis of the being of man, he has shown how the life of
faith, which is, on the one hand, the gift of God offered in the
kerygma, is, on the other hand, related to the possibilities of
man's being, and is, in fact, 'the fulfilment of his authentic
intention to life, to his true being'.[7] Not only are *kerygma* and
situation brought together, but the ontological foundations of
theology are laid bare, and the relation of the Christian to
the secular understanding of man exhibited, yielding as a
result a clearer understanding of the task of theology and
also of the concepts which it employs.

This part of Bultmann's work finds its best expression in
his exposition of the Pauline theology as a doctrine of man—
firstly, the understanding of man without faith, and secondly,
the understanding of man under faith. The exposition, as we
saw, is carried out within the context of existentialist ideas,
and is closely paralleled by Heidegger's own existential
analytic. The validity of Bultmann's work here is to be
judged by three considerations.

[5] *S. u. Z.*, p. 325.
[6] 'Die Bedeutung Martin Heideggers Philosophie für die Theologie', Bern, p. 14.
[7] *Th. des NT*, p. 266.

CONCLUSION

The first is an exegetical consideration, and concerns Bultmann's understanding of the term σῶμα. This is one of the few definitely ontological terms in the New Testament, and Bultmann, as we saw, understands it as roughly equivalent to Heidegger's concept of 'being-in-the-world', and as implying the concept of existence in the sense in which Heidegger expounds it. We already considered the evidence for Bultmann's interpretation.[8] If that evidence is deemed sufficient—and we argued that it is so—then the foundation for Bultmann's interpretation of the whole Pauline theology as a doctrine of man is securely laid, for everything else in his interpretation turns on this basic ontological concept.

The second consideration is an apologetical one. It concerns the relevance to my existence in the contemporary world which Bultmann has shown as belonging to the Pauline teaching. Archaic notions, whether of Jewish origin (as justification) or of Gnostic provenance (as the dominion of demonic powers), are existentially interpreted so that they become meaningful for the modern man. Common words which Saint Paul used in a technical or semi-technical way are likewise interpreted with the aid of existentialist concepts so as to become meaningful for existence today—the flesh, the world, and so on.

The third consideration is a logical one. It concerns the question of coherence of thought. It has already been pointed out how Bultmann has exhibited the various Pauline concepts within the framework of a systematic understanding of the being of man in relation to God and the world. He is not content to clarify isolated problems or to dwell on single aspects of Pauline teaching, but has set himself the greater task (in which he has been remarkably successful) of exhibiting the massive unity of Saint Paul's theological thought. For although Saint Paul expressed his theology fragmentarily in his epistles, Bultmann believes that it is a unity,[9] and his exposition of it has demonstrated that belief. Yet the key to this unity is the concept of existence, or the concept of σῶμα, as Bultmann has interpreted it.

[8] *Supra*, p. 41 ff.   [9] Cf. *Th. des NT*, p. 186.

A similar case could be put forward as regards the Johannine theology. There is here admittedly no key ontological concept corresponding to σῶμα and the ontological assumptions have to be inferred from the ontical statements. But the considerations of relevance and unity apply in full force, and attest the validity of Bultmann's interpretation based on the concept of existence.

Of course, it must always be remembered that Heidegger began his philosophizing with the study of medieval thought, and that his works are interspersed with references to Augustine, Aquinas, Luther, Kierkegaard and other Christian thinkers. It would be an interesting exercise if someone were to reverse the order of the present inquiry, and investigate the influence of Christian theology—and ultimately of biblical thought—upon the philosophy of existentialism. Such an inquiry would almost certainly show that, whether it is acknowledged or not, the secular and even atheistic existentialism of the twentieth century, with its insistence on the long neglected phenomena of fallenness, care, death and guilt, and its quest for an authentic existence, is nothing other than a partial rediscovery of some aspects at least of the biblical understanding of man.

We have here tried to indicate Bultmann's contribution to Christian anthropology or the understanding of man. He has based that understanding firmly on its ontological foundations, and has shown the life of faith to be nothing other than man's *existentiell* possibility of authentic existence. He has made the Christian understanding of man intelligible to contemporary philosophical thought on the one hand, while remaining loyal to its source in the New Testament on the other. This appears to me to be the most valuable part of Bultmann's work. And if, as was said, progress in theology consists in the clarification and fuller understanding of its basic concepts and presuppositions, then here we seem to have a genuine theological advance.

30. *Existentialism and Demythologizing*

We now turn our attention to some other points in Bultmann's statement of his theological position. The *kerygma*, he says, 'does not offer itself to critical thought, but speaks in concrete existence . . . and to begin with it is understood as question and demand'. The *kerygma* is not a world-view, not a system of timeless truths about the universe, as thinkers like Bradley seem to have supposed. It is not a statement about something but, says Bultmann, is first understood as question and demand. This line of thought becomes clearer when we remember that the *kerygma* rests on the Christian revelation. That revelation consisted in God's might acts in Jesus Christ, and so its truth is not the truth of a statement but the truth of a person. The revelation was expressed in action, not in propositions. Yet surely the revelation gives us to understand something? It does indeed, but the understanding which it gives us is an existential understanding which, as Heidegger shows, need not be expressed in words at all, but may issue in some practical consequences—to recall his illustration, I understand that the hammer is heavy not in making an objective statement about its weight, but in changing it for a lighter one. The *kerygma* is understood in analogous fashion as something which demands of me a decision. But what am I to decide? I am to decide between God and the world, or, expressed in another way, between the understanding of myself in the light of the cross and resurrection of Christ, and the understanding of myself as self-sufficient.

But if the *kerygma* brings me into a decisive question, and appears as demand, what about theology? As a science of some kind, it must express itself in descriptive statements rather than in questions. It would seem to follow, therefore, that theology cannot be a direct interpretation of the *kerygma*. Yet the *kerygma*, Bultmann says, 'never appears except as a theological exposition, and can never be expressed except in a human language formed by human thinking.' But if this theological exposition is different from the *kerygma* itself, what mediates it? 'Faith is the answer to the *kerygma*.' We saw already that faith is the decision to make the possibilities offered to men in the *kerygma* my own. But this means to enter into the new understanding of the self in the light of the cross and resurrection. And here we have something that is capable of being expressed in descriptive statements—namely, the new understanding of the self in faith. Thus for Bultmann theology is the systematic analysis of the understanding which is given with faith, or, as he also expresses it, faith explaining itself. It is not the direct expression of the *kerygma*, but, so to speak, the mediate expression—the analysis of human existence as it understands itself in faith, considered as the response to the *kerygma* in a concrete situation. This exposition of the content of faith, according to Bultmann, is Christian theology proper, as distinct from the pre-theological analysis of the presuppositions of theology.

That this view of theology has a certain attractiveness is impossible to deny. It has a firm ontological basis which relates it to the understanding of man in general. And further, in making theological statements proper to be statements about the understanding of the self in faith, that is to say, existential statements, it gives them a relevance to the situation which they could scarcely otherwise have. Theology becomes the exposition of an *existentiell* possibility of existence, namely, Christian existence, which is shown to be a genuine possibility within the existential horizons of existence. This appears to be also Heidegger's own view of the function of theology, as he expressed it in an unpublished paper on the relations of philosophy and theology, the substance of which has been made available by Schrey.[10]

But over against that attractiveness must be set the gravest dangers. If the business of Christian theology is to analyse an *existentiell* possibility of existence, then it is difficult to see how it can avoid being swallowed up in existentialist philosophy altogether. That is what we meant by our hint earlier on that one of the perils inherent in the existentialist influence upon theology is that existentialism might prove to be the Gnosis of the twentieth century.[11] The concepts of Christian existence could be taken over by existentialist philosophy without any reference to their origin in the cross and resurrection of

10 In his Essay, to which reference was made on p. 238.
11 *Supra*, p. 86 ff.

Christ, and Christian theology would disappear as such. We already discussed the question whether the existential approach to theology does not tend to detach theology altogether from any historical basis.[12] We have now struck on a more far-reaching question—whether this approach does not detach theology from any religious basis in the activity of God, so that, strictly speaking, theology itself would have ceased, and have passed over into philosophy. In a very different way, no doubt, but with pretty much the same result, we might arrive at something similar to the view sketched by Bradley[13] on which the ideas of Christianity, separated from any reference to Christ or to God in Christ, are incorporated into a secular philosophy.

It may be replied that this cannot happen, because Christian existence is only made possible by the *kerygma*, and ultimately by the mighty acts of God in Jesus Christ. That is perfectly true, and we noted it before in the discussion of demythologizing. But as soon as that claim is made, as soon as we speak of mighty acts or of grace or of revelation or of the uniqueness of Jesus Christ, we are making or implying statements which are not statements about human existence, and we have abandoned the concept of a purely existential theology. That is the inconsistency in Bultmann's own position. He puts forward a view of theology which calls for radical demythologizing, and the translation of all transcendent statements into statements about the understanding of the self. Yet at the same time he believes that God has acted decisively in Christ, and he does not appear to realize the incompatibility of the two positions. We do not find fault with him for holding to the latter position. Rather we might say—adapting Tillich's remark about Barth to our own purpose—that Bultmann's greatness here shows itself in his steadfast refusal to follow out his own ideas to the bitter end. But we can readily imagine that some disciple of his, with more consistency and less insight than his master, might run straight into the dangers which we indicated. The danger can only be guarded against by the frank acknowledgment

[12] *Supra*, p. 189 ff. [13] *Supra*, p. 190 ff.

that theology is concerned not only with statements about human existence but with statements about God and his activity as well—transcendent statements, if you like, which, because we lack categories for the understanding of transcendent being as such, can only be expressed in symbolic or mythical form.

Another danger, perhaps equally great, arises out of the selective emphasis which Bultmann's concern with existentialism has led him to place on those elements of Christian truth which lend themselves most readily to his method of treatment. We drew attention to several instances of this in the course of the argument. A further illustration would be the doctrine of the Holy Spirit, one of the obvious gaps in Bultmann's theological exposition. The existential significance of the spirit is interpreted—and interpreted very well —but of the divine Spirit as personal and transcendent there is scarcely a trace. But that is not to be wondered at in a theology which is based on the analysis of the understanding of the self.

When all this has been said, however, let us hasten to add that Bultmann's existential interpretation of theology has its own value. The attention which he draws to the existential-historical significance of the mighty acts appears to me a real contribution both to the understanding and communication of the truth which they give us to understand. Yet that existential-historical aspect must be understood in relation to the objective-historical aspect and above all to that irreducible transcendent element contained in the mythical aspect, as Bultmann would call it. The truth is that theology is not quite so simple as Bultmann's description of it would suggest. He deserves all credit for stressing the existential element, so often neglected and yet so vital, but room must also be found for that transcendent element which cannot be existentially translated, and which Bultmann, in spite of his theories, fully recognizes, so that he himself never really gets away from the symbol and myth in which it must find expression. Just as Heidegger intended to pass beyond the analysis of human existence to the quest for being in the widest sense, so theology cannot rest in existential statements, but must go on to speak of God and the transcendent—though in both cases the question of man's existence certainly appears to me to be the right starting-point for the inquiry.

Why is Bultmann so anxious to get rid of myth? If he says that it is inadequate to express what it is meant to express, no doubt he is right up to a point. But then our knowledge of God can never be perfect (in this world at least), and if that knowledge can only be expressed in mythical form, then the inadequacy of myth does not mean that therefore we must abandon it, for it is the only way of expressing such knowledge as we have. It is better to 'see through a glass darkly'[14] than not to see at all. If, on the other hand, Bultmann says that the myth must be related to existence, he is again right. The meaning of myth and symbol is misunderstood if they are not related to existence, but that is not to say that we can then translate them into existential statements and have nothing left over, for the religious myth may contain in itself a transcendent element which it relates to human existence but which can never be reduced to human existence.

Bultmann's strongest objection to myth appears to be that he considers that it is the chief stumbling-block to the acceptance of the Christian gospel in the modern world. Yet, as Professor Henderson pointed out in the passage which we already quoted, twentieth-century man has been ready to swallow myths that are much more improbable than any that are to be found in the Bible. Schrey has drawn attention to what he calls the mythical elements in Heidegger's thought, for instance, his idea of nothingness which is not lacking in positive content, and which Schrey compares to the Buddhist Nirvana.[15] Actually Schrey misses the obvious illustration which is Heidegger's use of the myth of Hyginus to elucidate the concept of care,[16] and the instances which he does quote might more accurately be described as mystical than mythical. Yet it is interesting to find him suggesting that Bultmann's attitude towards mythology is more negative than Heidegger's! When these points are

[14] I Cor. 13.12.   [15] *Op. cit.*, pp. 17 and 20.   [16] *Supra*, pp. 113-114.

taken into consideration, it seems clear that Bultmann's objections to myth are extravagant, and that he overestimates the intellectual stumbling-block which myth is supposed to put in the way of accepting the Christian faith.

The real stumbling-block is, of course, the surrender of self-sufficiency and the acceptance of the cross. And the real problem of communication confronting the Church is not the removal of myth but a much wider problem which is not confined to language alone, but implies the communication of the Christian life through the manifestation in the Church itself of faith, freedom, hope, peace, joy and love. In spite of all the existentialist warnings against excessive intellectualism, it seems to be a fair criticism of Bultmann that he has concentrated on a fairly narrow intellectual front and, like the liberal modernist of fifty years ago, attempted to present the Christian faith in a form not likely to give offence to the modern outlook.

But, on the other hand, theology is only one part of the Church's activity, and the theologian is no doubt entitled to concentrate on the intellectual—or conceptual—presentation of the Christian life, provided that he remembers that the Church as a whole has a much wider problem of communication to face. And it is only fair to add that if Bultmann has resembled the liberal modernist in an excessive desire to remove every intellectual stumbling-block, he has done so not to make way for a theistic world-view or a Christian ethic but for the presentation to man of his authentic possibility—to be forgiven and renewed through acceptance of the cross and resurrection of Christ.

GLOSSARY OF GERMAN TERMS

The page references show where an explanation of the meaning of each term may be found.

Abgefallen, 102
Alltäglichkeit, 91
Angst, 68
Augenblick, 194
Bedeutsamkeit, 49
Befindlichkeit, 67
Begrifflichkeit, 12
Beruhigung, 102
Besorgen, 39
Bewandtnis, 49
Dasein, 32
Durchshnittlichkeit, 91
Eigentlich, 39
Einebnung, 91
Einmaligkeit, 158
Entfremdung, 102
Entschlossenheit, 194
Entwurf, 60
Entwurzelt, 102
Erschlossenheit, 59
Existenz, 32
Existenzial, 34
Existenzial, das, 34
Existenziell, 34
Existenzialität, 34
Faktizität, 82
Fragestellung, 11
Fürsorge, 90
Gerede, 92
Geschichtlich, 160
Geschriebe, 92
Geworfenheit, 83
Hingabe, 152
Historisch, 160

In-der-Welt-sein, 39
Innerweltlichkeit, 39
Innerzeitigkeit, 160
Insein, 39
Jemeinigkeit, 33
Man, das, 91
Manselbst, 92
Mitdasein, 90
Mitsein, 89
Mitwelt, 89
Neugier, 92
Öffentlichkeit, 91
Ontisch, 30
Ontologisch, 30
Platz, 49
Schuldigsein, 144
Seiendes, 30
Sein, 30
Sein-zum-Tode, 119
Selbstverständnis, 65
Sorge, 113
Unauffälligkeit, 48
Uneigentlich, 39
Unheimlich, 70
Ursprünglich, 136
Verfallenheit, 101
Versuchung, 102
Verweisung, 49
Vorhandenheit, 32
Vorlaufen, 126
Wiederholbar, 162
Zeitlichkeit, 160
Zeug, 48
Zuhandenheit, 48

INDEX OF WRITERS

INDEX OF SUBJECTS

INDEX TO BIBLICAL
REFERENCES